Advance Praise

for

Homeschooling and the Voyage of Self-Discovery

"Every once in a while a writer comes along who really knows what writing is about, who understands how to use words and phrases effectively. A writer who knows how to communicate with the reader in a way that not only informs and entertains, but also blatantly restructures the reader's notions about life and how it works and how best to get along within it. A writer who encourages and empowers the reader to consider life-changing ideas, to step away from the confines of group-think, herd mentalities, and other schoolish notions ingrained from a tender age. John Holt was such a writer. David Albert is another.

"Through his books and articles David Albert explores the concepts behind education, parenting, social interaction—all that which makes us who we are. He engages the casual reader by telling charming stories about himself, his kids, his colleagues, the world to which we all relate. But then slowly, and convincingly, he shifts the focus, moves the perspective around to point out little and sometimes disturbing idiosyncrasies. He makes subtle connections most people would miss, but which, when pointed out, help to illustrate why things work the way they do, and what we can do about changing those things which need changing.

"David Albert's writing is dangerously effective: Don't sit down with *Homeschooling and the Voyage of Self-Discovery* expecting mere entertainment or elucidation. Instead, one should be prepared to have familiar and comfortable views and assumptions challenged, poked, and dissected, and to have a few sacred cows neatly skewered. I can practically see him grinning wickedly as he writes, and I end up reading his writings with a satisfied smile, ready to roll up my sleeves and get to work. What more could one ask of an author?"

—Helen Hegener, Editor and Publisher,
Home Education Magazine

"It is always a pleasure to read David Albert's essays. Albert's wit, enthusiasm, and insight challenge and enlighten homeschooling parents; they also help people considering homeschooling to discover the richness of living and learning that exist outside the confines of conventional classrooms."

—Patrick Farenga, Author,
*Teach Your Own: The John Holt Book of
Homeschooling,*
President, Holt Associates

"Thank you for publishing this beautiful book! As always, I'm filled with awe and gratitude by David's unique and thought-provoking insights on such vitally important, but often overlooked, issues that are at the very heart of homeschooling and parenting. I hope *Homeschooling and the Voyage of Self-Discovery* becomes standard reading for anyone involved with homeschooling."

—Lillian Jones, Editor,
www.BestHomeschooling.org,
former Book Review Editor,
Home Education Magazine

"One would think that David Albert's first book about homeschooling, *And the Skylark Sings with Me: Adventures in Homeschooling and Community-based Education*, could hardly be improved upon, but the deep insights and delightful prose in his new book, *Homeschooling and the Voyage of Self-Discovery*, are, if possible, even better. Albert understands the profound privilege and responsibility that homeschooling parents embrace. His thoughts on homeschooling and family are simultaneously pragmatic and philosophical as he encourages us all to seek and to celebrate the magical uniqueness of every child. Homeschooling parents everywhere will embrace *Homeschooling and the Voyage of Self-Discovery* for its permission to *enjoy* homeschooling, to stop apologizing for spending pleasurable time with their children, and to trust the curriculum of love as a compass for life's voyage."

—Lisa Rivero, Author,
Creative Homeschooling for Gifted Children: A Resource Guide

"A master wordsmith, David Albert stands unique among writers of homeschool lore. His insights offer us a new paradigm and an energetic approach to helping shape and direct the unique and potential-filled children who have come into our care. Don't expect the usual fare from this book: you won't find it. Building on his prior success with *And the Skylark Sings with Me: Adventures in Homeschooling and Community-Based Education*, David skillfully weaves wit and wisdom with sound and practical advice to produce a masterpiece of ideas in *Homeschooling and the Voyage of Self-Discovery*. Reading this book is like climbing a mountain on a clear day: one's reaction upon seeing the majestic vista is of awe and wonder. In this case, David has done the climbing for us, and has thoughtfully invited us along to share the view. His new book is as much an invitation to enjoy the journey of homeschooling as it is a fascinating and freedom-encouraging field guide to creativity and success in parenting. Even teens will enjoy this book. My daughter's evaluation after reading it was that "David Albert knows how to appreciate children for who they are and what they can become."

"Applying the ideas in *Homeschooling and the Voyage of Self-Discovery* challenges and encourages us to adopt a certain fearlessness in our educational adventures. I heartily recommend this book to veteran and novice homeschoolers alike—and that they share it with their children. David cogently reminds us that "learning must ultimately begin from within rather than from without"—a comforting concept to virtually all parents, and especially so to those who strive so hard to nurture and educate, and to exemplify peace, optimal development, risk-taking, creativity, and faith to their children. Thanks, David—you've done it again, and my hat's off to you."

—Marjorie Meyer, Founder,
School of Abraham,
a Homeschooling Resource for Latter-Day Saints,
www.schoolofabraham.com

"In *Homeschooling and the Voyage of Self-Discovery*, David Albert reaches out to every reader as if he is there with you enjoying a cup of tea or coffee, sharing delightfully with you about learning. Not a methodology, not a structure to incorporate, but a refreshing way of conceiving of things that liberates you to think freely about how you learn WITH your children. This book will help each of us capture that marvelous excitement for learning that we can pass on to children. Or better yet, help us discover that we as adults can capture that marvelous excitement for learning from our kids! This is a must-read book for new homeschoolers and old homeschoolers like myself."

—Sherry Stacy,
Olympia Christian Homeschool Support Group

"A unique, wise, witty, literate, useful, philosophical, and thought-provoking journey for homeschooling parents and thoughtful educators. There isn't a comparable work available for those seeking to enrich and expand their homeschooling horizons into a life-altering experience for themselves and their children. *Homeschooling and the Voyage of Self Discovery* carries the ideas brought forth by John Holt and John Taylor Gatto to another level. It is a wonderful combination of the practical—with ideas you can use—and an example of how to incorporate the aesthetics of family learning into the realm of daily living, with the world as your meeting house.

"David asks the most magnificent questions that will provoke you into turning ideas on their heads—but he doesn't always give you the answers. Instead, you are invited and challenged to find your own. He has the unique ability to find the kernel of truth in a quagmire and let it shine for us. *Homeschooling and the Voyage of Self-Discovery* will go right to the top of my list of books to recommend. I consider reading this book a major step forward in my own continuing education.

—Jean Reed, Brook Farm Books, and Author,
The Home School Source Book

"David Albert guides you through the narrow straits of conventional education, through some of his favorite ports, and then to open waters, where the winds of free thought will fill your sails and send you on an affirming and refreshing course to a destination of almost unimaginable beauty."

—Shay Seaborne, Writer, VaEclecticHomeschool
Discussion List,
Virginia Home Education Association

"David Albert has written a vivid, detailed account of his family's adventures in homeschooling, a story bristling with lessons for parents of children of all ages, and, perhaps paradoxically, powerful lessons for teachers and school people as well. *Homeschooling and the Voyage of Self-Discovery* is a gentle but persuasive indictment of the deadening effects most American schools have on children's minds and spirits.

"Albert shows us what a curriculum of love might look like, a course of learning and *living* based on listening, attending, and wondering together at the world we inherit. His approach resists the toxic habit of labeling children, and assumes that every child is an unruly spark of meaning-making energy on a quest for wholeness and competence, and that an engaged parent or teacher must also be on a quest. At an historical moment when "standards" are considered a necessary reform, Albert shows us how to uphold standards of empathy, generosity, compassion, and courage. David Albert's odyssey—so much more than a journey—is essential reading for thoughtful, caring adults who are trying to make a positive difference in children's lives."

—William Ayers, Distinguished Professor of
Education, and Founder, Center for Youth and
Society, University of Illinois at Chicago

"In an old-fashioned, unhurried style, David Albert gives us a gem: a provocative, vigorous, and illuminating encounter with the mad logics of the institutional mind—and some of the antidotes to their effects. This book is a pure delight! You must read it. Albert's intense thoughtfulness about every aspect of waking up to full humanity is a treat you should not miss."

—John Taylor Gatto, Author,
*Dumbing Us Down: The Hidden Curriculum of
Compulsory Schooling* and
The Underground History of American Education

HOMESCHOOLING

AND THE

VOYAGE OF
SELF-DISCOVERY

A JOURNEY OF ORIGINAL SEEKING

David H. Albert

Common Courage Press
CONNOLLY
Monroe, Maine

Library of Congress Cataloging-in-Publication Data is available from
the publisher on request.

ISBN 1-56751-232-1 paper
ISBN 1-56751-233-x cloth

Common Courage Press
Box 702
Monroe, ME 04951

(207) 525-0900; fax: (207) 525-3068
orders-info@commoncouragepress.com

See our website for e-versions of this book.
www.commoncouragepress.com

First Printing
Printed in Canada

"We must become ourselves before someone else does."

—*Robert Hunter*

For Aliyah and Meera–

my great teachers,

and

for Ellen,

who shares one of those little double desks with me.

Contents

Introduction

Warning:
This Book Could Change Your Life

Joyce Reed,
Associate Dean, Brown University

W hy would an academic dean at an Ivy League school (Brown University) be writing the introduction to a book about learning at home? I'll give you two basic reasons. The first is that I can bear witness to the fact that young homeschooled people who arrive in the heady atmosphere of such universities are usually well-prepared to succeed here...if success is measured by their ability to dig deeply into their materials; to seek out conversations with and supports from faculty; to become passionately involved in their academic and co-curricular lives; to reach out and support their fellow-students, and to model for them a satisfaction with their studies based purely on their enjoyment of the learning process, not on an outcome of grades. In my experience, homeschoolers are enthusiastic, self-motivated learners who are likely to write papers that fit the size of their interest in the topic—and not struggle for or hold to a 7, 15 or 30 page 'limit'!

The second reason is that, in my dozen years as a dean, I have come to know what makes a student successful in a challenging learning environment. Both my personal and professional experience as an educator have shown me that children who learned at home are likely to come to college equipped with all the right tools for the naturally joyous experience of learning—and few of the limitations imposed by formalized studies and standardized expectations. Usually, homeschooled students have *sought* their education; having learned eagerly about things that interested them deeply, they come to college with a hunger for and a delight in the learning process.

Home-learners frequently offer college admissions people a profile of the ideal applicant for whom we are constantly on the lookout. They are usually comfortable in cross-generational conversations, and thus eager to approach a professor when they are in search of a research opportunity, clarification on a point in a lecture, or a great conversation. They tend to have a better understanding of what their interests are, how they learn, what their particular challenges are, and, most importantly, how their learning fits into their life and goals. They are idealistic, and want their college experience to have personal relevance. Above all, they are fresh and eager. They are willing to make choices and take risks—to pursue new and different interests, without the fear of failure that so often hounds the "schooled" youngster.

But the second and more personal reason I am enthusiastic about introducing this book to you is that a generation ago (the '70s and '80s), I was a homeschooling parent. My five children now range between the ages of 25 and 40. They all graduated from excellent, highly-selective colleges; loved their learning experiences; have interesting (mostly cutting-edge, "techie") careers; and remain personally close to each other and to the other children and multi-generational friends with whom they grew up...though they all live in different cities, from Boston to LA. Boggle is still the family pastime at all gatherings and events.

So if you're anxious about the risks or challenges of homeschooling, take a deep breath and stay calm. My kids have succeeded *by any standards*—and we didn't do anything special...except NOT have required curricula, textbooks, or study time! We all did a lot of reading, and playing with Legos. The children helped with housework, gardening, and work in the wood shop (okay, sometimes they grumbled, but so did I!), and in general they were very aware that they contributed valuably to the necessities and the pleasures of our day-to-day lives.

Learning at home didn't come about for our family because I felt any personal antipathy towards school. On the contrary—I had enjoyed school so much that I have made a lifelong career as a professional educator. I had loved every moment of my own very traditional schooling, because from Grade 3 on, it gave me the opportunities to move beyond my rather narrow English Canadian upbringing. As an "only" child enduring many excruciatingly cold winters at home without playmates, I soon found my "best friends" in books...and I learned that if I mollified my teachers by doing my assignments rapidly and well, I could sneak a copy of Dicken's *Pickwick Papers* into my desk, and read and read...until I'd get caught for laughing. But oh, I was a good and successful (their standards!) and happy schoolgirl!

Not so for my first daughter. In 1969, when I was an administrator at the University of Washington in Seattle, and she was in school at ages 5 and 6, it was clear that she did *not* love the experience. Still an 'only' child at that point, Elizabeth was painfully shy around bunches of rowdy, physically boisterous children—but she was obviously very bright and curious. I cringed when I heard her teacher tell me that my daughter hid under the kindergarten table...but I did not yet imagine the simple solution...take her out of her distress, of course! School was, I thought, at least 'required.' Plus, I recalled loving it myself. Yet that was *because it met my own necessity.* It didn't meet Elizabeth's.

When we moved to the Big Island of Hawaii that year for a job at the University of Hawaii in Hilo, it just made no sense to force Elizabeth into school. We were doing so many exciting and interesting things in the little town. With a group of anthropologists and educator friends, we opened the Island's first health food store and restaurant, and taught at the U. of Hawaii and in the Peace Corps. What a revelation! Here Elizabeth and 3-4 other children were surrounded by a young and dynamic group of adults who were creating exciting community-based activities—why should the children be excluded and sent away to school? They did not want it, nor did the adults. Above all, we saw how clearly the children thrived when they were allowed to participate in our many creative adventures. They simply *learned* all kinds of things—no teaching required! They were eager, happy, contributing members of our community—it felt natural, and perfect.

When Elizabeth's first brother, Ben, was about to be born in 1971, our family moved 'up-country' to a magnificently beautiful, remote area where we lived for ten blissful years...with no electricity (no TV!), no telephone, no indoor plumbing...and no schools! Four splendid and happy children were born there. Within a few miles of each other's homes along the Ahualoa Road lived a community of wise, knowledgeable, indeed even learned people of all ages, so their/our children learned *naturally*, from each other.

People often asked me questions about my children's learning ("schooling", they called it!). The most common was, "how did I know what I was doing?" And my reply was always the same; I didn't. I only knew what we weren't doing—confining and limiting free, eager minds and bodies that were naturally determined to learn, every minute of every day! We never used the term "homeschooled" because it took us back to the concepts of "school" and "teaching", and these were the ideas we wanted to avoid. "Going to school" implies that there is a place and a time to learn; we were convinced by watching our children that that "time and place" were this lifetime, on this planet. Clearly, we are all always learning. The concept of "school learning" implies that somehow certain learning is worth more than another, AND it also implies that the learning process is not self-initiated. What a disastrous idea—as we are seeing it playing out in today's grade-conscious, test-oriented schools.

I knew that my husband and I had enough 'book-learning' between us, and augmented by the community around us, that we had a fair shot at answering the children's questions, or pointing them in the right direction to find their own answers and solutions. And I could see that my children (and any children I met) were as hungry and thirsty to learn as they were to eat. It seemed obvious, as I watched each child grow, that we are all *naturally* good learners...only sometimes we learn early that we don't match someone else's expectations and standards, and then our confidence in our ability to learn can be seriously damaged. Awestruck over and over again, I watched each very different child develop the massive number of skills that are generally acquired in one's first years of life; there were so many things they *learned* that I did not teach them!

We don't *teach* kids to walk—though we do *coach* them and cheer them on! We certainly don't stand, tight-lipped, on the sidelines—pen and notebook in hand, observing and grading them as we calculate how far they got in a given time, or how often they fell down! If that happened, we might all still be getting around on our knees. We respect and delight in a baby's learning process, acknowledging s/he will take many falls and bumps (multiple mistakes and errors) while learning to walk, and knowing that the process will create their unique stance and motion in the world. As a consequence, we can see a person walking from a block away, and know who they are. A child whose confidence in her learning ability has not been degraded or shattered (by someone else's judgments) will master reading or math as rapidly and successfully as she learned to walk, when she is interested.

What became clear to me was that each child had the right (and responsibility!) to approach any learning experience in their own individualized and positively-supportive fashion. Most importantly, as I saw one daughter developing artistic skills that were way beyond mine, and I helped one son read the directions as he built his first computer (which I could not use), I realized that to support their learning, I didn't have to know or do what they were trying to learn better than they could. Instead, I needed the patience and devotion to really, *really* observe their learning—to pay close attention to their style, stance, natural abilities—then give them whatever support I could to maximize their efforts in mastering what was personally relevant for each of them. Compare *that* to a standardized teaching experience—a situation where you cannot jump up and down and cheer the learning process, or hug the one who has just mastered his goal! We had fun.

Then, from a place of deep respect for each child's unique interests and attitudes, I was able to offer an array of information, perceptions, and modes of thought that opened enticing new vistas of knowledge. I could not say that my children had a well-rounded education, but each of my sons and daughters created a broad, deep and exciting learning experience. Their choices were often quite different, but they shared and talked about their interests. Their customized programs all proved to be excellent preparation for the broad range of studies they pursued in college.

Now what, you might ask, is a homeschooling enthusiast like me doing as a college administrator? The connection between homeschooling and college is a clear one for me. Unlike the "schooled" child who has been in age-graded classes in which everyone was expected to master the same material, the home-learner comes from a situation that is much more like college—a community of eager young people with very diverse interests, preparations, and goals. Furthermore, no one learns without making mistakes. Kids who learn at home seem more likely to develop courage from their errors, rather than fear of failure. They are eager to try again, to look for a fresh approach. They are confident that they can learn whatever they need and want to. Sometimes they discover a limitation in their learning spectrum. But rather than seeing this as a failure, they are more likely to view it as a clue to their natural abilities and calling. Consequently, they are usually "ahead of the game" when it comes to settling in and taking advantage of the abundant array of curricular and co-curricular offerings on a college campus.

Here's one of my family's stories that I like to tell when people ask me about our experience with homeschooling. When my children and I reminisce about learning at home, we always talk about the books we read: the ones they read voraciously to themselves through their teenage years—and the ones I read to them all. That was the crux of our home-learning "program". I read aloud to my children at least twice a day, and for at least two or more hours a day. I read everything—all the best of children's literature, of course; plus poetry, non-fiction, history, mythology.

Years later I discovered just how powerfully those reading sessions had honed the children's individual creative, visual imaginations. When they were in their late teens, I overheard them arguing about a movie they had seen when they were young. I listened for a while, and then pointed out that I personally had no remembrance of this movie...but I had read them the book. No, they insisted, they had seen the movie—and each proceeded to describe the hero and heroine, and some of the scenes. That's when the arguing really became strong! Their descriptions did not match—because, of course, each had actually *created* his or her own mind "movie"', while listening to the story being read. We checked the next day; the book had never been made into a film. But in my kids' minds the aural learning experience had triggered five uniquely creative multi-dimensional realities, which had stayed with them.

People ask, did I find home-learning successful? It's not "*did*", I tell them—I certainly *do*! Though they are now between 25 and 40, my children still call and talk to me (and each other) eagerly about the interesting new things they are learning—from how to build a business to how to design a museum exhibit. I love it—I am learning so much!

I want you to know how much I relished the book you are now holding. I found myself frequently calling my children or other old learn-at-home friends, to read passages to them. The joy and the satisfaction and the bewilderment of homeschooling are all here. David Albert shares with us a rich feast of personal anecdotes that are open, honest and revealing.

Yet the very satisfaction he is finding in his family's homelearning experience drives him to look deeply at the societal costs of the educational system that our nation clings to with increasing rigidity—and which he clearly shows holds our country in a lock-down pattern of social inequality.

Albert's well-researched, detailed, and long chapters called *Social Studies—The Courage of Our Questions* keep digging deeper and deeper and painfully deeper into the devastating roots of social inequality in America and find them clearly embedded in our national educational system. We should take special note of how his process in creating these chapters reflects the ways in which homeschooling can change the parent, as well as the child. David demonstrates how we, as parents, get a chance to hone our own skills in learning while we help our children grapple with the many questions they raise.

I greatly appreciate that this section is so long; as a homeschooler at heart, Albert was not going to stop at a thousand words, or ten pages, or any arbitrarily set limit on his topic, no matter how painful his research became—not until he had gone to the root of the matter. No pat textbook summations here—you'll have the challenging, often distressing satisfaction of following a pattern through to an obvious conclusion. The topic David wrote about in these chapters is disturbing. They revealed much about the history of social and economic inequality in America. There were times when I paced the floor while reading them. His deductions were so obvious and so painful—as demanding of full attention as a toothache—

nothing to do but pace, groan, and commit to do anything possible to address the situation.

This is a serious book, and it is also completely delightful and stimulating. I savored the warm and honest personal pictures of another family's home-learning experiences. But more importantly, I am deeply grateful for the clarity of David's vision and his deep sense of social concern. So be prepared, dear reader! You will not leave this volume un-chastened...or unmotivated!

Joyce Reed, December 2002

Joyce Reed completed her graduate and undergraduate studies in Classics and English at Brown University in the 1960s. She lived in Hawaii for twenty years, where she wrote and performed, created tutoring programs, did educational grant-writing, and taught at a private school—while her children learned at home. She returned to Brown in 1990, and as Associate Dean of the College, she has held responsibility for Brown's nationally-renowned peer academic advising programs for first-years; for advising programs for sophomores; and for tutoring and study skills programs. As a leader in alternative learning opportunities both inside and outside of the classroom, Dean Reed is retiring from Brown this year to create an innovative national educational consulting company...ConnectEdu, 'Connecting great kids with great colleges.' Her company's plan is based on Brown's highly successful model of peer mentoring. The advice that client/families will receive from educational 'experts' will be balanced by the information, inspiration and motivation that comes from regular contact with a Campus Peer mentor—an informed and caring college student.

Distinguished Visitors

I learned almost a year in advance that we would be having distinguished visitors coming to stay with us. No one seemed to know for how long, except to say that we should prepare for a lengthy visit, as they were being sent to learn absolutely everything they could about their host community and country, and they came with very little preparation.

People who recently had similar visitors suggested we should treat them as if they were honored guests, even though no one seems to know from whence they come exactly. Everyone agrees they don't speak the same language and know almost nothing about our culture, but they are very malleable and flexible, often—but not always—easy to get along with (in fact, they can be very demanding, I was also told), and, above all, fast learners. So quick we'd probably have to struggle to keep up. Luckily, they weren't all expected to arrive at the same time.

And so we prepared our house for the arrival of our visitors as best we knew how. We wanted them to feel comfortable, safe, and secure, as if this were their own home. And once we readied the space, we began to think about what we would want their sojourn to be like.

We'll want them to have the opportunity to explore. We'll try to introduce them to the best that we have to offer—the wonders of our natural environment and a community that will welcome them with open arms. We will share with them what we think to be important—our religion, our culture, our music, our creative arts—but we'll make sure to acquaint them with the religions, arts, and culture of our neighbors, too. We'll make a special effort to introduce them to people different from ourselves, so they can experience the rich kaleidoscope that makes where we are a great place to live. We might even get to take them to all those places we've always wanted to visit, but have put off in the crush of our day-to-day lives.

We'll feed them nourishing food. Not fancy every night—that's not the way we eat—but simple, nutritious fare, though we'll make sure they'd get to experience our festive foods as well. We expect they'll like some of it, and probably some items they'll move to the edge of the plate, at least for a time, until they get used to them. And maybe, for some of our foods, they may never develop a taste. Palates differ, and we'll respect that. People say they often come without any previous experience with a knife and fork.

I guess we'll have to remedy that as we go.

We'll respect their needs for privacy, for time alone and in nature, and give them enough space to express and pursue their own interests and desires. These may differ from our own, and indeed it would be surprising if they didn't, given that they come from another place and another time. They may even develop their own penchants in clothing and hairstyles, we've been informed, and their own musical subculture, blending what we have to offer with their own native sense of style. We'll try to learn to relax around them. I expect this will be difficult for awhile, but we'll learn. I'm sure we'll have as much to learn from them as they do from us.

We'll try to alert them to dangers they may encounter. I do not know if they are aware of our traffic habits, or the swift-moving tide in the inlet, or even how our gas stove works. They'll get comfortable soon enough but, as the maxim reads, "Safety First".

They might want to spend time with other visitors in our community, maybe just to compare notes and share common thoughts and feelings. We'll try to make sure they have opportunities to do so, though we'll be sure to check in with the other hosts first. We've also been told that our visitors may like to try out our sports with each other and, if we choose, they might even allow us to join in.

Of course, they'll have to learn something about our community's rules. We've developed them over time, and they have stood us in pretty good stead, though sometimes even we forget why we have them. Having to keep our visitors informed will be a good reminder. And since they will be living under the same rules as we do, as soon as they are fully familiar with our rules and traditions, we'll invite them to join us in improving upon them. Outsiders can sometimes provide us with new perspectives that we really can't supply ourselves.

We'll expect that our visitors will change over time. Whenever I've spent time in a foreign land, even for short periods, I've come back a changed person. How much more would I have been transformed if my stay had been a prolonged one!

We'll help them with languages—speaking, our forms of reading and writing, our sometimes strange ways of doing mathematics, our language of music—so they can open doors to our houses of wisdom themselves. After all, there's only so much we'll be able to teach them directly—there's so much, a large proportion of which I would be incapable of teaching anyway, and I know that I learn so much better when I choose the subject and pursue it on my own.

I guess I'm not too concerned about how many facts or concepts they take away with them. I really don't care much if they remember the state capital of Missouri, or who the Vice President was when they first arrived. If these enrich their visit and help them in the future, so much the better. But what I really hope they'll take with them is the recognition that our community and our nation, and with them our individual and collective happiness, are built upon the responsible exercise of freedom. This is really our greatest secret. It's a freedom we and they were born with, and I hope they will be able to take it along with them, unfettered by prejudice, their own or that of others, unhampered to the highest degree possible by others' expectations, or their own fears and self-doubts, or inhibitions they do not choose freely for themselves.

I know that I will grow to love my visitors, and expect that they will grow to love me. We will have shared so much together! Someday, of course, and I hope not too soon, they'll leave and continue on their respective journeys. I hope they'll drop us a card now and then, and call occasionally, and maybe we'll even be able to get together from time to time, and that we will be good friends. I hope they'll look back at our time together some day and, when faced with the prospect of distinguished visitors themselves, be able to say, "That's where I learned how to treat an honored guest."

Original Seeking
and the Voyage of Self-Discovery

That Divine light which enlightens all men, I believe does often shine in the minds of children very early, and humbly to wait for wisdom, that our conduct toward them may tend to forward their acquaintance with it, and to strengthen them in obedience thereto, appears to me to be a duty on all of us.

—John Woolman, "On Schools",
from *Considerations on Pure Wisdom and Human Policy (1768)*

I honestly can't say where my experience as a Quaker (to be technical, as a member of the Religious Society of Friends, or just "Friends") ends, and my commitment to homeschooling begins. As I reread this sentence, I am actually moved to smile, because it would seem more likely that one would be *committed* to a religious persuasion, and speak of the *experience* of an educational approach. But, no, as will become evident, I think I got the connections right.

In the interests of full disclosure, I have to admit that, despite the fact that I am a reasonably well-known (some might say notorious) homeschooling author, magazine columnist, speaker, and consultant, my commitment to homeschooling is wholly contingent. In other words, it gets me and my family where we want to go educationally speaking and otherwise, and if/when we believe there are more appropriate avenues for doing so, we will utilize them, and I would advise other families to do the same. But we haven't found them, and, for reasons that will become abundantly clear, I don't expect to, so I guess I'm still in business.

As I am now embarked upon the sixth decade of my interstellar sojourn, I've become keenly aware, as early Friends seemed to be, of the limits of human reason. As I read more and more, I have become increasingly distrustful of appeals to authority as sources of wisdom. (So here I am writing a book!) As my own expertise, both in my professional work and as a *professional homeschooler* (sic! doesn't that sound just awful?) has become more widely accepted, my sensitivity to what I don't know has grown more acute, and the list of caveats with which I feel called upon to address any particular issue has expanded.

Ultimately, having run through my paces, I have come around to the not-so-original conclusion, one that I could have learned from any two-year-old, that knowledge must ultimately be rooted in the light of experience. Early Friends might have called these experiences of light "personal encounters with the Divine", but, frankly, I lack the self-assurance to allow myself the luxury of such language. But whatever these encounters represent, it is clear to me that the revelations that result from such encounters are continuing ones, and are not confined by history, buildings, day of the week, or time of day, and certainly not to books, not even this one.

Friends like to speak of "the Light". The way we refer to it, this Light is not to be confused with the light of reason, but operates as the seed of wisdom or of conscience ("the Light within" or "the Inward Teacher", Friends are wont to say), which comes to be known and unfolds itself to us, to use the word of our shaggy-locked, leather-trousered founder George Fox, "experimentally".

This book is (thankfully, some of you are probably thinking) not a work of theology (if it were, my publisher would be having fits!). I presume you, dear reader, will come to whatever conclusions you choose about such matters, or already have. But what is relevant here to my commitment to home-schooling is that it addresses the "problem of knowledge". *Experimentally*, I have come to believe that learning must ultimately begin from within rather than from without, and indeed it does, whether we like it or not.

For as I looked into my daughters' eyes for the very first time, I saw that the seed of understanding—an inner light—was already there. I knew it, and know it, know it as well as I know what love means, even if I can't dissect it. I know it so well that it moved me to love. My experience presented me with the first curriculum, the curriculum of love, without which all other curricula are but so much dross. And my daughters had given me my first lesson. "Love," to quote the 18th Century Friend John Woolman and with apologies for the Quakerspeak, "is the first motion."

* * * * *

It is First Day. We are gathering, being gathered, falling into silence, as is our custom at our Friends Meeting. But the room is far from silent. A baby (pre-toddler?) is seated on his mother's lap. He drops his rattle, which clatters on the bare floor. The mother picks up the rattle and gives it back to the baby. Thirty seconds later, the baby drops (throws?) the rattle again. Again, the mother picks up the rattle and places it in the baby's hands. The process is repeated seven, eight, nine times until, finally, the mother gives the baby a bottle, and the baby falls asleep.

What exactly is going on? Is the baby experimentally testing the laws of gravity, the fact that no matter how many times he drops it, the rattle falls down rather than up? Wouldn't it be easier if he waited until he was a little older so that this could be readily explained to him? And what about the relationship between two colliding surfaces and the production of sound? Couldn't that wait as well for a time when this could be demonstrated in a more 'scientific' fashion?

Perhaps there is something more going on. Is the baby experimentally testing his mother's responses, learning that they are rather like gravity, only acting on the basis of laws not quite so immutable? Is he counting to see whether there is a pattern in how many times he must drop the rattle before his mother breaks the configuration of their relationship? Or is the whole point to get to the bottle to begin with, and this is a new way, short of crying, to achieve the desired result? Would Mom—being perhaps a bit slow on the uptake—learn to respond more quickly with the preferred action? Or, maybe, just maybe, is this a new form of communication being developed, the first steps toward sharing, beyond the simple demand of the baby's cry, or the unilateral actions of the mother in doing simply what she believes needs to be done?

Are there any ethics involved here? Should the mother respond to the Meeting's culture of silence and, if so, after how many rattle drops? Is it *ethical* for the mother to short-circuit the rattle relationship by buying the baby off with food? This *is* tiring—no wonder babies have to sleep so much!

Nature versus nurture. Perhaps it is a false dichotomy, or at least one a lot more complex than we usually speak of in common parlance. The parent nurtures the child. The nature of the child brings forth the nurturing of the parent. Or is that the *nature* of the parent? *The child nurtures the parent.* Is it possible to know where one ends and the other begins? Is it even a meaningful distinction? The child has a potential given her by Great Nature, which may or may not be fully actualized. The parent has the same. Nature is simply nurture actualizing itself over time. Nurture is nature manifesting itself in its fullest expression. It is nature that brings forth nurture. It is nurture that brings out nature. As the Sufi sage Ibn Arabi attests, creator and created give rise to each other, or, as Buddhists might testify, we are witnesses to *dependent co-arising*.

The important distinction—for homeschoolers, yes, and, I believe, for our entire society—is not between nature and nurture but between nature-and-nurture and a culture that systemically denies the potentialities of one and the integrity and possibilities of the other. In the meantime, the child has provided the second curriculum, and that is our learning to listen to him, and to act accordingly.

* * * * *

The educator William Ayers (*To Teach: The Journey of a Teacher*, New York, NY: Teachers College Press, 1993) suggests an exercise for teachers that I think worthwhile for homeschooling parents—or anyone else reading this book—to try for themselves. Brainstorm a list of things at which you are unskilled or can't do well, things you don't understand or don't care about, activities that make you feel incompetent or seem ridiculous to you. I can fill up a page really quickly. I can't program a computer, and have difficulty updating my website (www.skylarksings.com); I can't speak Italian (and I'm not particularly adept at foreign languages generally speaking); I've never done an oil change on my car (I'm semi-looking forward to this one) or tuned the piano; I don't really understand how my television works, or even the internal combustion engine; and I have a fearful aversion (learned or at least strongly reinforced in seventh grade shop) to power tools. To me, golf is a bad excuse for a good long walk. I can't play the oboe (I'd surely like to, but I don't have the years necessary to get me to the level that I'd really enjoy it); can't repair the refrigerator; my knowledge of calculus is a joke (got all "A's" in high school), and forget farming! Now all of these are likely useful things to know, might be very interesting, and certainly worthwhile. (And lest you think that the golf game is unimportant, consider how many corporate agreements are concluded on the links. It is certainly as vital to the average businessman as the Pythagorean Theorem!) Learning any of these things might admittedly have a chance of enhancing my quality of living.

Now imagine someone walked into your life with instructions to correct your deficiencies, and the authority over you to get it done. She is under no obligation to explain to you why this is necessary, no less to solicit either your input or consent. In my case, I might be required to attend remedial auto shop three mornings a week, and alternate television and refrigerator repair and piano tuning on consecutive days, sit through the slow-learners' Italian class every afternoon; and be required to wear a yellow golfing shirt and uncomfortable shoes four times a week when we'd go out to the driving range and hit balls into a net (the fifth day would be devoted to power tools.) In the evening, I'd come home and have to study the best way to grow rice (even though I live in a city in the Pacific Northwest), and complete 20 calculus problems.

The goal might well be to make me a more skilled and better person, "able to meet the challenges of the 21st Century," but the result would most likely be alienation, disinterest, and failure. I really don't have any interest in learning to fix televisions, and now that there are English translations flashed across an electronic board at the opera, much as I love Dante, I don't feel any compelling interest in reading Italian, no less in speaking it. And I wouldn't appreciate being laughed at in my yellow shirt (I look *terrible* in yellow!) when I'd totally miss the ball off the tee. Furthermore, I would likely grow to resent all these attempts to "fix" me, though I might hit on some psychological mechanism to deal with my dissatisfaction, either by being as passive as I could, or learning to anticipate and then do exactly as I was told, on schedule, even showing remarkable progress in my golf game. And it almost goes without saying that I would commit my own little acts of sabotage, quite irrelevant in the context of the larger enterprise.

You do have your own deficiencies, of course (you are looking at your list, right? shh! don't worry, I won't tell your kids about them, though chances are they already know), but they really don't say very much about you, do they? For example, in my case there isn't any distinction between those items that really do attract me (like piano tuning or calculus), and those that do not in the least appeal (refrigerator repair and the dreaded golf). And you really haven't learned much about me, either. You don't know that I like deep-sea fishing, play a South Indian musical instrument called the *veena*, know western classical music so well that I can usually name the composer after the first three or four notes, and am extremely well-read in both western and eastern philosophy. You don't know that I am (or at least can be) a good and creative cook, used to read both Biblical Hebrew and Sanskrit (but I'm rusty), dislike most country music (with apologies to those of you who do) but love gospel, played squash in college, have a great sense of direction, can compute large numbers in my head very quickly, and follow baseball. You probably don't know because you never invited me to tell you.

You also don't know that I am, on the whole, extremely level-headed and practical, and am a good problem-solver, even if I keep a messy room and desk. (A standing joke in our house is that we'd all make our beds more often if we ever learned carpentry.) You don't know that I've lived on three continents, and on both coasts of the U.S. as well as in the middle, and yet have a phobia about forgetting things when I travel. You don't know that I am also an amateur storyteller, and am completing two books on the uses of storytelling even as I complete this one.[1]

And without this knowledge, you would, if you tried, be in a poor position to teach me *anything*. The list of my deficiencies would make me feel awful about myself if I allowed it. I prefer to feel good about myself, strong and secure, independent, yet deeply committed to my family, my community, and my world. When I feel strong and hopeful, I can explore, take criticism and learn from it, accept nurturing, in short, *become more of myself*, or who I was meant to be. But of course, as a professional matter, you really wouldn't care about either my strengths or my deficiencies, as it is assumed that you know what they are, being the same among all 52-year-olds. You wouldn't know anything about my hopes or dreams or passions, and I wouldn't be allowed the time or mental space to develop any! I mean I am already so far behind on my refrigerator repair....

Now Ayers' job is to train future teachers. He knows that teachers are required to draw up lesson plans in the summer or fall without ever having met a single child they will be teaching. There is likely to be nothing in the child's record about anything that the *child* might care about, just a generalized list of deficiencies and how they match up against the state learning objectives.

An unspoken assumption behind the lesson plans is that the objectives couldn't have been met by the child before she enters the next grade. If she could, what would be the value-added of the year of education? In other words, each deficiency must be remediated *even if it doesn't exist* (there is no attempt to find out), and each child must withstand the most relentless and concentrated onslaught on his or her "weaknesses", real or imagined.

But, to continue the personal analogy, I would particularly resent it when someone would find cause to express fears of my "falling behind" and feel required to regularly test me for further flaws or infirmities, resulting in recommendations for even more "remedial" work. And the weaknesses can be created. A precise number of minutes per day, a particular number of days per week, and weeks per year in a specific timetable would be assigned to my mastering a particular skill, say, putting. My failings might simply betray my inability or my refusal to learn on this specific and wholly arbitrary schedule, and they would be certain to multiply. All of this would leave me entirely baffled as to what is really important (to me) and what is not, and wholly dependent upon the judgment of others in making this determination, and for my own self-esteem. I might even learn, with con-

---

1   Cox, Allison M., & David H. Albert, eds. *The Healing Heart~Familes: Storytelling to Encourage Caring and Healthy Families* and *The Healing Heart~Communities: Storytelling to Promote Strong and Healthy Communities.* Gabriola Island, BC: New Society Publishers, 2003.

⌐⌐ efforts including massive amounts of praise and gold paper stars, that I am "happy" within my yellow shirt and newly limited horizons, even if I have become wholly dependent upon others for my next "happiness fix".

Ayers teaches teachers to subvert this paradigm, to find ways to approach each individual child with courage, hope, and love, to see them all for the wonders that they really are. He instructs teachers how to navigate around the state learning objectives (even though he has to make sure the teachers are familiar with them), and how to assist their charges in dealing with the social and economic sorting mechanisms that mandated standardized tests have come to represent. And all this while struggling to ensure the kids can still feel good about themselves! In other words, he assists individuals in negotiating the inherent contradictions between the traditional role of the teacher, and the contemporary role of broker and delivery system for required information. And, I imagine, he's darn good at it, too! Some teachers actually learn the lessons he teaches, and get medals as outstanding educators as a result. More of them likely quit before their first five years are out. Most probably don't learn (or are quickly required to forget) what he has to teach in any case.

Those of you who are schoolteachers have chosen your own cross to bear, and I don't envy you for it. But those of us who are homeschooling parents, in homeschooling families, have no excuse to behave this way toward our children other than the failure of our own imaginations. We don't have to subvert the paradigm; the only question is whether we have the wherewithal to build our own.

* * * * *

I give talks to homeschooling groups about the inner lives of children, how they are influenced and shaped, how they develop, what are some signs parents can listen for, and how understanding and nurturing the inner life of the child can and should be placed at the center of the family's educational efforts. The talks have various names, sometimes humorous or catchy. "Learning About Learning: Conversations with My Violin" (included in this volume) examines the conversations children have with themselves as they grow and change. "Tackling Sushi" explores what it is like to encounter the totally new and strange. "Beans and the Curriculum of Creamed Corn" investigates the kinds of questions children at various stages might ask about the world and how to explore them together, and I demonstrate how I can create an entire K-12 curriculum—covering all state-mandated subjects—from a single can of cream-style corn.

I will spend an hour or so of making my points—using various metaphors, passing around props, citing favorite authors, talking about the experience of homeschooling my daughters Aliyah (now 15) and Meera (12), reminding mothers and fathers of their own school experiences, searching for the best way to connect with my audience. And then, about 20 minutes into the question-and-answer period, someone will ask me which math curriculum she should use with her seven-year-old son.

I am disappointed by the question, but I am no longer surprised by it. I am, for better or worse, a homeschooling "expert" and should therefore be able, at least in an advisory capacity, to provide the same kind of answers to a homeschooling parent that a school board provides to a second grade schoolteacher. (To my publisher's credit, he was in no position to offer me—a middle-aged man—a six-figure advance to write a book telling twenty-something women how to successfully become full-time mothers, and he probably wouldn't have wanted to, in any case.)

But I don't know anything about her seven-year-old or the context of her homeschooling efforts. I don't know if he even *wants* to be learning math formally just now, and, if so, why, or, really, if he should be. I have become convinced, by looking at more than my share of curricula and talking to enough people, that virtually every single curriculum ever published, even those I absolutely abhor, will 'work' (at some operational level, though there may be unintended consequences) with some individual child at some specific age in some particular school or family configuration. I might have my own particular favorites, or none at all, or some tricks or techniques to share, but they would be little more than personal predilections. I will and do share them if and when pressed, but filling the math hole in the little boy is just not one of my priorities.

And then, as would happen during the Q&A and happens again even as I write this, I realize how uncharitable I can be. For there was a time (there *must* have been a time, even if very brief in our case) when my wife Ellen and I (not to force her to share any of the blame), would have thought that what we had to be about was reproducing school at home, only *better* (and sans dodge ball!). Luckily for the kids, and for us, our children had drilled us well enough in the second curriculum (listening), we outgrew our infantile fixations, and we turned into listeners! And since neither Aliyah nor Meera had experienced school, they trained us in a whole new repertoire, one that placed in the forefront their need for learning and for being (including the use of curricula when *their* need seemed to call for it), rather than ours for teaching. I would like to see this book do its part to short-circuit that process for others, or I wouldn't be writing it.

The choice of curricula presumes the list of subject matter is fixed. With all due respect (and I have precious little) for the state learning objectives, E.D. Hirsch's books of lists of 'what your child needs to know in third grade' (if she wants to grow up to be E.D. Hirsch), or medieval theories about the training of the mind (at the end of which you are almost guaranteed to feel like a failure), my children have convinced me that there need not be a subject matter list at all (though I do believe there is a universal need for lots of time outside and in nature, and, in our culture, in the grocery store).

This doesn't mean there isn't anything that *must* be learned. On the contrary, my children have taught me that there is a single lesson that is absolutely essential for children, especially before the age of 10, and without which all the attention to subject matter counts for very little. Here it is (trumpets, or at least italicized typeface please)! [Aye, aye, Captain!— Editor's note]:

> *It is essential that children learn that fulfilling their quests for knowledge, and for mastery, requires time, energy, and effort, and that putting in the necessary time, energy, and effort can get them where they want to go.*

The subject matter at this point doesn't matter. In fact, a fixation on subject matter or learning a list of facts might actually get in the way of the lesson. Consider eight-year-old Susie. Dad took her to a ballgame, and she decides she wants to hit homeruns like Barry Bonds. Mom signs her up for tee-ball. Susie goes out onto to the field in her new tee-ball-team tee-shirt, new athletic shoes, and team cap, and walks up to the plate for the first time. She rubs her hands with dirt (as she saw Barry Bonds do), picks up the bat, and takes a mighty swing at the ball mounted on the tee. Nothing happens. She missed. She takes another swing, perhaps a little less mighty than the first. She hits the tee, and the ball falls meekly to the ground. And then one more swing, with all her might, and the ball slowly rolls off the tee toward second base. "Run!" Susie's teammates yell, and she runs towards first base. The second basegirl bobbles the ball, and Susie beats the throw to first. "Safe!" cries the umpire.

If things go well over the period of the next several weeks and months, Susie will try to copy the better hitters, many older than she, mostly by watching them intently. She will take a little direct instruction from the coach, and from her dad. But, mostly, she'll hit the ball off the tee a couple of hundred or thousand times, with the encouragement of her friends, until, finally, she manages to hit it beyond the infield for the first time. No, it won't go over the fence...yet. But Susie—and she could have been a budding country fiddler or a classical pianist, a birdwatcher, a stamp collector, an Irish stepdancer, a poet, a Lego builder, a gardener, or all of the above—has internalized the most important lesson she will ever learn, and that is the satisfaction that can come with a knowledge quest self-chosen, and of putting in the necessary effort to fulfill it. And, with a little encouragement, and with repeated experiences of this kind, Susie will have learned *experimentally* that this lesson is transferable to other aspects of her young life.

If you think there is something more important going on in our nation's classrooms, or in any curriculum guide you have ever seen, I ask you to reconsider. Don't take my word for it. Take a few minutes to sit quietly and examine the voyages toward knowledge you have undertaken in your own life, how the boat was launched, and what was necessary to steer you safely into shore.

* * * * *

Butterfly larvae don't have wings, and chrysalides don't fly. And if you cut them open early enough, you will see little that is 'butterfly' about them. But the nature that inhabits them is already there.

Now environment will impact the condition in which butterflies will emerge: whether leaves were green and plentiful for the larvae to nibble on, whether branches for the cocoons were sturdy enough to withstand a strong wind, and whether or not they were subject to potential predators. But regardless of what happens, what emerges will never be a moth. A misshapen or stunted butterfly perhaps, but never a moth.

Children, of course, are not butterflies. They must contend, as must we all, with the surrounding culture, and we are all at least partially shaped by it. But the seed within, informed and nurtured by that Light (call it nature if you will), is already there, even as it is prepared to make its appearance as a unique and entire expression of what it means to be human. The child is not a collection of deficits, nor a set of missing facts, much as the larva is not a butterfly without wings. She is a singular whole, revealed to us in the present, and a source of continuing revelation in the future. And most of all, if the voyage of self-discovery is a fruitful one, engaged awareness will provide an avenue for continuing revelation for herself.

The child's voyage of discovery and self-discovery is not without effort. Indeed, no matter how old-hat the world has become for us, it is recreated anew, spanking new, in all its wonders and terrors and miracles, for each and every child, each time a world created just for her. And the challenge is to master it and, in doing so, to master oneself.

I have come through experience to embrace a concept called

 ~~~~~al seeking". I think I may have heard it for the first time in Quaker circles, but it is by no means a term that is special to Friends.

We are born upon this earth to seek. We witness this seeking behavior the first time the newborn infant reaches for its mother's breast, and we see it continue through childhood, and throughout our lifecycle as humans. Indeed, the utter fearlessness of childhood, the willingness of children, at least before it is quelled, to set sail bravely into a pristine world, is an expression of this inner propulsion. We put all of our resources into this seeking—the keenness of our five senses (and maybe more), the force of our intellect, the drive at the core of our being. This seeking can be shaped and transformed by our families and culture, dulled by time, misshaped by tragedy or circumstance, freed up by nurturance, but of one thing I am certain: it is impossible to stamp out. For it is, in my judgment, the very defining characteristic of human beings.

But at the same time each journey of seeking is absolutely original, even as each and every child is unique. We are made this way. Diversity is nature's way of caring for the species. No two journeys are identical, nor are our characteristics as they display themselves during our seeking in our individual habits, proclivities, behavior, personalities, and gifts, the outward manifestations of our own *original* nature. There are no *average* children, only people forced to conform to particular, and not very well-thought-out, management schemes, modeled on a 19th Century Prussian military where soldiers were interchangeable, and one dead enemy was as good as another.[2] Recognition of the utter originality of each and every journey, to my way of thinking, remains by far the single most important reason to homeschool.

Such an understanding of this truth about human beings is ancient. The Greek philosopher Aristotle coined a term for a philosophy which incorporates some of this wisdom—*eudaimonism* (yoo-di-mon-izum.) The term itself is rather difficult to translate, but Aristotle posited eudaimonism against *stoicism*—the idea that happiness is best achieved through an attitude that results in the avoidance, or at least the mitigation, of pain—and

---

2   Horace Mann, founder of the modern school movement, visited Prussia in 1843, and was awestruck by what he saw. Overrun by Napoleon in 1806, the Prussians were determined that such defeat would never happen again, and bent their entire social, economic, and educational system toward their national and military goals. As Mann's biographer Jonathan Messerli (*Horace Mann: A Biography*; New York, NY: Alfred Knopf, 1972) writes, "Ruled by an absolute monarch whose will was carried out by a ruthlessly disciplined army and a narrow-minded and highly efficient bureaucracy, in an age of incipient nationalism, Prussia was admired as a model by other aspiring nation-states. Its citizens were well fed and clothed, literate and absolutely loyal, even if this meant they were also cogs in a

hedonism—the idea that happiness is best actualized through maximizing pleasure and pursuing narrow self-interest. Against these notions, eudaimonists hold to the view that well-being consists of fulfilling one's own *daimon* or inner nature. Eudaimonism distinguishes between those needs and desires that are subjectively felt and whose satisfaction leads to momentary pleasure, and those whose realization is conducive to human growth and produces *eudaimonia*—well-being.

Eudaimonism should not be confused with narrow self-interest. A broad view of this philosophy would hold that it may be one's nature to serve others or the common good, or to commit oneself to religious service, or simply to realize a concern for the self-fulfillment of others as a necessary condition for one's own self-fulfillment. But eudaimonists would strictly adhere to the stance that what life should be about is the actualizing of human potential, and that well-being makes its appearance when people's life activities are most congruent with their own deeply held values and are holistically and fully engaged.

Carol Ryff, a contemporary eudaimonist psychologist and thinker, has isolated six components of well-being: autonomy; personal growth; self-acceptance; life purpose; mastery; and positive relatedness with others. One might call these the *curricula of original seeking*. For from this viewpoint, it would be the task of every human being to seek out that which provides for an inner sense of each of these six components and thus fulfill one's unique

---

national machine whose lives took on meaning largely in terms of some manifestation of national purpose. Work, sacrifice, and patriotism were Prussian ideals, all synthesized into an unquestioned obedience to the state. ...Credit for their accomplishment rested with the most organized system of education on the continent. ...The schools were an instrument of the state and their curricula were first and foremost a matter of national political policy. Through them, schoolmasters carried out a program of instruction which systematically, efficiently, and unswervingly aimed at achieving national rather than individual, familial, or local goals."

This was to become Horace Mann's model for Massachusetts (this despite the fact that, during his visit to Prussia, Messerli notes, almost all the schools were closed!) The military model was pretty clear from its inception: train a small elite in thinking/leadership skills, a slightly larger class with technological skills, and the rest in obedience. Later, with the system spreading widely throughout America, and having made clear his own distrust of democratic ideals and the placing of political power in the hands of the people, Mann was to write, "We who are engaged in the sacred cause of education are entitled to look upon all parents as having given hostage to our cause."

I would only add that the ubiquity and fundamental sameness of modern school systems—regardless of nation, economic system, political ideology, or form of social organization—indicates that this hostage-taking has now achieved the status of a universally accepted, essentially religious enterprise.

inner nature, and the job of every educator is to help each child find it. This is what the voyage of self-discovery is, ultimately, all about. At the end of the day, be it at the end of their life, or at the end of the education of their youth, our children need to be able to answer the question, not "What do I know?" but "Who am I?" Not "What did I learn", not "What did I buy", not even "What do I need", but "Who am I?" And, with our nurturance, they should be able to find for themselves the inner vision of a life, and the courage to pursue it.

* * * * *

It has been asserted that we are destined to know the dark beyond the stars before we comprehend the nature of our own journey...but we also know that our inward destination lies somewhere a long way past the reef of the Sirens, who sang of knowledge but not of wisdom.

—Loren Eisely

The great wonder is that we are on our voyages together, but not in the same boat. Our little barks have met up under this great expanse of cloud and sky, and, for a time at least, we journey forth in tandem.

I am grateful for the opportunity. And here I speak of homeschooling for its gifts to us as parents, rather than as a burdensome obligation of the parent to the child. It doesn't last all that long. I have chosen to use the opportunity to be warmed by my children's light, even as my own shadow grows longer and stretches forth into the evening. Or perhaps, more accurately, to see my own reflection in it. And I have embraced the opportunity, to use the words of Janusz Korczak, the great Polish-Jewish educator who ended up running an orphanage surrounded by the carnage of the Warsaw Ghetto, to "Seek in that stranger who is your child the undiscovered part of yourself." My children help me discover, or rediscover, my own *daimon*, my inner nature.

I don't want to over-romanticize here, but homeschooling provides us with the opportunity to embrace the world through our children. We are blessed with a second chance. But to do so requires a repertoire that goes beyond what most of us experienced in our own education. In school, rather more than we ever learned how to learn, most of us learned how to *teach*. We learned, despite the often admirable intentions of our teachers, that teaching means dispensing denatured, non-contextual knowledge that often intimidates, confuses, and lulls as often as it awakens, informs, and animates. We learned that teaching involved the prescription of moral platitudes and the preaching of cheap virtues, with respect and obedience imposed through manipulation, admonition, and compulsion. We learned that the Golden Rule has no place in the world of education, for teachers would regularly engage in behaviors in "educating" us that they would never countenance if directed at themselves.

And so what I hope you will find in this book—whether you are just contemplating homeschooling, are a new homeschooler, or have been on this voyage for a long time—is the resolve to expand your repertoire. There will be few blueprints, maps, or charts of the ocean upon which you and your child find yourselves, but I do hope you will discover a gyroscope to help keep your little boat righted, and an occasional lodestar to provide you with a few moments of comfort when the waters are swirling. And maybe, just maybe, the courage to explore the further sea-splattered reaches of the heart and mind.

Don't take anything I write for granted. Test it against the light of your own experience, *experimentally*. We are all big kids here, and we've earned the right by shouldering the responsibility. Take as your own the words of Rumi, the great Sufi poet-mystic:

> *But don't be satisfied with poems*
> *And stories of how things*
> *have gone with others.*
>
> *Unfold your own myth,*
> *Without complicated explanation,*
> *so everyone will understand*
> *the passage, "We will have opened you."*
>
> *Start walking toward Shams.**
>
> *Your legs will get heavy*
> *and tired. Then comes a moment*
> *of feeling the wings you've grown*
> *lifting.*[3]

---

*   The Great Teacher.

3   Rumi, Jalal Al-Din, *The Illustrated Rumi*, translated by Coleman Barks, illustrated by Michael Green. New York, NY: Broadway Books, 1997.

* * * * *

This book is a collection of pieces I have written since the publication of *And the Skylark Sings with Me: Adventures in Homeschooling and Community-Based Education* (New Society Publishers, 1999), though some have earlier roots. Some have been published previously in my "My Word!" column in *Home Education Magazine*, while others have appeared in *Home Educator's Family Times*, *The Link*, *Growing Without Schooling*, and *California Homeschooler*. While a few appear almost unchanged from their original publication, others have been edited or significantly expanded, reflecting new thoughts on previously introduced subjects.

Several of the pieces began life as lectures and workshop presentations. In the past three years, I have spoken with homeschoolers in Washington, Oregon, California, Florida, Virginia, District of Columbia, Maryland, New Jersey, New York, Connecticut, Massachusetts, Maine, Utah, Ohio, Indiana, Texas, and British Columbia, and have found homeschoolers both a source of inspiration and challenge. Still others took shape as dialogues on various e-mail lists, most notably the Quaker Homeschooling Circle, to whose members I am especially grateful.[4]

Finally, there are some materials being published here for the first time. Often they have had a long gestation period, and have been the product of dialogues with friends and colleagues ranging well beyond the homeschooling community, and well beyond the borders of this continent. The long three-part meditation on social studies, for example, arose initially in brief correspondence I had with a sixth grade teacher who wanted to find better ways to teach about the very diversity that existed in her own classroom, but felt actively constrained by the history textbook. To all of you I convey my thanks.

More than a few schoolteachers, educators, and parents with kids in public schools have indicated to me that the materials to be found herein would be of great utility if available to a wider public. Of course, I hope this book finds a ready audience wherever it can be of use. But after substantive deliberations with my publisher, I have decided to stick to my knitting, and have kept this book focused on what I believe I can do best: reassure would-be or new homeschoolers, and help expand the repertoire and thinking of

---

4   If you are interested in checking out the Quaker Homeschooling Circle, you can find us at www.topica.com under our name. We welcome Friends and fellow travelers, homeschoolers and other seekers. For more information about Friends generally, you can find just about everything at www.quaker.org.

more experienced ones. However, please don't hesitate to give a copy to your schoolteacher mother—I gave one to mine!

Themes will be found to repeat within this volume. I have not attempted to edit out the repetitions, but rather to maintain the completeness of each individual essay. If you are a busy homeschooling parent (or, for that matter, *any kind* of parent), one essay per sitting might be the maximum for which you have time. So I have worked to assure that each piece can stand on its own.

I take full responsibility for everything that is written here, and none whatsoever for how you decide to use it. You must act according to your own Light, not mine. Make sure to take the pizza out of the box and remove the wrapping *before* you put it in the oven, and remember to heed the cautionary note on that jar of nuts you just purchased: "Warning: May contain nuts." *Raisa ipso locutor*. Things are often as they seem.

Unlearning All the Time

A homeschooling mom of an obviously precocious ten-year-old writes me with a problem:

> We read in *The New York Times* that scientists have now discovered that the universe is flat. Among the implications of this cited is that the Big Bang theory (of the creation of the universe) is almost certainly wrong. I wondered wryly what they'll do down the street at the brand-new, multi-million dollar Space Center at the American Museum of Natural History, which is very cutting edge and has a whole room dedicated to the Big Bang. Today's *Times* carries an article about physicists who have reportedly proven that light can be accelerated beyond the speed of light, thereby calling into question all of Einstein's theories.
>
> So how do we go about teaching our gotta-know-it-all kids even the basics of something like physics when suddenly some of the underlying assumptions have gone kaflooey? When every book that's out there is almost certainly wrong? Where do we begin? I don't want to give them materials that they're going to have to unlearn. Where do we find educational materials that are as timely as needed....

So there it was staring me in the face, a subject for my inaugural column for *Home Education Magazine*. But where to begin? My first impulse was to giggle. Flat universe. I could form a religiously anachronistic "Round (or "Spherical") Universe Society", where we could get together, eat red M&Ms, get high by sniffing ditto machine fluid, type silly messages on our Kaypros and Commodore 64s (without, of course sending them to each other), and watch old "Son of Flubber" movies on Betamax. Those of us who tend toward the rotund would be pleased to learn that our 'amplitude on the horizontal plane' is really only an illusion, and that we are all really flat along with the rest of the universe. (Weight-loss tycoon Jenny Craig will have to employ an astrophysicist in her public relations department if she hopes to stay in business.) Light traveling faster than light I can only appreciate poetically, or reminisce about Flash Gordon. My older daughter

Aliyah never bought the Big Bang to being with.

Three different kinds of responses immediately began to crowd in on me. The first temptation was to go to the Internet and find all the most wonderful up-to-the-minute websites, connections to research institutions and science-by-mail programs associated with universities, and the latest in journals, etc., etc. But I quickly realized this wasn't going to help much. Neither my friend nor her son was ever going to keep up with what is out there except in highly circumscribed areas, if that. The dizzying rate of progress in science these days seems to match or exceed the font of information to be found on-line. It will put her well ahead of the science teacher in the local junior high school, but it wouldn't address her underlying question: how do we provide the most timely materials and theoretical constructs, much of which neither she nor the junior high science teacher could be expected to understand?

My second inkling was to respond, "Just read *The Times* and have your son read it, too. After all, they pay people to keep up with this stuff, and to write it in language that (with some work) we might all be able to understand. It will set off a new round of questioning and knowledge quests in our children, and we too might learn a thing or two along the way."

When Aliyah was working through her high school biology (which we did via a distance learning course with the University of Missouri—cdis.missouri.edu), she'd find errors all the time (based on her reading of *Scientific American*) and would come to me with her complaints. What she was learning about, even if she didn't immediately realize it, was the process of scientific revisionism, and how textbooks (and teachers who parrot them) aren't holy writ. A good lesson! We'd reinforce the lesson by having her write the publisher whenever she'd come upon an error. (Never received a single response.) To turn a title of one of John Holt's wonderful books on its head, my daughter came to understand through this experience, as almost no children ever do in school (and especially not the "good" students), that education is really about "unlearning all the time"!

So I wouldn't hesitate to give the kids that old 1962 *World Book Encyclopedia* currently spontaneously generating silverfish in the attic of your 'flat' house, or those wonderful Jules Verne 19th Century science adventures, or H.G. Wells' *The Time Machine*. Just make sure you talk about how times change. Your kids will learn to understand and appreciate that—they're changing, too!

Like a little project? Sit down one afternoon with your child and brainstorm with her (without correcting!) what she currently believes and thinks she knows about the world—nature, science, society, history, etc.—make it fun. Then agree to put the list away to be pulled out again next year on the same date, and let her see how her beliefs and knowledge have been altered. (If you're into assigning writing projects, "How My Knowledge of the World Has Changed" is a great topic, and will help your child on the road to greater self-awareness.)

But I confess—I was an English major. That's no particular qualification for writing this column (Helen and Mark, the editors and publishers of *Home Education Magazine*, never asked for my degrees), but it does affect the way I think about learning science. For it has always seemed to me that what children really need to know is that science is not just a series of "facts". Rather, it is the ability to tell a good story, based on available evidence. And when the evidence changes, the story gets transformed along with it.

I think of it rather like a game of Clue, although instead of "who done it", where, and with what weapon ("Colonel Mustard in the billiard room with a candlestick"), science is a "what done it", "how done it", and "why done it". Now I'm not sure there is any direct connection between succeeding at Clue and winning the Nobel Prize for physics, but the principles are the same. And anyone who has spent time in a doctor's office has observed a physician construct an illness narrative based on the available evidence, change the story based on new evidence, and concoct a prefigurative tale of pharmaceutical employed, behavior changed, and health restored. (A little bit of prayer in the mix probably wouldn't hurt.)

So, homeschool mom, thanks for your question, and here's the answer I've been encircling. The key to a good science education is not ensuring the availability of the most up-to-the-minute facts, which by definition will change in the next minute. It lies in helping our children understand the process of science, the stories it tells, and why and how those stories change.

The basis of this scientific storytelling, indeed the basis of all scientific inquiry, is freedom. You can fill your kids up with facts and concepts, but if they never experience the freedom to construct and take responsibility for their own stories, they will never be able to appreciate what the process of science is all about. Don't make them memorize the Linnaean classification—kingdom, phylum, class, order, family, genus, etc. (most will be able to do so when they need to anyway)—have them make their own, based on colors, or size, or number of legs, or speed, the permutations are endless. Do the same with the four food groups—the accepted chart from the USDA is all a marketing ploy anyway, and everyone knows that one should always eat more of the foods at the top of the pyramid (like chocolate ice cream!)—that's why they're at the top! The kids' charts may not reflect accepted scientific understandings, but what the process will do, even more critically, is help them organize a clear sense of their own experience. And that's what doing science is all about. Or should be.

Invite your child to join you in expanding your joint powers of scientific observation. Don't worry about lacking the latest in equipment—the most advanced scientists are always complaining that they don't have it either! Maria Mitchell, the first female American astronomer and first woman elected to the American Academy of Sciences, who at age 12 started setting ships' chronometers for sea captains by the stars, once said "A small apparatus well used will do wonders...Newton rolled up the cover of a book; he put a small glass at one end, and a large brain at the other—it was enough." In other words, all the fancy equipment does is extend your five senses. If you can't use your unaided senses to discriminate now, the apparatus won't help one bit. Join the local Audubon chapter and go bird-watching. Plant wildflower seeds on your front lawn and see what comes up (maybe even map it!). Go to star parties sponsored by the local astronomy club or the regional astronomical league—you'll find hundreds or even thousands of astrophysicists, auto repairmen, Internet-surfing teenagers, childcare workers, and short-order cooks all united in their knowledge quests. (You can find a list in *Astronomy Magazine*—www.astronomy.com) Get some high boots and walk through marshes and splash in puddles. Weigh and measure your pets.

Have fun. Scientists do.

The Code Cracker and the Information Hound

Reading. Sigh. Let me let you in on a dirty little secret. *All* children, in a literate culture, learn to read.

Okay—let's get the exceptions out of the way. Children with some type of organic brain syndrome (including fetal alcohol effects or genetic disorders), undiagnosed and uncorrected vision problems, and those suffering from some type of post-traumatic stress disorder—including, but not limited to that occurring as a result of child abuse or neglect, or scapegoating and emotional abuse inflicted upon them in the school environment—tend to have more difficulties than others. Of course, there are exceptions to the exceptions, too.

But putting aside this admittedly sizeable portion of the pre-adult population, all children learn to read. I must have spoken with 5,000 home-schooling parents—with more than 10,000 kids—over the past three years, and I can't remember a single instance of inability to read extending into the later teen years. (I'm sure they exist, but I can honestly say I haven't met up with any.)

Learning to read is like learning to ride a bicycle. Some kids are presented with training wheels at an early age. Some receive formal instruction. Some watch older siblings. Some are given shiny new bikes for Christmas, just the right size, and some forage some old beat-up balloon-tired Schwinn from a neighbor's dilapidated garage. Some peddle along on the sides of bicycles made for adults, the only available two-wheelers, so large they can't reach their leg over the cross-bar or otherwise get to the peddles. For some it takes months to get up the nerve to try. Others just jump on without any preparation whatsoever and ride away. Some are younger, some are older; some end up loving it, and others decide they have more important things to do with their time and energy.

The kids learn to read if there are lots of children's books in the house, adult books, or just a few old magazines. They learn to read if they are read aloud to from the time they can sit up, or if storytime is ignored. They learn to read if they watch Sesame Street, or the X Files, or if television isn't allowed in the house. They learn to read even if they are obsessed with computer games that require no reading, or if all they seem interested in is gymnastics or dance or the successors to Pokemon. They learn to read if they have powers of concentration that would put adults to shame, or if they never seem to be able to sit still.

Schools don't want parents to know this dirty little secret. If they did, school administrators wouldn't be able to trumpet school "successes", or mount campaigns for more funds for "failing schools", or hold mom and dad nervously enthralled to hear the report on Susie's progress on parent-teacher night, or blame the parents for the lack of it. Standardized tests would be known to measure the variables they actually do reliably gauge—neither student nor teacher performance, but average parental income and average years of parental education in the geographic area surrounding the school. If school districts really wanted to improve test scores, they'd deal with school air quality, which some have suggested may be the greatest single determinant of student performance. (In 20% of schools across the United States, as I learned in almost ten years of working for the Washington State Board of Health, indoor air quality does not meet industrial labor standards *for adults*, and the federal Occupational Safety and Health Administration won't issue pediatric indoor air standards for fear they might result in the closure of half the nation's educational institutions, or more.) The dirty little secret keeps parents emotionally and intellectually dependent upon the schools, a dependence they first learned when sitting in those little chairs behind those little desks themselves.[1]

Most teachers don't want to admit the dirty little secret to themselves. After all, their self-esteem depends upon denial. But give the teachers some credit: to be fair, they are often called upon, rightly or wrongly, to deal with the consequences of poor family or community life. They, like parents, take delight in watching their charges take their first few steps through the doors opened up by reading into the houses of wisdom. And they should, for it is no less a wonder, even if teachers are not in the least bit responsible for it.

---

1   William Torrey Harris, U.S. Commissioner of Education from 1889 to 1906, and probably the individual single-most responsible for the standardization of American education, saw the links between poor school environments—including bad air—and the 'rightful' purposes of education some hundred years ago. In *The Philosophy of Education*, published in 1906, Harris wrote: "Ninety-nine (students) out of a hundred are automata, careful to walk in prescribed paths, careful to follow the prescribed custom. This is not an accident but the result of substantial education, which, scientifically defined, is the subsumption of the individual." He wrote further, "The great purpose of school can be realized better in dark, airless, ugly places.... It is to master the physical self, to transcend the beauty of nature. School should develop the power to withdraw from the external world." See Gatto, John *The Underground History of American Education*, Oxford, NY: Oxford Village Press, 2001, 105-106.

The prevailing "wisdom" asserts that both the teachers and children must be held accountable. So if the child is not "ready" for reading, they must be ready for "reading readiness". Or, if not, the kids must be scrupulously prepared to get ready for reading readiness, if they haven't learned their consonants *in utero*.

No one, of course, expends a lot of energy talking about "bike readiness", and the idea that there is "early" bicycling or "late" bicycling would be considered utterly ludicrous. Teachers are themselves taught that children best learn to read, much as they learn everything else, on their own individual timetables. But when the standardized tests and related hype come down the pike from headquarters, the theory quickly goes out the window.

There are "methods" to the teaching of reading. The ones we hear most about are *phonics* and *whole language*. And here lies another dirty little secret: regardless of the method *taught*, I have never in my entire life met a single child who *learned* by either method to the total exclusion of the other. Never happens. Anyone who has ever listened to a conversation in a foreign language and noticed that the language has *sounds* that make up *words* that make up *sentences* that are used in *context* that result in *communication* (in some languages, like Italian, accompanied by some critically important hand gestures) can quickly understand why.

Whole language has been around for more than four decades, phonics quite a bit longer. I performed several database searches for articles regarding both methods published in the last 20 or so years, and came up with more than 6,000 of them, and a startling conclusion. Not a single study has ever been conducted on what I would consider to be the *only* important question: which method of instruction is most likely to result in *adults* who enjoy reading, and who are best able to use the skill in pursuing their vocational or avocational interests? Not one! It is not a difficult study to undertake (the Framingham health study has followed the behavioral habits and health indicators of thousands of nurses for more than 40 years). But researchers and teachers and administrators seem more concerned with whether six-year-old Jimmy knows his vowel sounds. This, and this alone, is what has come to be considered as accountability.

* * * * *

The fact is that learning to read is not particularly difficult, provided one has a reason to want to do it. Indeed, I'd suggest tentatively that the best method of helping your homeschooled child along in acquiring the skill may have most to do with *why* she wants to acquire it in the first place. (Schoolteachers never get to ask this question, or if they do, they seem trained to disregard the answer.) In watching my two kids, and in talking with dozens of homeschooling parents and their children, I have found that would-be readers seem to come in two garden varieties (of course, these proclivities exist along a spectrum rather than pre-packaged as frozen foods): *the code cracker* and *the information hound*. There may be other varieties, I imagine, but they've never appeared in my garden.

My younger daughter Meera was a code cracker. We never could read to her, as she never would sit still long enough to listen to a story, and besides, stories didn't contain anything worth knowing anyway. She learned the letters somewhere along the way—we don't remember how, but *Sa, Pa, Fa,* and *Ma* (the little phonics quadruplets in the overpriced workbook) didn't strike her as information worth having either, and so, from her perspective, it was a waste of time.

What Meera wanted was *power*, specifically the power available to adults as a result of *our* reading skill. She didn't like being told what she could eat in a restaurant, and believed that we were holding out on her when it came to the available choices (we were). So she wanted to read the menu for herself. We'd travel to Seattle and back, and when she would ask how long it would be before we reached our destination, she was tired of hearing "fifteen minutes" or "soon"—she was convinced we were lying (and, from her perspective, we were). So she needed to figure out the names of the various exits on the highway, and plot time/velocity/distance ratios in her head. (Five- and six-year-olds do this, one quickly learns.) She wanted to be able to read the food labels in the grocery store so she could better participate in the decision-making process—after all, she'd have to eat this stuff. What did the sale flyers say that came inside the newspaper? (Given the opportunity, she still loves to shop.) Could she help pick out our next video rental, sort the mail, or figure out where to call to learn how to "lose 30 pounds in 30 days"? (At age 5, she weighed all of 33 pounds.)

She simply wanted to crack the adult code. None of this, she quickly figured out, was going to be found in books. That's not where power lay. And *Sa, Pa, Fa,* and *Ma* was not going to be an especially efficient way of getting it. Meera learned to read music about the same time she learned to read English. She didn't need to, as being a very gifted pianist, it was easier to learn all of her Bach and Beethoven by heart, but she was tired of being looked at as the baby at her teacher's student recitals. All the other kids, much less gifted, brought music up to the piano, and she wanted to as well. Now, of course, she can sight-read almost anything. Her reading of English was helped along by the fact that her book of Gershwin songs had the words printed along with the piano music, and if she could follow along quickly enough, she could double the entertainment power of her musical prowess with her family, relatives, and friends by singing along with her playing.

For the code cracker, a little phonics might help, but it is not a particularly effective way for her to get where she wants to go. So she trained us to give it to her straight. The more efficient way is to memorize whole words, and the context in which they are likely to appear. This will lead to some interesting reading malapropisms as new words are mastered. After polishing off a short biography of Helen Keller, Meera told us insistently that following four years at Radcliffe College, Keller "grad-a-too-tooed with horns" (graduated with honors), and grew into a beautiful "duck-a-tack" (an educated woman?). The main point is that the approach she took to reading (with our assistance) needed to satisfy her need for meaning (and for power!) rather than ours for teaching (an expression of the same).

My older daughter Aliyah was an information hound, although it took us awhile to cotton to it. She (and we) enjoyed the warm and fuzzy family togetherness as we read the incomparable Vera Williams' trilogy *A Chair for My Mother*, *Something Special for Me*, and *Music, Music for Everyone*, would add the necessary missing words as we recited Maurice Sendak's *Chicken Soup with Rice*, and was captivated, at least initially, by the library videotapes of "Reading Rainbow". We would make little books out of her own stories, which she would spend many happy hours illustrating.

Looking back on it, Aliyah, Ellen and I had a wonderful time in the "reading readiness" years, but other than watching us exercise our literacy skill, I'm not sure it had any significant effect on Aliyah's future reading whatsoever. I suspect she actually didn't want to read for a time because she (correctly) figured out that she would lose the closeness of the storytime experience; she also realized that the stories she made up in her head were at least as interesting (to her) as any to be found in the volumes we lugged home from the library.

What pushed her over the reading edge, finally, was a keen awareness of our ignorance. She came to the hopefully not-too-harsh realization, having executed an exhaustive environmental scan of our impoverished brains, that we knew absolutely nothing about wolves or wildlife habitat, birds, trees, or marine life. Having come to the conclusion that her parents, for all their good qualities (thank you), were pretty hopeless for the kinds of things she wanted to know, she went from no reading at all at six to college textbooks on cetaceans at six-and-a-half. Aliyah enjoyed some fiction, too, but wouldn't take on a book until she read (or had us read to her) the last chapter first. Why put in all that energy if you are only going to be disappointed? In hindsight, instead of (or in addition to) reading to her Helen Lester's hilarious *It Wasn't My Fault* or Mitch Inkpen's *If I Had a Pig* (both of which my wife and I adored), we should have been paging through *Scientific American*.

The information hound often has a rich conversational life (and vocabulary) developed at whatever age (but before extensive reading), so she can put a little knowledge of phonics to good use almost immediately as words are placed in contexts she can understand. Unlike the code cracker, who may be satisfied with the knowledge to be gained through the reading skill once the desired power is achieved, the information hound is more likely to want to luxuriate in feeding her head. While the code cracker tries to find the required information as quickly as possible, uses it, and moves on (my wife Ellen used to call Meera a "Dragnet" reader, and it still well applies), the information hound simply seeks input, often for its own sake. The code cracker needs exactly the right book at the library, and utilizes the encyclopedia to obtain facts. The information hound will often enjoy being given the elementary, middle, high school, and college versions simultaneously of whatever subject matter she is interested in (and we early took to this practice when we brought Aliyah to the library), and will sleep with miscellaneous volumes of the encyclopedia open to seemingly random pages next to her pillow. The code cracker will always press the "search" button; the information hound, "browse". The code cracker will enjoy playing "Jeopardy", while the information hound may easily become offended at being asked questions for which she knows you already have the answer.

The information hound may also find values in written material neither intended by you nor even by the author. My favorite example of this in our household occurred when Aliyah was ten. We both watched an entrancing show on public television about fractal geometry and the Mandelbrot sets, those wonderful repeating spiral designs that apparently can be found throughout the natural world. Following the program, Aliyah asked me to get some books from the library on fractal geometry. All the available ones were college textbooks, well beyond my own current mathematical capacities and certainly beyond hers. Nonetheless, she took one of the textbooks to her platform bed, where it remained open for the next six weeks. When the library began to pester me, I asked her whether I could take it back. Aliyah burst into tears, pleading with me not to return it.

"Ali," I said, "You really didn't understand much of it, did you? I mean, I sure didn't."

"No," she agreed.

"Well, why then can't I bring it back to the library?"

"Because," she sniffled, "Because it reminds me of how much I have to look forward to."

Eventually, of course, if all turns out well, the code cracker sees there is more to reading than a hammer to be used in power relationships, and the information hound figures out that knowledge may have more uses than personal entertainment. And off they go on their merry ways. So we learn to relax and enjoy it, and realize that, in the ultimate scheme of things, we—parents, teachers, or simply adults who take delight in children—already had our turn, and are only along for the most glorious of rides.

* * * * *

No consideration of reading is complete without a nod and a wink toward Frank Smith's masterful *Reading Without Nonsense* (New York, NY: Teachers College Press, 1997). There is probably no single book that is more widely purchased and read by future public school teachers, and more thoroughly forgotten and ignored in teaching practice. Dr. Smith's thinking can be summed up in four simple sentences: 1) All methods of teaching reading can achieve some success, with some children, some of the time; 2) Children seem able to learn to read *despite* the method of instruction that is employed; 3) Children *cannot be taught to read*; at best, we make it possible for them to learn to read (and that's probably being charitable); and 4) We do not have to train children to learn, or even account for their learning; all we have to do is avoid interfering with it.

Hebetudinous

Spell 'hebetudinous'!"

I had just fallen out of bed and, with eyes not yet fully functioning (ah, the evils of middle age), had staggered my way to the stove to put on water for my morning coffee. There was Meera, my 10-year-old, already awake (a rare event), and she didn't even say "good morning!"

"What did you say?" I mumbled, trying to get my ears in focus.

"Spell 'hebetudinous'."

I thought I heard a percussive sound. *Hepatudinous*. Maybe to do with an enlarged liver. Something like "splenetic"? New one on me.

"Can you use it in a sentence?" (I really wasn't stalling for time. Well, to be honest, maybe a little....)

"He was hebetudinous," she replied, impatiently waiting for me to blunder.

Fat help that was. And so I went ahead and misspelled it, based on my extensive knowledge of Greek body parts.

She laughed in glee. Stumped the chump.

My wife Ellen gave me the story behind how "hebetudinous" came to be in our household. While at work, Ellen received a call from Meera.

"Ali called me stupid!" complained Meera about her 13-year-old sister.

"Put her on," said my wife. "Aliyah, if you are going to call your sister names, at least use more interesting ones."

There. That would put an end to that! Isn't it great when you can end squabbling among siblings so easily?

"You're hebetudinous," said Aliyah, having found a literal way around the implied prohibition.

"What's hebetudinous?" asked Meera.

"Go look it up," replied Aliyah.

"How do you spell it?"

Aliyah spelled it for her. Meera got out her dictionary. There it was. Hebetudinous.

Adj. Lacking in intelligence; blockheaded, dense, doltish, obtuse, lethargic. Dull and stupid.

* * * * *

Meera (left) and Aliyah (right), Autumn 2002.   Photo: David H. Albert

Spelling is wrapped up in a societal myth. For those of you who have for-gotten your freshman sociology class (or never had one), a societal myth is a story or premise (whether it is true or false is irrelevant) that guides our attitudes and shapes how we make concrete life arrangements or enable social institutions to function.

The societal myth embodied in spelling is a simple one: "Spelling is a signifier of intelligence. Good spellers are more intelligent; bad spellers less so." The salient feature of this particular societal myth is that we all know deep down that it is untrue. In fact, when declared as baldly as I have just done, it is downright laughable, isn't it?

If you ever have the opportunity, take your kids to the wonderful Revolutionary War history exhibit at the Smithsonian Institution in Washington, DC. There you will find on display documents and letters from our nation's founding fathers. Don't be surprised, however, if, after examining two or three of the display cases, your 12-year-old turns to you with his latest discovery. "Hey, Mom," he'll say, in a voice loud enough that everyone in the exhibit room can hear, "These guys can't spell."

And you'll look more carefully yourself and see that your son is cor-rect. Washington and Hamilton, John Jay and Samuel Adams, Patrick Henry and Richard Henry Lee, they all spell, well, shall we say, "different-ly". It's not only a matter of half the "s"s looking like "f"s, or noting histor-ical changes that have occurred in spelling since the last half of the18th Century. No, it is evident that what was important was communication, pure and simple, and regularized spelling had nothing to do with it. It gives new meaning to the slogan, "good enough for government work," for, indeed, it was good enough for the creation of a nation.

The whole idea of regularized spelling and "spelling" as a school sub-ject was the creation of Noah Webster and, later, the rise of public educa-tion. (Though at least if we had adopted Noah Webster's reforms, we could have been rid of all those ridiculous silent "e"s.) And the goal of the school people had nothing to do with communication. It had everything to do with compliance and control, pure and simple, the antithesis of the Revolutionary spirit. With it came the creation of the societal myth. Since the largest portion of immigrants to America in the late nineteenth and early twentieth century—at whom public education was largely directed—came from countries where spelling is truly (or at least close to being) pho-netic, and in which languages they may already have been literate, spelling was a simple mechanism for judging their children to be intellectually infe-rior, not deserving of educational opportunities, and, in the final analysis, socially unfit; in short, *hebetudinous*. Except the greatest fear was not that they were congenitally dull and stupid (like the images already projected onto African-Americans, who were already being denied decent education), but rather that (like the fears surrounding African-Americans), they might be untamed and, in the end, untameable. Public education quickly became the bulwark of a "civilized" society against the alien savages whose bodies, ironically, were essential to keeping the industrial combine humming. (The same people who gave us public education also brought us early twentieth-century eugenics, and you know where that ended up![1])

If we peel away another layer, we find another societal myth at the core of American public education: while it exists ostensibly to create new opportunities (which it arguably does for the few), the major purpose of public education, at which it was spectacularly successful in the nineteenth century and remains so to this day, is to *limit* these opportunities ("ration-

---

1   There is much written on this subject, but a good place to start would be Selden, Steven, *Inheriting Shame: The Story of Eugenics and Racism in America*. New York, NY: Teachers College, Press, 1999. Also see Sotskepf, Alan, "The Forgotten History of Eugenics," *Rethinking Schools*, 13(3), Spring 1999.
www.rethinkingschools.org/Archives/13_03/eugenic.htm
        From 1900 to 1930, virtually every major educator in the U.S. other than John Dewey (and notably including David Starr Jordan, president of Stanford University; Charles W. Eliot, president of Harvard University; University of Wisconsin President Glenn Frank; University of Chicago educator Charles Judd; Henry Fairfield Osborn, president of the American Museum of Natural History; Edward Lee Thorndike of Columbia Teachers College; and Robert M. Yerkes, Harvard professor and president of the American Psychological Association) supported a program of eugenics, or "selective breeding", as imperative to defend and improve the quality of the national character. This was the source of much of Adolf Hitler's thinking on this issue. In 1931, the New York Commissioner of Education asked (in the publication *Eugenical News*) whether since "the greatest care is exercised in the breeding of live stock, is it not vastly more important that the human race be improved?" and shouldn't teachers do whatever is in their power to prevent the "haphazard mating of human beings?"
        Often repeating the slogan popularized by Princeton University biologist E.G. Conklin that, "Wooden legs are not inherited, but wooden heads are," a strong belief in biological determinism and eugenics (as well as the futility of environmental changes) was taught through biology textbooks in junior high and high schools well after Hitler came to power (some of them actively praised his efforts), and even as late as 1948. In the widely used textbook *Animal Biology* written by University of Wisconsin biologist M.F. Guyer (Fourth Edition—New York, NY: Harper Brothers, 1948), we find the following gem: "The greatest danger to any democracy is that abler members and less prolific types shall be swamped by the overproduction of inferior strains. This has been the fate of past civilizations—why not America?" So much for assuming sex education in the schools is a recent development!

alize" would probably be a better term), while training people to accept these limitations.[2] Spelling is just one of the many screening mechanisms. We refuse to accept the institutions' limitations in meeting our children's intellectual, emotional, and spiritual needs—isn't that ultimately why we homeschool?

* * * * *

As a professional writer and editor, what I want my kids to learn is that communication has power. Of course, they began to learn that as infants— the right combination of crying and smiling enables them, in most cases, to get them what they desire! Later, it becomes a bit more complicated.

The tools of written communication have their own power, and can be wielded as weapons in and of themselves, as first Aliyah and then Meera, like millions of other kids, have learned. Uninterested in spelling for the first ten years of her existence, Meera now totes around a diction- ary like some people I know carry a Bible, and sleeps with it next to her pil- low. She has become infatuated with *soul*, "n. The immaterial essence of an individual life; the spiritual principle embodied in human beings or the universe," she reads aloud to a neighborhood playmate. "It's quite a bit dif- ferent than a flat fish or the bottom of my shoe," she urges upon her friend Courtney, who has no idea she has wandered into Meera's House of Homonyms. The game doesn't last for very long, though. The problem with wielding the tools as weapons or exercises in one-up-man-ship (rather than using them for what they are intended) is that some people can get hurt, and, as we know from our own school days, all-too-often they do. Left to their own devices, the kids, if not budding sociopaths, will end their game once there is too much experience of pain; unfortunately, the school administrators, who have not been socialized properly, cannot be expected to do the same.

So how do we teach spelling? Well, we don't. It is not because we seek to express solidarity with the organizers of the Boston Tea Party by not

---

Such thinking was still to be found in the biology textbooks in the 1960s. I remember being taught about the inherited feeblemindedness and criminality of the Kallikak and Jukes fam- ilies, and the inherited superiority of the Edwards. Growing up in New York City, I never met any Edwardses, but my 9th grade homeroom teacher was name "Kavelak", and behind his back we used to joke about his name incessantly.

2   U.S. Commissioner of Education William Torrey Harris, who could be said to have overseen the birth of the modern public education system in America, wrote in 1889, "Our schools have been scientifically designed to prevent over-education from happening.... The average

encouraging the kids to make the best possible use of the tools. On the contrary, we make a special effort in our family to ensure that our children understand the societal myth: if their written communications do not reflect conventional spelling practices, others are likely to take that as a

---

American [should be] content with their humble role in life, because they're not tempted to think about any other role."

Beginning around 1905, a new organizational scheme for public education—the Gary Plan (named after the town in Indiana in which it was first implemented)—was initiated. Under the Gary Plan, school subjects were departmentalized, entailing the constant movement of children from class to class—thus inhibiting any deeply engaged exploration of any subject—and requiring schoolteachers to teach the same subject and same lesson again and again, like factory workers assigned to tightening a single bolt. (There were other, more appealing elements, such as ongoing links between the schools and community life, which, however, were never integrated into other Gary-like experiments taking place throughout the rest of the country.) A 1916 analytical report by the New York educator Abraham Flexner found the Gary Plan to be a total failure, "offering insubstantial programs and a general atmosphere which habituated students to inferior performance."

There were protests. In New York City, thousands of children and their primarily immigrant parents protested their children being given "half-rations" of education. Thousands of demonstrators shut down Public School #171, which had adopted the Gary Plan, and riots spread to schools and neighborhoods throughout Manhattan, Brooklyn, and the Bronx. More than 300 children were arrested, most of them Jewish. The cause of the protest was that the Gary Plan deliberately dumbed down the school, thus limiting the opportunities available to low-income children. While the Gary Plan itself disappeared, its worst aspects—a 'platoon approach' to scheduling designed to allow double enrollment of pupils in a single building and hence save money—was quickly adopted by school systems throughout the nation.

Closely following on the heels of the New York School riots, the chair of the Psychology Department at Princeton University and the nation's leading psychometrician, Henry Herbert Goddard, published his public policy opus *Human Efficiency and Levels of Intelligence* (Princeton University Press, 1920). Noting that government schooling was about "the perfect organization of the hive," Goddard argued that social and economic inequality was both good and necessary because some people are smarter (and hence more deserving) than others. Intelligence testing would be a useful tool to convince the lower classes of their inferiority, and discourage them from attempting to rise above their rightful station. Through the training of hundreds of the nation's educational psychologists, Goddard's thinking quickly became a guiding force in American education. Nowadays, parents, no less than teachers, school administrators, or college admissions officers, think nothing of limiting the opportunities available to children solely on the basis of test results, and based on tests employing questions that they haven't even seen, all confirming the self-fulfilling prophecy that the kids (and the parents!) receive both the education and opportunities they deserve!

sign that they are hebetudinous, *even though both parties to the communication know this is not true.*

In our experience, good spelling comes from lots of reading. It doesn't matter (for this purpose) whether this reading capability came to be as a result of the *sa pa fa* method or from recognizing whole words. (As I've already indicated, I have trouble imagining kids who don't actually use both, regardless of how we teach them!) No amount of attempted explanation will derail them from believing that "i" before "e" except after "c" makes no sense except as an educational instrument of torture.

When the kids are writing, we have a rule (which means I'm sure we've broken it, of course): give them that for which they ask! If they request that a word be spelled, we give it to them straight—none of this "oh, what does it sound like?" or "do you know any words it rhymes with?" or "use your phonics" or "look it up". (I always thought this last was the most dimwitted suggestion, as dictionaries aren't designed for spelling inquiries.) No, we just give it to them, like we would to any adult who wasn't too embarrassed to ask (when was the last time you told your co-worker to use her phonics, or sounded out a word for him phonemically? And, indeed, how many of your colleagues or friends won't even ask for spelling assistance because they remember being shamed at school when they did so as children?)

I fully understand the usefulness of teaching the kids to use their knowledge of phonics or rhyme or dictionaries in figuring out how to spell a word, *but when they are writing is not the proper time.* When you interpose this extra task, you are upsetting the far more critical and delicate operation, which is their finding ways to communicate by effectively transferring thoughts and feelings from brain to paper or computer screen.

We do help the kids with their spelling, punctuation, grammar, and syntax *after* the words have been committed to paper, *if they ask.* If writing is part of the assignment we have agreed upon, joint editing will be a piece of the process. Doing the phonics or dictionary thing at this stage might be okay—just don't necessarily assume that it helps very much, at least for all children. But the editing, rather than the writing, stage is the time to equip the kids with new tools, which they then can decide to utilize or not as they choose.

We edit most "public" communications. This provides the perfect opportunity to talk about social conventions and societal expectations, and the differences between the public and private world. Yes, your seven- or eight-year-old can understand this (chances are she already does), but it will provide you both grounds for much future amusement.

Spelling games? It's time for a new one. The old one—"spell x-y-z"—is one of those school games cruelly aimed at uncovering a deficit, with a smug pat on the back, unnecessary word of praise, or $10,000 college scholarship awaiting when the deficit does not reveal itself in a competitive situation. Don't get me wrong: I take as much delight in homeschoolers' recent monopoly of the National Spelling Bee as the next homeschooler! (When I wrote this essay, I was enjoying the Seattle Mariners, too, even if I think of the ballpark as a taxpayer-subsidized, corporately owned-and-operated tavern with a ridiculously high cover charge and overpriced hotdogs.) But isn't the Spelling Bee really, as a *Washington Post* staff writer recently wrote, "an archaic exercise in brutality"? Viewing it on television, is the fascination much different from "Survivor II", as hundreds of prepubescent geeks (having been one myself, I remember the feeling) reveal their fatal flaws and are banished ignominiously from the island? I mean it's almost five hours of morbidly watching kids fail!

Try another game. Assume the kids already know how to spell it *right*. Ask them to figure out how many different alternate "creative" spellings they can come up with, based on analogies in sound with other words they know. Phonics. Phonix. Phanix. Phonnicks. Fanicks. Fonnix. Phaknicks. Fonicwz. (?) Educational value? Your kids will never forget how to spell the word correctly, and will have learned a little bit more about the absurdity of their mother tongue.

Need something for the car? Portmanteau words are the ticket. "Portmanteau", originally a large suitcase that opens up into two hinged compartments, was first appropriated to signify a new word formed by merging the sounds and meanings of two others by Lewis Carroll, who in this vein brought us *chortle* (chuckle+snort) and *galumph* (gallop+triumph), but failed with *slithy* (lithe+slimy). (Remember what Yogi Berra said about luggage? "Don't buy expensive luggage. After all, you only use it when traveling.") You already know plenty of portmanteaux: *motel* (motor+hotel), *brunch* (breakfast+lunch) (*lupper* never caught on, as it couldn't replace High Tea); *smog* (smoke+fog); *tangelo, dumbfounded, twirl, cockapoo, motorcade*. New ones are being created all the time: *simulcast, dancercise, frappuccino, netiquette, Medicare, breathalyzer*, and *Reaganomics* (which I think has something to with running up large public debts to pay for obsolete military equipment.) Now, it's your kids' turn: help them create their own. You may end up with your own private language. Your kids will learn that languages are always changing, and that words take on a life of their own.

Once they get the hang of it, don't be surprised if they find it totally *fantab-ulous*. (If you need some help getting started, visit Wonky Words at: learningedge.simpatico.ca/recess/fl/ww.html.)

You will be humbled in this process. It won't be long before your child is correcting you, or at least trying to. It will keep you on your verbal toes—keep the big dictionary in hiding for your own private use for a while; it will be your secret weapon! But not for long: your kids will find it and accuse you of trying to keep them barefoot and hebetudinous, and you'll have absolutely no defense.

At least, though, I'll be able to say I've done the dirty deed, for, if this essay does its work, *hebetudinous* will now have made its way into home-schooling kitchens across the nation, and breakfast may never be the same.

Potato-Heads

He that uses many words for explaining any subject, doth, like the cuttle-fish, hide himself for the most part in his own ink.
—John Ray, Naturalist (1627-1705)

Mr. Lucas, my sixth grade teacher at Public School # 131 AND Three-Quarters in New York City (I've changed the number to protect, well, I'm not exactly sure what I'm trying to protect, but it seemed like a good idea) had a plan. We were all going to leave his sixth grade class with absolutely perfect handwriting, and he was going to make sure that it happened *his* way. You see, he understood that our current state of imperfection wasn't our fault. It was a result of poor teaching and a lack of attention to detail in the earlier grades, and he, being in charge of us before we made the great leap forward to junior high school, was there to ensure the incoming students from P.S. 131 3/4 were not going to be found wanting. Or least not if he had any say in the matter.

Mr. Lucas was a former military man who fought in North Africa in WWII. One of his preferred activities was to regale us with stories of imbibing diverse varieties of African bug juice, thus making all the girls, including Stacy Schwartz who was already too hot from her new training bra (did they really need to be trained?), extremely uncomfortable. (Would "bug juice talk" now be considered a form of sexual harassment?) So his plan was simple: handwriting was to take place 45 minutes every day. During this time, beginning with capital "A", we were each to write ten lines of ten perfect letters (100, all the same), in Roman military formation, and once we had accomplished this and had them checked by him, we would be promoted on to the next letter.

Now my last name begins with "A", which had condemned me to the front-row righthand-side desk near the door for the past seven years, and made it difficult (but not impossible) for me to stare out at my favorite tree in the schoolyard. Occupational hazard, that last name beginning with A, and I was lucky not to have developed a permanent crick in my neck from perennially being forced to look left, or to have been permanently disfigured as a result like a galley slave chained in perpetuity to a single oar on the left side of the ship.

So, anyway, I did my ten lines of ten capital "A's," all with my

Waterman cartridge pen as neatly as I could (quite a trick, as most of the ink used to leak out all over my shirt pocket), and brought my paper up to Mr. Lucas' desk, behind Johnny LoSassini, the class artist, who was onto the capital "J"s before I could manage his name once without a lisp. Mr. Lucas, pen in hand, began to put big red "X"s (capitals or smalls, I couldn't tell) over a third of my "A"s, mumbling "Potato-head" or "Looks like a squished pear" or "Needs to go on a diet", and sent me back to my desk to create another *century*.

Days, and then weeks went by. At first, I used to approach Mr. Lucas' desk with some concern, hoping that my "A's" would finally pass muster so I could go on to "B"s. But no such luck. There were always potato-heads or beer-bellies or squished pears and lots of red "X"s on my paper. After about three weeks, with everyone else in my class moving ahead except me and my friend "A"rthur (wouldn't you know it? and Stacy, still in training, was already on "P"!), I began to become embarrassed, and then ashamed. After six weeks, the shame turned to barely concealed anger, and then, maybe three months into this exercise, I discovered that I didn't care anymore, and that it was really all right. After all, no matter where you were in the alphabet, you still had to spend your 45 minutes in handwriting.

In four-and-a-half months, and including more centuries assigned in daily homework, I drew a total of 27,923 capital "A's". The reason I know the count to this day is that my friend Arthur and I started to keep tabs, and wore the number of our red-stained "A's as badges of honor (I can't claim to have read *The Scarlet Letter* yet, but when I finally did, I imagined a black, cursive capital "A" with big red "X" on it. We were, however, deeply immersed in *The Red Badge of Courage*, which may have been more on point.)

I never would have escaped capital "A", except that in January, Mr. Lucas, normally a man of iron—a veritable Cal Ripken of the school-teaching world—who ruled the schoolyard during recess like the army lieutenant he was, and without a winter coat, got sick for two days, and a substitute came in who didn't quite know the rules. She, rather shapely as I remember, would walk around the room in a haze of cheap toilet water (I told this to my older daughter, and she burst out laughing, and the term still makes me inwardly smile), and as she passed your desk, if you'd hastily scribbled barely a line or two she would check your paper and you were on to the next letter. In two days, I went from capital "A" to lowercase "m".

I honestly don't remember if I ever finished the alphabet, but I do know that from that year forth, my handwriting has deteriorated into the inscrutable, and most of the letters between capital "A" and small "m" are a veritable wasteland. Oh, and what of Arthur, my partner in this tale of scrawl? He became a famous Park Avenue cardiologist, and I think he now uses a self-inking rubber stamp for his signature.

* * * * *

"Cases of dysgraphia in adults generally occur after some trauma," reports the National Institute of Neurological Disorders and Stroke of the National Institutes of Health. Hmm.

* * * * *

Q: *"Do you teach Zaner-Bloser or D'Nealian handwriting?"*

A: *"I think Zaner-Bloser and D'Nealian are perfectly capable of learning handwriting by themselves."*

My older daughter Aliyah had dysgraphia. The reason we knew is that she told us so. "The problem is," she'd say after staring at a blank piece of paper for what she would agree was a ridiculously long amount of time, "is that my headwriting is faster than my handwriting." Of course, I could have looked at this as a simple case of *asynchronous development*—like the Little League shortstop who could field, but hadn't yet learned how to hit a curve ball—and simply assumed it would come with time.

But since I'm supposed to know a bit more about writing than I do about baseball, and since Aliyah can neither field nor hit a curve ball, could care less about either and I don't expect that to change, my kids' writing commands my attention. *Dysgraphia*—and let's not get fancy here: all it means is "difficulty in writing"—is actually four separate problems: thinking clearly; finding subject matter and getting words from head to paper; the physical act of making meaningful ink appear; and editing. In working with both of my kids, we have found that isolating which of the four is the problem is half the solution. Then by refocusing, much of what we have come to call dysgraphia, over time, simply melts away. Or so has been our experience.

The first thing to do is to throw out "writing" assignments altogether. Once the kids regard what they are doing as "writing", and have come to the conclusion that writing is difficult, the emotional charge increases radically, and unnecessarily. If the purpose (yours and, you hope, that of your child) is to think about something and have it committed to paper, we've discovered the best way to go about it is to let your child do just that. If she has something to say, let her dictate it to you while you sit at the computer (you could do it in long-hand, but the computer display bestows instant results that a beginning reader can more likely read.). "Writing" has happened—and that's the most important thing.

There is a terrific advantage in starting this way. As a professional writer, editor, and writing coach, I teach that, with very few technical exceptions, good writing mimics speech. What better possible demonstration of this could there possibly be than having your child contemplate out loud and have her thought appear, complete with correct spelling, punctuation, and grammar, on paper! Let her admire her own handiwork. (She can reread it, of course, and with the gentlest of coaxing, decide whether she wishes to change any of the thoughts.)

Having trouble deciding on subject matter? For some kids, subject matter seems to come naturally; for others it is a grave stumbling block. Solution? In our house, it has always been thank-you notes. Our kids write thank-you notes for just about everything—to music teachers at the end of the year, to grandparents for birthday presents, to gymnastics coaches, to summer camp directors. Sometimes these notes are full three-page essays, and we have found they are received with great delight, thus reinforcing in our kids the understanding that writing occurs in a larger context of human social relationships.

Handwriting? Clearly, as a result of my school-induced trauma, this is not my cup-of-tea. But a good way to go, if this is the dysgraphical disorder, is to have your child copy out that already perfected thank-you note in long-hand. Since the thinking, grammar, punctuation, etc. are already taken care of, she can concentrate solely on making the card or letter as beautiful as she can. Allow your child to decorate the communication with colored pencils or paper cutouts. And if she has come to believe that her handwriting is too dreadful to be read by the recipient, offer to send the typed copy along with it. The point is to eliminate as many possible sources of trauma as can occur as a result of the writing experience.

But, for some, penpersonship may remain painful for a long period. This is the time to consider introducing the computer typing program, perhaps for ten minutes a day. Some of these are quite wonderful (we've especially liked Mavis Bacon in our house, but there seem to be plenty of good ones out there.) A suggestion? If your child takes piano lessons, append the typing program to piano practice, rather than to anything to do with "writing". The skills required are similar, and like the piano practice, where correct playing is instantly rewarded by the sought-after sound making its way to the ear, the typing computer games and scoring will provide similar feedback.

Is the dysgraphical disorder related to grammar, spelling, punctuation, capitalization? In my experience as a writing instructor working with adults, poor writing has two major causes. The first is unclear *thinking*—when the thought to be expressed is unclear, one form of written expression is as good as any other. The second is school-induced trauma in which mind-numbing attention is paid to the mechanics of writing at the expense of expression. I have been well paid to undo the damage. For some children, copious amounts of *good reading*, to the exclusion of any work on the mechanics of writing whatsoever—and sometimes for a period of years—will be all that is necessary for the mechanics to eventually fall into place, especially for a visual learner. For others, learning a foreign language may turn out to be a great help.

The concern here is not about writing at all, however, but about *editing*. We've made it a fairly strict rule in our house that we don't edit the kids' work unless they ask for it, or unless the work is public communication (i.e., will end up outside the house). I have the advantage, of course, of having them watch me edit my own work, often *ad infinitum*, and, with my older daughter, showing her the various drafts and discussing with her the reasons for the various editing decisions I have made. Children need to know that well-crafted written work does not emerge in stellar perfection among adults as from the head of Zeus.

There is nothing worse than spending serious time and energy committing one's thoughts and feelings reluctantly to paper and having it come back covered with big red "X"s, circles, cross-outs, and unreadable comments in the margins. (I only use green pen at work, but I don't think it helps much.) The goal for all writers is to become self-editors, and the best way to get there is by editing the work of others. In our house, the "Editor-in-Chief" Series from Critical Thinking Press (www.criticalthinking.com) does the trick. Each page has a short story supposedly written by a newspaper reporter, and a captioned picture containing important information. The editor (your child) has to find the number of errors specified, and then gets to physically rewrite the story so as to eliminate them. The kids will learn all the mechanics of writing, and fact-checking as well, without the need for any formal instruction—which may have "environmentally induced" the dysgraphia to begin with, whatever the underlying cause.

Aliyah became a national prize-winning poet (first published in a book at age 11), and essayist, and a decorated musical composer. She still "writes" slowly, and her handwriting, she would agree and hereby allows me to state, is still abominable (though I think it is closer to Arthur's than to my own.) We can live with that, and so can she. My younger daughter Meera has a stunningly beautiful hand, and her cards and letters are much appreciated by all who receive them.

What we didn't require along the way was the usual "positive self-talk" that goes along with much of what passes for dysgraphia remedia and remedial approaches to other learning disabilities. Perhaps Aliyah's condition was not as severe as those experienced by other kids—it is difficult to know. The only reason that we "diagnosed" the condition at all is because Aliyah told us she had it, and that it was upsetting, though I suspect (based upon no medical expertise whatsoever) that dysgraphia with a neurological etiology is somewhat rare. We simply assumed that if she had a disability, it was one that we could effectively work around. Otherwise, we likely would have simply assumed that her in-built compass wasn't ready to take on the writing challenge, and we might have ignored it entirely, with perhaps equally good results. What we do know is that by dumping the "writing assignments" (coupled with the fact that there were to be no comparisons either with schoolkids or through testing), working through the difficulty simply became a natural part of growing up. In fact, the entire experience reminds me most of Meera's *dysnexia*[1], and her almost futile attempts to learn how to swim. As a gymnast, she, like most greyhounds I'm told, has absolutely no body fat and hence physically can't float, and no amount of positive self-talk will add to her lightness of being.

---

1   "Difficulty in swimming". I made this one up, which doesn't mean it isn't a perfectly good word, with assistance from the folks at Bolchazy-Carducci Publishers. They, however, don't want to take any credit for it. If your kids decide to learn Latin or Greek, this is a great place to start: www.bolchazy.com. Please note, however: dysnexia is not to be confused with dysNexia©, which is one of those copyrighted corporate words referring to "a pandemic cultural learning disability" that prevents leaders and executives from seeing "The Big Picture". (I like mine better.)

A Travel Excursion of the Mind

A group of homeschooling mothers gathered together in a circle to discuss unschooling approaches to their children's education.

"I can't get mine to do any math," moaned one, and heads began to nod.

"Mine neither," whined another. "She never wants to."

The heads rolled and shook more vigorously, and soon I found myself sitting—metaphorically, of course, and with no offense intended—amidst a Greek chorus of heartrending laments, sighs, and whimpers, perhaps something like a modern homeschooling rendition of Euripedes' *The Trojan Women*.

"I've tried to convince her that math is a skill she'll really use later in life, but she isn't buying it."

I've pondered this for some time now. Perhaps the kids have a sixth sense about them. They somehow know it is a lie. Most of the math I learned in school I have never used. Not once. Nary a differential equation, nor a logarithm, nor the area of a scalene triangle has wriggled or waddled across my path in more than 30 years, and I use a significant amount of quantitative analysis in my day job. My carpenter friend Bill, who flunked geometry and dropped out of high school, makes use of angles and sides all the time; I am yet to encounter a colleague who still uses a sliderule.

Consider the dukes and duchesses, counts and countesses, marquis and marquises, earls and earlesses of earlier times. They didn't learn math so they could balance their checkbooks (there were no checkbooks!), or so they could become accountants—they hired people to do that for them. They didn't use math in shopping; they had stewards for such mundane activities, who paid the grocer's and haberdasher's bills. And unless they were real misers (or getting ready to flee), they didn't spend a lot of time counting money. They didn't study their Euclid so they could become architects. They did so because it added meaning and beauty to their existence, rather like the required "continental tour", only this one a travel excursion of the mind.

Preaching future utility is futility (for math, or for any other subject)—it is a wrong-headed approach. It's not only based on a lie, one of many my teachers told me (they may have believed them, too, for all I know), but an ineffective one to boot. The young child comes into the world as a princess. The whole world is there, and is hers, waiting to be revealed, fully investigated, and, ultimately, inhabited. She is a "stout Cortez when with eagle eye/He star'd at the Pacific—/Silent, upon a peak in Darien." What use worrying about some wholly inscrutable future time, when this glittering oyster of a world lay opening before you!

Don't attempt to brainwash your kids into contemplating something that is ultimately unknowable. All that can be known with certainty about the future is that it will be unlike today (and checkbooks will probably have gone the way of sliderules.) Teach them (yes, unschoolers, I'm using the forbidden "T" word) that mathematics is one of the most beautiful creations of the human spirit. String necklaces of colored beads in varying mathematical patterns, and wear them with pride. Provide allowances in wampum (convertible to hard currency, of course). Get out the old magnifying glass and count centipede legs (are there really 100?) Give your child a set of pattern blocks (as soon as you are sure she won't swallow them)— chances are that if you provide them at 3, she'll still be playing with them when she's 12. Count the sections of oranges and tangelos, plot them on a graph, and see if the distribution falls in any particular pattern. Read books about Archimedes and see how a lever, properly placed, can move the world (don't let the kids try this without adult supervision).

When they are ready, show them the Fibonacci numbers, and where they can be found throughout the natural order: in the spirals of shells, branching plants and leaf arrangements, flower petals and seed heads, pineapples and pine cones. (Check out the book *Fascinating Fibonaccis: Mystery and Magic in Numbers* by Trudi Hammel Garland, and her wonderful posters—www.iguanagraphics.com/fibonacci/.) Make beaded bracelets in the pattern of the Fibonacci-related Golden String (1011010110101101.... You can have fun for hours on the best Fibonnaci website: www.mcs.surrey.ac.uk/Personal/R.Knott/Fibonacci.). If you know the Fibonnaci series, you may be able to sit in a field of daisies and figure out whether "she loves you, or loves you not" without picking a single petal!

Go to the library and get a copy of the extraordinary Arthur C. Clarke video "Fractals: The Colors of Infinity" on the Mandelbrot sets, those extraordinary patterns of fractal geometry to be found in nature that may remind you of the wall projections during a '60s Grateful Dead concert (my age is showing, but the soundtrack really is by Pink Floyd!). (This was the public television show I referred to in "The Code Cracker and the Information Hound.")

Find a set of Zometools (www.zometool.com), sophisticated tinkertoys updated for use by architects, research biochemists, and hobbyists, and which are just plain fun! (Your daughter or son may end up making "truncated icosahedrons", also known as "Buckyballs" after Buckminster Fuller, or "clustering Kepler solids"—whatever they are!) Be forewarned, however: Zometools are outrageously addictive, and will quickly supplant all other forms of youthful human activity.

Okay—sold on beauty but still want to ensure that the usefulness of mathematics seems like a plausible hypothesis? Well, you probably learned that one in Unschooling 101. But to review: bake cakes. Go to the supermarket and figure out the per ounce costs of all the breakfast cereals; convert the ounces to grams, too. Compare distances to various friends' houses using the odometer, and compute how much the gas costs to get there and back. Does your son want to purchase something with his savings? Construct bar charts with the goal, and calculate and plot the percentages of how much has been socked away thus far. Have your daughter balance the checkbook as one of her chores (she might learn to do a better job than you would anyway, and she'll have learned a vanishing art.) Figure out how many jars (by volume) it's going to take to can all the peaches from the tree in the backyard. Concerned about your weight? Have your son manage the calorie counter—he'll keep you honest!

Do your kids surf the Internet? Help them explore the Boolean logic operators behind their searches (AND, NOT, OR), and use them to solve some of the marvelous puzzles by Charles Dodgson, otherwise known as the author of *Alice in Wonderland*. (For a primer, try www.albany.edu/library/internet/boolean.html.) Choose a neighborhood tree and try to find three ways to figure out its height without climbing or employing the aid of a helicopter. Sort potatoes—see if you can come up with a volume rule for Mr., Mrs., and Baby PotatoHead. Measure absolutely everything—from the size of the living room rug that needs replacing to the relative girth of olives, from small to super colossal (that's the kind with St. Louis stuffed inside it.) Use this one as an introduction to "fuzzy set theory" (ever see a fuzzy olive?).

Oh, I know. You still want them to understand that the math they learn today might be of use later in life. Mrs. Blum, the 9th grade algebra teacher with the voice of one of the Harpies, has infected your bloodstream and there's no known cure. Well, don't preach—visit! If your child seems interested, meet with an architect, an air traffic controller, a computer software designer, an epidemiologist, an astronomer, a baseball statistician, a physicist, my mother's stockbroker Larry, anyone who uses math as part of her daily work—anyone, that is, but Mrs. Blum! Don't know any? That's okay, that's what phone books are for. Work with your child to develop a list of questions she might actually like to ask. If you're still stuck, go visit my friend Bill the carpenter.

Whenever we are stuck in our homeschooling routines, whether it be around math or anything else, I am learning not to be frustrated with my children, but to step back and ask myself three questions: Have I provided what is necessary so that my kids can discover the beauty in what they are learning? Have I given them opportunities in the present to use it? Do they have models in front of them to which they can aspire if they put in the necessary learning effort? And, my experience has shown me that when I can answer these questions affirmatively, there's not an awful lot left to worry about. My kids, bless them, can take care of the rest themselves.

Except maybe for the centipede legs....

* * * * *

All right—I understand—the first part of this essay worked for some of you, but others of you read it and started to sweat. Admit it, your blood pressure went up, your heart began to race, and you began to worry. First of all, what went through your heads was that if it doesn't seem like *real work*, how can you be sure the kids are learning anything? After all, that was the way you had to do it, right? And then you flashed just briefly on how in your own school career, joy was systematically leeched from mathematics, and fear instilled in its place. From your first memory of "This little piggy went to market" forward, it was all a downward spiral, from which you've never entirely recovered. They kept on trying to find out what was *wrong* with you, probing and testing for all your mathematical weaknesses, and finally—with SATs—presenting you with a test where they expected you to get a whole passel of wrong answers, and that no matter how well you prepared, you were going to feel inadequate.

So you've decided to use a curriculum. Nothing wrong with that, if such is your proclivity. We've used them ourselves—tried various book versions (Singapore Math—www.singaporemath.com—being by far the least offensive), and ended up having the kids do their high school math through the Federal Way Internet Academy (www.iacademy.org). We liked the Internet Academy primarily because it gave the kids a pretest before trying to do any instruction—that way if the kids already knew the material, they didn't have to repeat it. No busywork! And following a "test", the computer would isolate only those areas where problems were still occurring, and only require a review of these. Slick and efficient, and it left time for us, as parents, to focus on the all-important context in which math education occurs, which is what the first part of this essay is all about.

But *how* one uses a curriculum, we've discovered, is just as important, maybe more important, than the curriculum itself. I can remember those hours—long hours!—of mindless homework, when I already knew what I needed to know, and really—for educational purposes—I should have been out playing stickball. Or, worse, on those rare occasions that I didn't absorb a concept quickly enough, there would be pages and pages of rote, boring, *plaguing* problems that made me remember how much I would have preferred a trip to the dentist.

The wonderful folks at the Sudbury Valley School—a democratically managed, child-directed learning environment in Massachusetts that has now been operating for more than 30 years (www.sudval.org)—have demonstrated rather conclusively that all the mathematics taught in public schools from kindergarten through twelfth grade can be learned by average, normal, healthy kids in about eight weeks, *when the child has expressed a real interest in doing so.* (No kidding—check out some of the books on the School.) They use curricula for this purpose, but the real issue is not whether or what curriculum to use, but one of interest and motivation and timing. So now I've got your palms wet.

Of course, some of us insist, against the entire tide of our own personal experience, that the way a child should be made to learn a particular mathematical operation with which she has struggled is by assigning several dozen additional problems where use of the same skill is required. Well, maybe, or maybe not. I remember once being told an anecdote related by the great anthropologist and systems thinker Gregory Bateson. Bateson had met an experimental psychologist who had substituted a ferret for laboratory rats in his learning experiments, as ferrets in their natural state, unlike rats, do actually hunt for their prey in the maze of rabbit warrens. The psychologist placed the ferret in the maze and, after turning down every blind alley, the ferret found the haunch of a dead rabbit in the reward chamber and promptly chowed down. The next day, the psychologist placed the ferret in the same maze. This time, the ferret turned down every blind alley, but the one place he did not go was the same location where now a new rabbit haunch had been placed. This, concluded the psychologist, proved that the ferret had not learned anything. On the contrary, said Bateson, no self-respecting ferret is going to expect to find dead rabbits in the exact same spot twice on consecutive days. Do I detect a nervous facial tick or a little bit of tremor in your lower limbs?

My wife and I happened upon a strategy that we've now used with both children. It might on the surface seem counterintuitive, but it works! Meera would master multiple-digit multiplication, but then all of a sudden when faced with a problem involving multiplying decimals, it would be as if the final decimal point would fall from the sky like a meteor, and wherever it landed would be where it ended up. Ellen and I would look at each other and, based on our experience with our older daughter Aliyah, instantly knew what to do. Failing fifth grade math? Give her seventh grade math! Sure enough, Meera would move on to the new, more interesting concepts and, usually sooner rather than later, the difficulties in accomplishing particular mathematical operations would clear themselves up of their own accord, with little help from us whatsoever.

You'll never see this attempted in a public school environment. Imagine the parent-teacher conference: "I'm sorry, Mrs. Johnson, but Susie is failing fifth grade math. However, instead of making her do extra homework, or signing her up to work with a tutor while the other kids are enjoying themselves in the schoolyard, or suggesting you take her to the nearest Sylvan or Kumon Learning Center while her friends are out riding their bikes, or leaving her back or putting her in the "slow learners group", we've decided to give her seventh grade math instead. Is that okay with you?"

This begs the whole question of what exactly is "fifth grade material" and what "seventh"? I'm sure the "scope and sequence" people are convinced there is a logic to this business—it is, after all, an entire industry!— but what difference does it make if the children, who are, after all, the "end users", lose interest along the way? I find it is the exception rather than the rule to find children who learn math in a linear fashion, which is one of the reasons so many of us ended up hating math, isn't it?

Using the school model for our homeschooling endeavors generally speaking is extremely limiting. Gregory Bateson's daughter Mary Catherine Bateson once wrote that, "Trying to understand learning by studying schooling is rather like trying to understand sexuality by studying bordellos." The reason the "skipping" method worked for both of my children was not that they moved "ahead" in material, but rather that they left concepts they had already mastered for a new, more interesting mathematical universe, one where the rote operations they formerly had been struggling with now had a larger purpose, embedded as they were in an area which fed their expanding mathematical view of the world.

Now I've got some of you feverishly mopping your brows. "This is just too challenging. I can't deal with it, much as I couldn't deal with math when I was in school back in the dark ages." Okay. I'll keep it simple: the single most important thing you can do for your kids around math is to help them avoid "math anxiety". And one best avoids "math anxiety" by preventing "math trauma". Be a physician, and apply the first principle, "Do no harm". Without trauma, anything remains possible. With trauma, your kids may end up with certain skills, but they will also end up with wounds that may take a long time to heal.

The June 2001 issue of the *Journal of Experimental Psychology: General* includes an article titled "The Relationships Among Working Memory, Math Anxiety, and Performance" by Drs. Mark Ashcraft and Elizabeth Kirk. In their study, the authors found that, "Fear of math can cause a temporary brain glitch that may explain why an otherwise glib person stumbles and stammers over the simple matter of adding two numbers." In experiments with university students, the researchers found that those with "math anxiety" suffered a fleeting lapse in working memory when asked to do some mental arithmetic. These memory problems failed to crop up in tests that did not involve numbers, meaning that the phenomenon is "very specific to math.... It's a learned, almost phobic reaction to math," explained Dr. Ashcraft. He noted that research indicates that people need not be anxious types in general to harbor a fear of math. The mere specter of doing sums has been shown to send a person's blood pressure and heart rate skyward.

Math-phobic students were often stumped when it came to remembering basic math rules like "carrying over" a number when adding, or "borrowing" from a number when subtracting. An explanation for the memory problem, Ashcraft proposed, is that when math anxiety takes hold, a rush of thoughts goes through a person's head. This leaves little room for the task at hand. And this makes for a "vicious cycle" for students. Once they develop math anxiety, the fear gets in the way of learning, which leads to waning self-confidence in their ability to ever conquer arithmetic. Part of the problem, according to Ashcraft, may rest in how math is taught—at least in the U.S. Students may be taught math rules, but they rarely know why a certain approach to a math problem works. Giving students a "deeper understanding" of math may help fight phobias, he suggested.

Getting kids to develop deeper, problem-solving skills in school may be important, argues Ashcraft, but that may be easier said than done. In one study of math anxiety among college students, he noted, fear of math was most rampant among elementary education majors.

Hmm.

Glad we're homeschooling!

Dodge Ball

"I only remember a really confusing episode where someone grabbed me and shoved me into the middle of a circle of people, and they were throwing a hard ball at me and wouldn't quit. I was trying to run away and they kept shoving me back into the middle. I have a real paranoia of things flying at me, especially balls; I don't know if I had it before that episode or not. I was tiny and skinny and a misfit and new to the school, and I got hit in the head and face several times. Thankfully, most of the rest of my memories of the episode seem to be blanked out, but I do remember that I was very traumatized. And the teacher, whom I loved, she just stood there and watched!"

—Homeschooling Mom, California

"Where you stood depended on how smart you got. Being fat and not particularly athletic, I always chose the back, because it was harder to get the ball back there and easier to dodge. This of course only works for the first part of the game because, as it progresses, fewer and fewer kids are there to act as a barrier. I remember kids pushing others in front of them to get whacked first, but eventually we all got hit. That was the whole point!"

—Homeschooling Mom, Massachusetts

"I was small and agile, and managed to evade quite well. I was never ashamed. My only downfall was that I loved to talk. One time, in the 3rd grade, I got so absorbed in a conversation with my friend Lisa Shackleton (I still remember her name!), I never saw the ball coming and it slammed me in the head. I was standing sideways and the impact sent me reeling against the wall. Next thing I knew Lisa was freaked, shaking me and telling me to get up. The game never stopped...no one but Lisa noticed. I had recently had my ears pierced and the side that hit the wall, that ear developed a huge bruised swelling, I had a 104 fever and had to have the swelling lanced. The teacher never even asked about it."

—Homeschooling Mom, Texas

"I don't recall the rules of dodge ball very clearly, but it seems to me that if you got hit, you were out, which meant you got to stand off at the side and not have to participate any more. So that was okay; the torment was time-limited. Whereas with other sports, the torment lasted and lasted.

*"I think they explained how you play softball when I wasn't there.
All I knew about softball is that you were obligated to swing the bat
a few times, and then you could step aside. If you managed to hit
something, you were supposed to run someplace, but no one ever
told me where, so I just ran some place while everyone yelled at me.
And if the other team was at bat, you just stood somewhere in the
far-off end of the playground and tried not to be anywhere near the
ball, because if it came near everyone would yell at you."*

—Homeschooling Mom, Canada

I was, I must admit without bragging, really adept at dodge ball.[1] It wasn't
anything I was taught. I was possessed with some speed, a reasonably strong
arm, good eyes, and a natural shiftiness and cunning that stood me in good
stead. People liked having me on their team. I felt confident, secure, and
strong, and I think my confidence helped others overcome their fear.

Initially, though, I hated it. I had to attack and be attacked, and it was
easiest (and encouraged) to choose the fat and clumsy and nearsighted
(and, especially, the girls with glasses) as my first victims. They would usually cower against the wall, awaiting the inevitable, as the balls clanged
against the grates on the windows above them. Rockets red glare! There
was nowhere to run, nowhere to hide (as Martha and the Vandellas—
dodge ball champions of northeast Detroit?—reminded us), and they
wouldn't have been fast enough or wily enough to effect an escape in any
case. Their one hope was that, when their time came, it wouldn't hurt too
much. They came to believe they deserved it. One or two would stand in
the middle, offering up their bodies with the hope that they would be hit
during the first assault so they could go sit on the sideline.

At least at first I didn't like attacking the fat and clumsy and nearsighted, or even the girls, and it was pretty lame to molest the sacrificial
lambs. They (not the girls, of course) were often my friends, for awhile. I
wanted to spend time with them, share common interests, or have some
one with whom to walk home. But this didn't last long. The divide between
predator and prey began to widen. I guess it was hard to remain friends with
someone who pummeled them three times a week with dark red (was the
color of dried blood intentional?), super-pomelo-sized missiles, though, on
second thought, being associated with a pummeler—even as a victim—
might actually raise one's social status. Perhaps I was just "over-sensitive".

---

1   At P.S. 131 3/4 there were actually two games called "dodge ball". I have since learned that,
in other places, this second game, played with multiple balls, was called "bombardment".

My sensitivity, however, wasn't allowed to last long. I learned, under the watchful eye of my trained and certified and caring schoolteachers (who instructed us in the rules), that "taking out my aggressions" (which I didn't I know I had) in this way was doing the right thing, and the results were both fair and just. I learned that my former friends were somehow lesser beings who received their just desserts, much like those first-graders who were sent off to the "Robins" for reading (I being all puffed up at being a BLUEBIRD!), almost never to be encountered again by me in the next seven years of my public school education, or even (heaven forbid!) to special ed (which is where they seemed to send all the Black kids). And having been confirmed in my obvious superiority and being able to express it—whether at reading or dodge ball—it really was a lot of fun at the time, though with significant negative consequences experienced later in my life.

Now I did in fact have a real friend among the lower castes, my friend Richie. Richie was slow-moving, clumsy, stuttered, and was 40 pounds overweight in third grade. His mother took him to the doctor (I don't know if the fear, shame, and pain associated with dodge ball was the final straw) who promptly put him on a diet and amphetamines three times a day. Richie had to eat yogurt and carrots for lunch (in fact, it was from him that I got to taste yogurt for the first time!). He lost the 40 pounds, but it didn't help him at dodge ball at all—he was still slow, clumsy, and nearsighted—and he still stuttered, and six months after being taken off the amphetamines, he put on 50 pounds! Richie's mom was always excited, perhaps ecstatic is a better word, when I came to visit (now, mind you, Richie's house was more than two miles away from mine, all the way on the other side of St. Gregory's Catholic School—did they play dodge ball there, too?), perhaps because playmates for Richie were really rare. I think he became a nuclear scientist, and I have occasionally worried about what might happen if he ever had the opportunity to take out *his* aggressions.

Still, Richie aside, I think it took me 20 years to recover the emotional maturity stolen from me by public education so that I could imagine with empathy what life must have been like among the pummeled or Robinish. It was simply not part of my life experience.

The only argument put forward by the defenders of dodge ball is that it is a *fun* representation of what life is really all about. Homeschooling Mom, Massachusetts got the message: "I remember kids pushing others in front of them to get whacked first, but eventually we all got hit. That was the whole point." Fun for whom, *kimo sabe*? But I don't think it can easily be denied that dodge ball is, at bottom, an accurate and chillingly dynamic depiction of the sorting and culling mechanisms, built on a foundation of systemic violence, at which American public education excels.

Of course, I've also heard it said that dodge ball is illustrative of a *Lord of the Flies* mentality that children will manifest without provocation. I beg to differ. Not only does dodge ball actually have to be *taught* by our trained and certified public servants, but I have never seen a game of dodge ball played anywhere except in school. Of course, there *are* adults who actually believe that children are like pit bulls, and shouldn't be allowed in the neighborhood.

And as for *Lord of the Flies*, while I'm on the subject (read the sign around my neck: "I rant for food"), it is interesting to see it turning up on eighth grade reading lists again. The point seems to be to teach the kids that violence and oppression are children's natural state (original sin?), from which they can only be rescued by adults who have learned to control the kids' antisocial tendencies. Yeah, right. As far as I'm concerned, *Lord of the Flies* could only have been written by an adult who had been bred through several generations of attending English boarding schools (dodge ball 24/7! in the case of William Golding, it was the Marlborough Grammar School, where his father taught as well). In fact, wasn't it the real point of the novel that these boys, having had their minds "well-trained" as they received their "classical educations", were now poorly equipped for the *Survivor* series? Oh, where was Harry Potter when we needed him?

For the "undodge ball alternative", there are two excellent books by Josette and Ba Luvmour, *Everyone Wins! Cooperative Games and Activities* (Gabriola Island, BC: New Society Publishers, 1990), and the spanking new *Win-Win Games for All Ages* (Gabriola Island, BC: New Society Publishers, 2002). The Luvmours run EnCompass (www.encompass-nlr.org), a holistic learning center for families (many of them homeschoolers) in northern California, and have pioneered a family-oriented approach to human development called Natural Learning Rhythms.

From the Luvmour's perspective, games should be part-and-parcel of a healthy approach to a child's well-being, and should enhance self-esteem, help resolve conflict, aid in communication, and empower people to understand and appreciate one another. Children do not usually make compartmentalized distinctions between games and other facets of their learning selves. They either feel a positive sense of who they are or are in the process of becoming, or find barriers placed along the way. The institutional dodge ball advocates probably feel exactly the same way (scary, but true), which suggests to me that this is no minor matter.

Just a ball game? or a small theater in the struggle for our children's souls? You decide.

Stickball

It wasn't all dodge ball. There were other lessons I got from sports while growing up, and they have played at least as an important, if not more important, role in the way I have come to think about education. They raise questions for me regarding both *where* learning actually happens, and *what* is actually being learned, regardless of what is ostensibly being taught. I imagine if you allow yourself the luxury, you might find yourselves in the midst of similar reflections.

* * * * *

I grew up playing stickball on a New York City street. Played with a sawed-off broom handle and a pink rubber ball (either a Spaldeen or a Pennsy Pinkie). That was all the equipment required, which certainly didn't endear stickball to the sporting goods manufacturers.

We all played, from age 7, until the time any of us moved away, be it at 17 or 20. The seven-year-olds, if they weren't allowed in the street yet, became automatic first basemen for both teams (first base being a fire hydrant), until they were old enough to be let off the curb. Uncles who had moved out of the neighborhood might play when visiting. Dads, too, for that matter, though rarely did we see fathers come down to the corner to do anything but call us in for dinner or homework. No girls, though, and it never struck me at the time that girls would even consider playing stickball! Times have changed. (My wife, though, who grew up in Washington, DC, recounts similar experiences to these, playing street soccer.)

Four sewers was a homer. To translate: a ball hit the distance of four manhole covers on a fly ("personhole" covers hadn't been invented yet) was an automatic homerun. We made up our own ground rules. Any ball hit into Mrs. O'Brien's yard was an out—it was commonly believed as part of our neighborhood lore that Mrs. O'Brien was an ogre and didn't appreciate us or our stickball games, though I can't remember any personal experience confirming this. Mr. Federman's automobile was in foul territory—we all liked him and didn't want to hit his new car. He liked us, too, and took to parking around the corner. Other cars were in fair territory—a fly ball that bounced off a car roof and was caught was an out.

We could play with any number of kids from 5 to 18 players, without

pitchers if fewer than eight, and each team would supply their own catch-
er if fewer than ten. We chose up sides every afternoon or evening, depending on who was available. Everyone always got to play—no exceptions.

We didn't have any problems with bullies. Of course we had them.
But the thing was that Sheldon, (one of the bullies, who dropped out of
high school, drove a cab, and ended up, last I heard, pursuing a Ph.D. in
history at Columbia University), knew that the kid he was doing a number
on from the opposing team might be on his own team tomorrow, so he
learned to moderate his behavior or no one would want to play with him.

There were no umpires. We had our disputes, and we handled them
by a boisterous consensus. If one person insisted loudly enough that he
was safe at second base, but the majority thought otherwise, we would
more times than not let the individual get his way, as it wasn't worth
fighting over.

There was rarely a set number of innings. We played until it was too
dark to play, or too many players had to go in. There was, however, a
twenty-minute timeout around 5:15, when the "Sperries" came. For years,
when I was really young, I imagined dark, shadow-like figures, spectres of
death or destruction, passing by on 82nd Avenue. I soon learned that we
were avoiding the rush-hour traffic coming out of the nearby Sperry
Gyroscope plant, which would stop play too often.

We all—even the little ones—imagined ourselves as Willie Mayses
(definitively known to be a four-sewer guy), Duke Sniders, Mickey
Mantles, or even Ed Kranepools (a member of the 1969 "Miracle Mets" and
a New Yorker like ourselves, who also grew up playing stickball). We'd
practice, too, endlessly. Two of us were enough. We'd go to the local concrete handball wall by the school (actually, any unwindowed wall would
do), chalk in a strike zone (until the Parks Department painted one on for
us), and play a Yankee-Dodger World Series, complete with announcers,
lineups, and batting averages, all memorized and then liberally embel-
lished. We were Sandy Koufax (a Dodger from Brooklyn), Joe Pepitone (a
Yankee, also from Brooklyn), and Mel Allen (the "Voice of the Yankees",
from Alabama?), all rolled into one.

Frankly, we pitied the Little Leaguers. Some of us, uncharitably,
thought of them as sissies. They never got to play with kids older than
themselves. If they weren't good enough, they rode the bench and barely
got to play at all. Parents watched every move, and argued loudly, embar-
rassingly, over calls at first base. Coaches played favorites; umpires, too, or
so it seemed. Losers felt like losers, and they might be losers for an entire

season; and those left out, well, they were left out. Managers did whatever it took to win; that's what the parents wanted, and everybody knew it.

Now, I don't want to over-romanticize. Many of my friends' families couldn't have afforded Little League even if the kids had wanted to play there. Our equipment was what it was and what there was of it, our coaching non-existent, and, (Ed Kranepool and Joe Pepitone being the exceptions that proved the rule), the chance that stickball would lead to something greater virtually nil. (Joe Pepitone, it is worth noting, later went on to become a petty criminal.) Today, I love watching children participating in gymnastics or karate (pacifist though I am), individual sports where, while organized in teams, the kids actually compete against themselves, and learn that mastery, and self-mastery, only come with the necessary time, energy, and requisite effort and focus, and are always constantly exposed to other participants—potential mentors—who are both older and more adept than themselves. What I don't like is the amount of emotional energy, expended by adults but picked up by the kids, that goes into testing, measuring, and comparing, rather than celebrating our children for simply being who they are.

There is no stickball in my neighborhood today, nor anything resembling it. After school, the schoolyards and parks are virtually empty, except for an occasional two-on-two basketball game. The latchkey kids are instructed to stay inside until mom gets home from work. The government enters the house uninvited at the same time in the form of homework. Of course, some kids, having not been sufficiently obedient or passive during the school day, are punished with more of the same, either in the form of detention or extra homework. (A true oxymoron: here is revealed in a flash how educators really perceive education—*as an acute form of punishment.* School is punishment, homework is punishment, and extra school and extra homework is simply a larger dose.) The other kids go to "afterschool" activities, planned by adults, closely monitored, rigidly controlled, or to competitive sports, with more of same. Parents who feel safe letting children come out into the front yard simply to mess around seem to be a vanishing breed, and certainly not on the street! But, to be fair, most of the parents just aren't home.

So what brought us back to stickball, day after day, month after month, year after year? Well, what it certainly wasn't, for any of us as far as I could tell, was fear- or anxiety-producing. There was no chance of public humiliation. We could simply be ourselves, and grow into the game. In our own sweet time, we would find ourselves in the flow. And we did.

Meanwhile we learned a series of lessons, without benefit of adults—managers, coaches, referees, organizers, parents, or teachers. Kind of a reverse *Lord of the Flies*. We profited greatly from benign neglect. Indeed, looking back on it, I think adults would have just mucked it up. I'm convinced I would have learned these lessons much less well if I thought that adults were teaching them!

We learned to accept people—players all—of differing ages, religions, national origins, and natural abilities, and make use of whatever skills each of us possessed. In doing so, and in knowing that there would always be someone better than we were but understanding our own contribution to the game, we learned to value ourselves and our own progress. We learned skills from each other, mostly by watching those older and more proficient. We learned to respect the property of others without, however, making a fetish of it. We learned to respect the feelings of our neighbors. We learned to make decisions informally, democratically, and consensually. We learned to set our own rules and boundaries, and abide by them. We learned to improvise, and make effective use of available space, people, and resources. Above all, we learned to play fair and to be fair and to understand that when we did not do so, we harmed ourselves in the process. And, over time, we learned to value friendship above winning.

What's more, it was fun—or we wouldn't have done it. We were, after school, above all, free.

Ah, freedom. That's the place where learning happens....

P.S. To learn even more about stickball, peruse photos, read stickball poetry, or visit the Stickball Hall of Fame, go to www.streetplay.com/stickball

Perfection

Your six-year-old daughter picks up a crayon and draws three lines on the paper. She looks down, screws up her eyes, then discards the piece of paper, reaches for another one, and repeats the process three or four times. While her younger sister continues to scribble happily away, she walks away from the table and sits down disconsolate on the carpet. No matter how hard she tries, it won't *really* look like a dog.

Your son has been waiting for this day for months. This is the day you go to get the new rental violin at the music store. He picks up the violin, puts it firmly under his chin, places the bow on the strings, and you can see his jaw sag. This doesn't sound anything like the fiddler he heard at the county fair during the summer. In fact, it sounds awful! This disappointment will repeat itself intermittently, month after month, year after year, even as the cat scratches begin (finally!) to change to music. At some point, assuming he is not the reincarnation of Yehudi Menuhin, he will decide it is truly worth the effort and that he is good *enough*, or he'll sabotage the learning process until you'll agree he can stop. If the latter, you'll feel like you've made the right decision, but still experience twinges of guilt in the process.

Your daughter learned to read at age three. But at seven, she will only read the same book over and over again. You've filled her room with books about dogs and horses, her favorite things in the whole world. You know she can read these books, but she won't, and especially not to you, fearing there are words she will stumble over.

You insist that your ten-year-old son write, something, *anything!* You are at the end of your rope. You've cajoled, you've instructed, you've offered what you thought to be sympathetic and helpful assistance, you've threatened, you've screamed. You know he can do it—he reads voraciously, *everything!* and never forgets anything he's ever read. But he stares at the page or computer screen, totally frozen. He is afraid to misspell a word, or misplace a comma, or fears that his handwriting isn't good enough, or that he'll simply be unable to find the right words to capture the complexity or the intensity of his thinking. And why write at all, when he knows from his extensive reading that it has already been written better by someone else?

If you haven't done so already, sooner or later you are likely to tell your son or daughter, "Don't be such a perfectionist!" as if this will solve the problem. It won't, it never has, but you'll say it anyway.

You may experience another phenomena with these same kids, one that may not immediately strike you as related. It often first makes its appearance in the car. Your dd or ds ("darling daughter" or "darling son"— I'm finally learning the e-mail jargon) asks question after question, almost at random, or so it seems to you. "How do the buttons at stoplights work?" "Where does the wind start?" "Why are thundercloud plum tree leaves purple?" "What is a transmission?" "When you lose 30 pounds in 30 days, where do the pounds go?" You answer some of them, until you get totally exasperated. You offer to help him look up the answers at the library, but most of the time he's not interested. You suggest that she call her uncle to ask the same question, or read a book on the subject or, using that clever little ruse you learned from a child development expert on *Oprah*, you ask her what *she* thinks. None of these work; you'll still be faced with another raft of questions.

Chances are ds/dd is not really interested in the answer. Oh, she'll register the new information all right, and sometimes put it away to be drawn upon when the appropriate occasion warrants. But what she is really doing is testing you. She is learning the limits of your knowledge, where the holes are and where your knowledge resources are deep and, if lucky, the sources of your knowledge and how it was acquired. You think she is just seeking answers, and she is, but more importantly, she is engaged in a kind of information mapping, conducting experiments in knowledge ethnography, and you are the primitive subject. She is laying down the data coordinates of your mind!

Young children experience their parents and other caregivers as "perfect beings". They have no reason to believe that mom and dad, and those who teach them, haven't always known everything there is to know, and always been able to do all that they are now capable of doing, seemingly without effort. On the one hand, we are fonts of wisdom, the fountain seemingly inexhaustible, able to rise to all occasions, capable of meeting all their needs and desires. (Are you feeling tired yet?) On the other hand, since your child has no idea from whence your knowledge, skills, or wisdom spring, or how it was acquired, chances are she'll think it is innate, or comes naturally as part of what it means to be human, or, at least, older. In short, the perfectionist child who can't achieve perfection may come to think of herself as *disabled*, and, from the perfectionist point of view, she is.

In my experience, there is only one solution to this conundrum. Luckily it is happy one. Okay now, put on shield and buckler and prepare to defend yourself: here comes a homeschooling "should". *Learn something new yourself.* Is your daughter taking piano lessons at least partially because you always wanted to as a child, but your mother never allowed it? Well, now's the time—the *best* time in your life—and you'll make time to do it because it is the best thing you'll ever do for your daughter (after loving and listening). You'll end up pestering her less about practicing, and she'll get the point just as well by watching you. (I recommend this especially for families who have just taken their child out of school and are going through the normal process of "deschooling". Mom—it's almost always mom—just has to do something while waiting for the kid's natural curiosity to return, or she'll drive the poor thing nuts!)

Always felt stuck in a gender rut and never found a way to break out? *Corragio*, now's your chance. Mom—take up auto mechanics, or woodworking, or plumbing (yes, I know, many of you already do this last one, whether you like it or not). Maybe a little something with power tools. Dad, ever had that urge? Put on an apron and learn to bake, or go to a knitting class, or even, imagine, buy a pair of tights and take up modern dance! And maybe the both of you always wanted to learn Japanese and never really understood physics and forever have dreamt of making a stained glass window and....

Don't feel you can spend the money on yourself because you need it to spend on the kids? Well, let me tell you—this is a "two-fer". You may be surprised how out of touch you may have become with the habit of learning. Your empathy with, and humility around, your children will increase exponentially. You'll teach them through example that mistakes are a part of the learning process, whether when you burn the brioche, hit that real clunker of a note, or stick yourself with the sewing needle. This is a lesson they'd never receive from even the best public school teacher, so you really have an edge.

Just as importantly, your kids will see that learning anything new always begins with some level of discomfort, and that it's really okay. They will watch you progress and come to understand that mastery of any subject matter—be it mathematics, crocheting, baseball, or singing—and self-mastery only come by developing sound learning habits and putting in the requisite time, energy, and effort. And then by doing so, self-confidence grows. And what is self-confidence, really, but the feeling that one is prepared to tackle a future replete with exciting new adventures!

So give your children your greatest gift: strive to become the person you always wanted to be. This should also put an end as well to any strange notion you may have had that your homeschooling efforts have to be perfect. Call it "reality therapy". Someday your kids will thank you for the lesson. But not right now: there's too much other stuff to learn!

* * * * *

My favorite of all of John Holt's books is *Never Too Late: My Musical Life* (Boston, MA: Addison-Wesley, 1999), an intimate portrayal of his adventures in taking up the cello after age 40. This book is a friendly reminder that serious learning, and the love of it, do not have to be reserved to the young.

Geese

We were pleased when Meera told us she'd like to learn Spanish. Seemed like a good idea to us. The census people tell us that by the year 2010, the majority of people in the three western states (California, Oregon, and Washington) will be native Spanish speakers, and they are in many places already. They will be the majority, and maybe—just maybe— we'll see a change in the history textbooks as well to reflect the experience of the original European Americans to settle in what is now the United States.

"Pilgrims—to the back of the bus," might be an interesting switch. I'm not holding my breath. "Move over Pilgrims, and sorry, Miles and Priscilla, hate to burst your bubble. For the Pilgrims did not come to the "New World" seeking religious freedom, but to escape from it, and the threats that such freedom posed to your beliefs. You had already found religious liberty in the city of Leiden in Holland where, under the leadership of Pastor John Robinson, you had worshipped openly in complete freedom for more than 12 years. But you couldn't get along with other English dissidents, and didn't like your kids constantly rubbing elbows with Dutch people, and you decided to come to a place where you would be afforded free reign for the expression of your own religious intolerance."

"Time to make room in the history books for Luis de Torres, the first European settler in the New World. De Torres, a Spanish Jew, who came over with Columbus as his interpreter, settled, happily it turns out, in Cuba to escape the Spanish Inquisition 130 years before the grounding on the Plymouth pebble. Sorry, Sir Walter Raleigh, de Torres is also responsible for the first European importation of tobacco (as well as the word 'Turkey', which in Hebrew means 'peacock')."And, lest we forget, the journeys of both Columbus and the Pilgrims were made possible by one Abraham Zacuto, another Spanish Jew, who invented the astrolabe. Let's start marking up those textbooks."

At any rate, it would be *useful*, I thought, if all children were able to converse in the language of the majority and, since I have long been an advocate of working with the public schools (on *our* terms) when appropriate, we started contacting them to see if there was a class Meera could take. Now the educational research on this issue, with literally hundreds or even thousands of studies behind it, is clear: language instruction should start before the age of 10 (some believe that ages 5-8 are prime; others 3-5). Meera was, age-wise, coming to the end of the window.

We discovered, somewhat to our amazement, that in our school district, which is richly financed, with 11 elementary schools, four middle schools, three high schools (one brand-newly renovated), and a vocational skills center, and every possible sports team short of tiddlywinks, there isn't a single class in Spanish offered before ninth grade. In their rush to ignore educational research and instead to provide every standardized test known to humankind, the school district has condemned my entire community to conversational illiteracy in the language of the majority for yet another generation.

But perhaps, given my own experience, I shouldn't have expected any better....

* * * * *

I grew up in New York City at the height of the Cold War (the '50s and '60s) and had (or so it was believed) an IQ of more than 88, which meant my education was to be dictated by the national purpose. As "Sputnik babies", we were all to grow up to become nuclear physicists who would invent the magic weapon that would defeat the Soviet Union once and for all. After all, hadn't the Premier (doesn't the word "Premier" sound evil even when you just say it?) of the Evil Empire banged on a table with his (evil-smelling) shoe and declaimed "We will bury you?" (Actually he didn't quite—what he actually said was, "We will bury you under an avalanche of industrial production," but no one seemed to understand enough Russian at the time to translate fast enough to get beyond the first four words.[1]) I have never seen any Russian-made shoes on this continent as far as I am aware, but I am convinced we shipped all those indestructible Corfam shoes featured at the 1962 New York World's Fair and that made our feet hurt to the poor people of Afghanistan, and they've been right ornery ever since.

Shoes, like ballpoint pens, were the objects of conspiracy, or so it was intimated to me. I always had to wear leather shoes, with "cookies" in them, and I was told in no uncertain terms that if I were to wear my sneakers for more than one hour a day, it would definitely ruin my feet. But was this connected in any way with the great pen conspiracy? I vaguely

---

1   Seems that most people now deem the same thing happened to God, Blessed Be He, when He proclaimed His famous four-worder, "Thou Shalt Not Kill." Of course, given His Wisdom, it is generally agreed that there *must* have been at least some qualifiers!

remember this had something to do to with ballpoint pens, BICs to be specific. They came from France, even if invented by a Hungarian with the unlikely name of Biro now living in Argentina, as I later learned, and had something to do with Communists, and would definitely ruin our hands. I think Mr. Lucas, my sixth grade teacher, actually said "hand", but all I can reliably remember is that sneakers and ballpoint pens would undoubtedly destroy the youth of America, hands and feet together. Ballpoint pens were forbidden in school. Once we graduated from pencils, it would be real fountain pens that leaked out all over our pockets. Of course, within several years, I knew the Communists would win: *Premier* Khrushchev had banged his leather shoe with a cookie in it on a leaky American-made fountain pen, and Crystal BICs mostly eliminated the need for pocket protectors, only 'mostly' because the ballpoint pens leaked too, and plumbers and real estate agents found an advertising alternative by putting their names and phone numbers on cheap pens rather than on pocket protectors. It all turned out just the way the Communists had planned. (?) (Note that virtually all the contemporary methods of torture, oops, I mean "teaching" the accursed cursive were designed with free-flowing fountain pens in mind. No wonder so many of our kids have difficulties—it's a Communist plot!) If you didn't understand a word of this, know that you are in good company because I didn't either, and am still, four decades later, trying to piece it together. This always gives me pause as to what the world currently looks like to present-day children afflicted with public education.

Anyhow, for some reason, the national purpose required that I learn Russian. I'm not quite sure why. We weren't going to peruse Soviet scientific papers, and we wouldn't be allowed to travel there. I'm sure our national leaders didn't have a lot of interest in our reading Tolstoy and Dostoevsky in the original. And Russian culture? Well, to be fair, "Midnight in Moscow", as I remember, was a hit pop song around 1963:

> *Stillness in the grove, not a rustling sound,*
> *Softly shines the moon, clear and bright,*
> *Dear, if you could know*
> *How I treasure so*
> *This most beautiful Moscow night.*

The song might have been part of another Communist plot, hatched by some shoemaker, and composed with a ballpoint pen. Maybe those of us who didn't become nuclear physicists would make it as spies. I thwarted the national resolve by turning into an English major (which is not how I came to write this essay).

But the national purpose required that we learn the language of the enemy, and so we did, sort of. I had two years of Russian in junior high, and another three in high school, and can barely remember a thing. We had reel-to-reel tapes from official-sounding organizations that we listened to through the world's most uncomfortable earphones (most assuredly *not* made in Communist China), and learned Russian children's songs, and I seem to remember being taught a Soviet Army marching tune in which young girls sob (?). Never did learn to converse, couldn't read any "litera-ture", and I would have made a terrible spy anyway. Became oddly fasci-nated with Ivan the Terrible—I think if you mention his name (or at least what he did) in a public school these days, you are likely to be suspended or expelled. Got all "A"s.

About 13 years ago, I did actually get to make use of what remains. It was a dinner party for a group of scientists from the Soviet Union (still) who came to the U.S. to solicit help in cleaning up Lake Baikal, the earth's oldest and deepest lake, home to the world's only species of freshwater seals, and one of the most polluted bodies of water on the planet (see www.earthisland.org/baikal/baikal2.html). "Dinner party" in Russian trans-lates as "lots of vodka", though I didn't learn that in school. I don't drink, but they sure did, four really beefy guys, looking for all of Siberia like Russian bears, all beards and big shoulders, toasting whatever they could think of, and polishing off bottle after bottle. Somehow, it came out that I had studied all of this Russian but couldn't remember anything, not even "please" or "thank you", but then it came to me, I remembered a poem! It was a sonnet by the poet Lomonosov (I don't remember who he was), and with very little cajoling, I consented to recite.

Perfectly, too, all fourteen rhyming lines, without a hitch, and with feeling. Tears streamed down the faces of the scientists. They all wrapped their arms around me and hugged me, beards and big shoulders, and had several more toasts, to me, and to Lomonosov, whoever he was, and to poetry in general. But, and here's the thing, I didn't know what the poem means! Still don't, though I know it has geese in it. Anyhow, I am equipped: if I ever find myself in Moscow, I may not be able to ask where to find the bathroom, but I probably can stand outside and recite my poem that I do not understand and earn a few rubles. Regardless, it was the first and only time in my life that my school Russian came in handy.

Now I hope it is understood I have nothing against the learning of

languages, and wish I were better at it. I would love to be able to read
Chekhov in the original, as well as Homer and the New Testament in
Greek, the Bhagavad Gita in Sanskrit (once, I could almost do that), talk
to my neighbors in Vietnamese, and bargain vociferously in Italian—complete with hands—for the best price in a violinmaker's shop in Cremona.
Sigh. Next lifetime, perhaps. I have one daughter learning Latin (better
than I did in college!), and another dabbling in Spanish, and I suspect if
the Pope or some migrant farmworkers lived next door, both kids would be
way ahead of the game.

But learning a language has to have a purpose, and it has to be a purpose embraced by the learner, regardless of the teacher's (or the nation's)
intentions. The purpose may simply be to have something show up on the
transcript intended for the Yale admissions office, but at least there has to
be one.

In the meantime, childhood has a better curriculum, the curriculum
of nature and wonder and of everyday life. It may or may not speak to the
national resolve, but as homeschoolers and as citizens of the planet, I
believe we would do better if we were to heed it.

After founding the Commonwealth of Pennsylvania, the Quaker
William Penn took a few spare moments over a course of years to jot down
what he thought was really necessary for the education of free citizens in a
new land. He published it in a little book titled *Some Fruits of Solitude* in
1693, and we would do well to consider his words:

"The first Thing obvious to Children is what is sensible; and that we
make no Part of their Rudiments. We press their Memory too soon, and
puzzle, strain, and load them with Words and Rules; to know Grammer and
Rhetorick, and a strange Tongue or two, that is ten to one may never be
useful to them; Leaving their natural Genius to Mechanical and Physical,
or natural Knowledge uncultivated and neglected; which would be of
exceeding Use and Pleasure to them through the whole Course of their
Life...

It were Happy if we studied Nature more in natural Things; and acted
according to Nature; whose rules are few, plain and most reasonable. Let us
begin where she begins, go her Pace, and close always where she ends, and
we cannot miss of being good Naturalists. The Creation would no longer
be a Riddle to us: The Heavens, Earth, and Waters, with their respective,
various and numerous Inhabitants: Their Productions, Natures, Seasons,
Sympathies and Antipathies; their Use, Benefit and Pleasure, would be
better understood by us: And an eternal Wisdom, Power, Majesty, and

Goodness, very conspicuous to us, thro' those sensible and passing Forms: The World wearing the Mark of its Maker, whose Stamp is everywhere visible, and the Characters very legible to the Children of Wisdom.

"And it would go a great way to caution and direct People in their Use of the World, that they were better studied and known in the Creation of it. For how could Man find the Confidence to abuse it, while they should see the Great Creator stare them in the Face, in all and every part thereof?"

Indeed, if we were to take Friend Penn's advice, there wouldn't be any more Lake Baikals. Then it will be time to celebrate, Russian-style.

I'll be ready with my poem.

* * * * *

I would appreciate hearing from anyone else who knows a sonnet by Lomonosov with geese in it.

ADT̲D™ (No, It's Not a Typo)

W̲e realized early that if we put Meera in public school, they'd probably drug her. They'd claim she never sits still (even though she could easily sit at the piano at any early age for an hour at a time), doesn't pay attention (though she can spend four hours a day at the gym following detailed
directions and training each and every muscle in her body), and is disrup-
tive during story time (she does tend to ask a lot of questions.) And she
never shuts up (at least this was true when she was younger)!

They would have played upon our maternal and paternal instincts.
Ignorant parents we, and they would remind us how much we wanted her
to *succeed* (presuming that we'd bought the line that success in school
always translates into happy and healthy adult living), and try to create the
shared assumption that we too saw her many *deficits* as requiring psychopharmacological intervention.

Perhaps we would have bit. The school psychiatrist, on the recom-
mendation of the first-grade teacher, would have been all-too-happy to
write a prescription. They would not have told us that psychotic symptoms—including paranoia and hallucinations—have been reported in up to
9% of children diagnosed with Attention Deficit Hyperactivity Disorder
(ADHD) and placed on psychostimulants, or that, following these episodes,
physicians often prescribe medications that are FDA-approved only for the
treatment of psychotic adults, including anti-depressants, mood stabilizers,
and neuroleptics.[1] And they certainly wouldn't have told us that if we chose
to discontinue use of the drugs, we could be reported to Child Protective
Services by the school district for alleged child abuse. (I'm not making this
up! This has happened at least twice recently in New York State.[2]) The
result might require a lengthy and expensive family court battle to ensure

---

1 Cherland, E. and Fitzpatrick, R. "Psychotic Effects of Psychostimulants: A 5-Year Review."
   Canadian Journal of Psychiatry, 44 (October 1999), 811-813. Shawn Cooper (responsible for
   the 1999 school shootings in Notus, Idano), T. J. Solomon (1999 school shootings in
   Conyers, Georgia and Kip Kinkel (Springfield, Oregon 1998) were all taking Ritalin; Eric
   Harris was under the influence of Luvox (a prescribed Prozac-like drug) at the time of the
   1999 Columbine, Colorado shootings.

2 *Times Union*, (Albany, New York), "Ritalin Use Splits Parents, School", May 7, 2000
   (www.breggin.com/schools); and *New York Post* (New York, NY), "I Was Told to Dope My
   Kid", August 7, 2002 (www.nypost.com/news/regionalnews/54243.htm). In this second case,

that Meera would not be removed from our home.

Because I am not a doctor, I hesitate to comment on whether there are children who, because of some genetic disorder, can and do benefit from the regular administration of psychotropic substances, though I would note that the emerging scientific consensus points in another direction.[3] The Europeans (whom I generally find more enlightened in these matters) do prescribe Ritalin (methylphenidate), Adderall, and other psychostimulants to school-age children, though less than 4% as often as Americans do. I also do not doubt, given my own school experiences, that there are millions of school-age children who, given the tyranny of four walls set at right angles and the "dreary shower" (thank you, William Blake) raining down upon them from the front of the classroom while spring beckons through the windows (if there are any), probably think they are happier (or at least experience less pain) when ingesting psychopharmacological agents than doing without them.

Writing in 1971, Ivan Illich could not have been more prophetic:

> If we do not challenge the assumption that valuable knowledge is a commodity which under certain circumstances may be forced into the consumer, society will be increasingly

---

a first grader, drugged with Ritalin, was placed on a second drug after he displayed anti-social behavior, including chewing on his own shirtsleeves, collars, pencils, and tests. Having told his mother that he was hearing voices, his mother stopped the medication, and school officials filed a complaint against her with the state child-abuse hotline. The mother was cleared after independent pyschiatric evaluations indicated that the boy's condition was caused by the drugs themselves. The boy is now suffering from a heart murmur, a known side effect of drugs similar to Ritalin. The superintendent of the school district within which the boy resides has refused to comment because of the need to "protect the individual rights of the students."

3   A blue-ribbon National Institute of Mental Health Consensus Panel was convened by the National Institutes of Health in 1998 to end the controversy regarding the use of Ritalin in the treatment of Attention Deficit Hyperactivity Disorder (ADHD). The 13-member expert panel—including psychiatrists, pediatricians, neurologists, epidemiologists, and educators, and thought to be favorably disposed toward the use of psychostimulants—found, "After years of clinical research and experience with ADHD, our knowledge about the cause or causes of ADHD remains largely speculative." They also found, based on hundreds of peer-reviewed studies, that, after 20 years, Ritalin has no proven positive long-term effects. In the short-term clinical trials that have been undertaken (three months or less), the Consensus Panel reports there is "demonstrated ineffectiveness of current treatments in enhancing academic achievement," and "little improvement" in social skills. For the full report, see http://odp.od.nih.gov/consensus/cons/110/110.

dominated by sinister pseudo schools and totalitarian managers of information. Pedagogical therapists will drug their pupils more in order to teach them better, and students will drug themselves more to gain relief from the pressures of teachers and the race for certificates. Increasingly larger numbers of bureaucrats will presume to pose as teachers.... The totally destructive and constantly progressive nature of obligatory instruction will fulfill its ultimate logic unless we begin to liberate ourselves right now from our pedagogical hubris, our belief that man can do what God cannot, namely, manipulate others for their own salvation.[4]

In the year that the paragraph above was first published in Illich's book *Deschooling Society*, there were 150,000 U.S. children on Ritalin; today there are over four million. In 1991, the U.S. Department of Education informed schools they could access additional special education grant funds for every child diagnosed with ADHD. The totally predictable result is an epidemic. The number of ADHD diagnoses since then has grown at a rate of 21% per year, and Ritalin production has increased by more than 700%. (The Swedes, in contrast, citing the documented evidence of side effects, banned Ritalin use among children in 1968, and have seen no reason to lift the ban.)

I know from my professional work (as Senior Planner and Policy Analyst for the Washington State Division of Alcohol and Drug Abuse) that the illegal sale and use of Ritalin now ranks third among drugs for which adult arrests are made in Vancouver, British Columbia. The number is rapidly increasing state-side. It would not be a stretch to suggest that the recent epidemic rise in the manufacture and use of methamphetamine (a powerful psychostimulant), mostly among individuals in their 20s, is directly related to the development of drug habits formed among these same individuals as children as early as age five.

But maybe we are treating the wrong people.

* * * * *

I'd like to propose, only half tongue-in-cheek, that I have discovered a new learning disability, which I am giving the name "Effective Education Deficit Disorder™" (EEDD™), though it closely correlates with another condition, "Attention Deficit Teaching Disorder™" (ADTD™), the difference being that the second disorder is specifically tied to the class-

---

4   Illich, Ivan, *Deschooling Society*, New York, NY: Harper & Row, 1971, 72-73

room, while the first may manifest itself more widely in other venues as well.

Both disorders (which only seem to afflict adults within the teaching occupation when they are trying to interact with children for purposes having to do with "education") can be diagnosed by the presence of at least four of the following six conditions:

1. The patient is unable to focus on the learning needs or desires of any individual child (or at least not for more than three minutes at any given time—hence the "attention deficit").

2. The patient is unable to interact flexibly with the learning timetable of any individual child. On the contrary, the patient expresses irritability (sometimes extreme) when children cannot or will not conform to his or her teaching timetable. "Jumpiness" and "impulsive behavior" are two of the hallmarks of EEDD™/ADTD™.

3. The patient suffers from a minor form of dementia or other "thought disorder", and believes that learning takes place through the unadulterated transfer of information from his or her own head to that of another, physically smaller one. At its worst, this thought disorder may express itself in feelings of grandiosity regarding one's own thought, and a belief that little is gained by allowing children to express their own. It may manifest itself in belligerent tones of voice, or unnatural facial expressions.

4. The patient suffers from obsessive-compulsive disorders. These may take the form of requiring regimentation in arrangement of furniture, rigorous requirements regarding handwriting or form of address, the lining up of objects or other human beings in size places (only according to vertical, and never horizontal, size) or alphabetically, a lack of regard for the personal space of others, the overly fastidious arrangement of materials on walls and bulletin boards, and a sometimes fanatical regard for the importance of what he or she regards as "neatness". The disorder may also manifest itself in repetitive speech. Disruption of expected spatial or chronological patterns or routines may result in symptomatic expressions of irritability, anger, difficulty in focusing, and other attention deficits and, in some cases, may result in the patient choosing to self-medicate, usually with alcohol, tobacco, or the illicit use of prescription drugs.

5. The patient believes that most effective learning takes place within his/her own highly controlled environment (despite all

evidence to the contrary), with strict grouping of human beings according to chronological age, and reduced contact with other human activity taking place outside the small indoor cubic space to which he/she is confined.

6. The patient has grandiose opinions regarding the importance of the activity in which he/she is engaged, despite the opinions of others as expressed in financial remuneration or social status. Having lost perspective, the patient may also lose any sense of humor or proportion, and may be subject to secondary bouts of delirium and/or depression.

Treatment:

EEDD™ and ADTD™ are difficult to treat effectively, especially as Stages 2 and 3 of the disorder are often accompanied by denial. There may be genetic predispositions to the two related disorders, though symptomology is most often environmentally induced. It is important to recognize that both EEDD™ and ADTD™ are chronic diseases, characterized by frequent relapses, and must be treated accordingly. Pharmacological interventions are under development. It is recommended that the patient be removed from the environment where symptoms manifest themselves, preferably for the long term. Group therapy and self-help groups such as EA™ (Educators Anonymous™) and TIR™ (Teachers in Recovery™) have shown promise, especially with attention to the first two steps in the 12-Step Process. ("1. We admit that we were powerless over our disorder, and that our lives had become unmanageable; and 2. We came to believe that a Power greater than ourselves could restore us to sanity.") Compassion, rather than ridicule or stigmatization, should be shown toward the unfortunate sufferers.

Large amounts of outdoor exposure during daylight hours are recommended. It is also highly advisable that contact with children be carefully controlled, and limited to recreational activities, preferably to those in which the patient has no expertise or experience. Once symptoms are under control, patients should be encouraged to engage in therapeutic learning activities, preferably those which may have been denied to them during their own childhoods.

We are delighted to have kept Meera home.

Learning About Learning: Conversations with My Violin

Nothing is so beautiful, nothing so moving, as the observance of a mind at work.

—Ruth J. Simmons, President,
Brown University, Inaugural Address,
October 14, 2001

At the beginning of my homeschooling talks, I usually inquire how many people in the audience are homeschooling parents or guardians. Virtually all the hands go up. (People are very well trained!) Then I ask how many were homeschooled themselves. In four years of asking, three hands have been raised.

The poet William Wordsworth made famous the catch phrase "The child is father to the man". Try as we might, we—as homeschooling parents—are unable to escape the reality that our picture of the world and of education is highly colored by our own school experiences, perhaps coupled with whatever efforts we have made to outgrow them. For many of us, these occasionally all-too-vivid memories, sometimes just lurking below the surface, are at least part of the reason that we have chosen a different path for our children. Yet many parents, sometimes unconsciously, often replicate methods or ways of addressing subject matter with their kids that resemble failed approaches that they themselves had to endure. Our experiences have left their scars, and our repertoires are sometimes limited by our personal histories, or our circumscribed ways of seeing the world, and we have learned how not to "be all that we can be", either for ourselves or for our children. Homeschooling can be an invitation to new potentialities and new possibilities, but only if we are willing to appreciate the lessons of our own pasts, and move beyond them to truly engage the unique inner wisdom of each individual child.

And so I like to spend time with homeschooling parents reflecting back upon those happy or unhappy days, as we try to assist each other in coming to a common understanding of what they were really about, and then use this understanding to move forward in our collective family educational journeys. This is half of what I call "learning about learning". The other half, which I will share in the second part of this essay, is what I've been learning about learning in our homeschooling experiences.

* * * * *

There was a child went forth every day;
And the first object he look'd upon, that object he became;
And that object became part of him for the day, or a certain part of the
*   day, or for many years,*
Or stretching cycles of years.
                    —Walt Whitman, "There was a child went forth", from
                                                              Leaves of Grass

I grew up in New York City. I usually tell people "it's a great place to be from." Actually, I don't remember it as being a bad place. Most kids grow up believing that their hometown must be like everyone else's hometown, only to be rudely or pleasantly surprised by later experience.

Anyway, as already noted earlier, I attended Public School #131 AND Three-Quarters. I don't believe it had a name. I didn't think of that as particularly strange at the time and, until much later, assumed that all public schools were known by number rather than name. Now having lectured from coast to coast across North America, the only other place that I have discovered with schools numbered rather than named is Buffalo, New York. But at the time, I would have needed some convincing.

The school was a Works Progress Administration building from the 1930s. It was four stories tall, all in red brick, and topped by a Roman triangular pediment in granite, with the words "Public School #131 AND Three-Quarters " carved into the frieze. They were apparently very proud that the schools had numbers rather than names, and probably saw the numbering as an expression of progress—if one could numerize and quantify something, chances are one could improve it, and something of importance was likely to be taking place inside.

So when I try to focus back on what went on for me there, the first thing that instantly jumps out is that we "did" Eskimos in the third grade, Egyptians in fourth, and South and Central American Indians in fifth. Here we were, in New York City, sons and daughters and grandsons and granddaughters of immigrants. This would be even more true today: Jews from Russia and Lithuania and Romania; German Lutherans; Italian and Polish and Puerto Rican Catholics; Indian Hindus; Buddhists and followers of Confucius from China; African-American Baptists; a few Moslems with roots in the Middle East; even, might I dare say it, a rare Episcopalian! Now my school wasn't quite that diverse at the time—the wonderful polyglot of cultures and colors that is New York City—but we would all have loved the opportunity to learn about each other, or about our own roots, or at least to have had some connection or something to contribute to the learning enterprise.

But, no, we "did" Eskimos, Egyptians, and Central and South Americans in that order. All classes the same, always in that order. Year after year, or so I've been told, the order never changed. The third grade teacher, old wonderful gray-haired Mrs. Epstein (all names have been changed to protect the guilty) could only "do" Eskimos, and I bet she didn't know anything about Egyptians. And fat, marble-mouthed Mrs. Bonein only knew how to "do" Egyptians—and then, only dead ones—but she would have been totally out of her depth with Incas and Aztecs. (And all the dead Egyptians in the books and pictures were white, too, which never got explained to me—I think I may have been the only one in the class to figure out that Egypt was, currently, in Africa, according to the map on the wall, and I kept on imagining that maybe Egypt was in a different location in the old days? I mean (as I later realized), wasn't there a Thebes in Greece (Aeschylus even wrote a play about it!), and isn't Graceland in Memphis? And didn't Cleopatra look like Elizabeth Taylor on her second husband? But then I'm not sure most of us had learned yet that Black people originally came from Africa either—it wasn't part of the curriculum. Come to think of it, I had no idea at the time how *any of us* ended up at P.S. 131 3/4!)

Much later in life, I discovered that a lot of the information my teachers served up was wrong. Until I was 40 or thereabouts, I thought that Eskimos (until then, "Inuits" and "Aleuts" hadn't been invented for me) lived in igloos. I remember making igloos in Mrs. Epstein's third grade class. We took sugar cubes and pasted them together in the shape of a dome onto a piece of stiff cardboard, with puffy cotton snow pasted all around, and, at the entrance, a little plastic Eskimo dog, too big of course, so big that the dog might have eaten the igloo! And parents of all the kids came on open school night and admired our Eskimo housing developments—they got educated, too!

I quickly came to believe that the only people who lived in Canada were Eskimos, and that it was covered in snow all year round. The following summer (I being age 9), we took a trip to Toronto to visit a very distant relative. He resided on the fourth floor of a 15-story apartment building, and it was broiling hot, in the highs 90s. This really couldn't be Canada, I remember telling myself, because he wasn't an Eskimo, there was no snow, and there was nary a sign of an igloo anywhere.

Forty years later, I now know that Inuits and Aleuts lived in houses made of stone, earth, and what little wood and whalebone could be found. The igloos were only for fishing and hunting expeditions. When I told this to a colleague of mine from North Carolina some months ago, she said it was a life-changing experience!

I also seem to remember the fifth grade teacher Mrs. Millard telling us that the Aztecs had "died out" (no explanation as to why). I took that to mean *died* of course, so it came as a surprise to me when I got to meet my first Aztec about ten years ago. Now I can't blame my teachers, really, as I'm sure they'd never met either an Eskimo or an Aztec, and I'm positive they hadn't met any dead white Egyptians! And it wouldn't have mattered if we had done Romans, Greeks, or Hebrews instead.

But more critically, I have often wondered what might have happened in my poor brain if they'd changed the order or, heaven forbid, asked us who *we* really wanted to learn about. And the same was true for all my subjects. Why should I want to learn long division when what I really wanted to do was figure out the height of the big oak tree outside the classroom window. Cursed with a last name beginning with "A" and thus condemned to the front row, righthand seat in the classroom for more than a half a decade ("Ah, yes, Row 1, Seat 1," my retired schoolteacher mother remembers officiously), my wandering attention was too obvious.

"David!" snapped Mrs. Bonein, "Would you mind sharing with the class what is so interesting out there?"

"David," Mrs. Millard would utter in sweet sing-song manner, "Do you think you could grace us with your presence a little longer?"

"Mr. Albert," barked gruff Mr. Lucas, the sixth grade teacher, former military man, who doubled as the schoolyard monitor, "I hate to inform you of this, but the windows were put there to allow light into the building, not so you could look out!"

We all have our own tales to tell. I invite you to remember them, and share them with your kids when appropriate. It is how we have come to recognize that the Emperor of public education has no clothes. The main reason we all have these wondrous stories to tell about schools, sometimes comical, sometimes tragic, is that they reveal the first two of three fundamental principles of public education, namely:

1. Children are to be taught a content not of their own choice; and
2. They are to be taught this content on a timetable not of their own devising.

These two fundamental principles put schools at a tremendous disadvantage in trying to provide anything that might responsibly be called education. Teachers recognize this, which is why the good ones feel compelled to come up with all sorts of tricks to make content that should already be inherently engaging "interesting" to all, and why they chafe under the strain of the new standardized tests. It is in harnessing the empowering potential of other possibilities than makes homeschooling, in my judgment, such an attractive option.

The late John Holt, considered by many to be the founder of the modern homeschooling movement (though he was himself a schoolteacher, and with no children of his own), once compared the administrative machinery of public education to a cannery. It should be remembered, of course, that public schooling as we now know it rose in tandem with the modern industrial system, and for the explicit purposes of serving its needs, as John Taylor Gatto (in *The Underground History of American Education*) has so amply demonstrated. Frank Smith, in his superb *The Book of Learning and Forgetting* (New York, NY: Teachers College Press, 1998), among others, also points to the Prussian military as the other major foundation of the public education system.[1]

At any rate, the imagery of the cannery is apt and easy to see. The empty cans are mounted on the conveyor belt at age five…whoops, maybe at age three through Head Start….age two through Early Head Start—I wouldn't be surprised in the future to see phonics being taught *in utero*. At each grade level, identical ingredients are poured into presumably identical cans. In my day, it was Eskimos in third grade, dead white Egyptians in fourth, Central and South American Indians in fifth, etc. Standardized tests are taken which make it possible to bump the dented or leaky cans off the line—either by moving them backwards on the line so they can be refilled, or by placing them in "special ed" racks (where they are highly prized for the extra revenue they bring in). Paradoxically, the school district would be quite pleased if they disappeared entirely (if the cans are removed from the school district, they will no longer bring down the school's test score average). The line continues and once the cans are more than half full, they are provided with micro-doses of new material—the "spices"—48 minutes of this, 52 minutes of that, 49 minutes of etc. The

---

1   Smith notes that, "Numerous relics of the militaristic origins of modern educational theory survive in the language we use today. We talk of the *deployment* of resources, the *recruitment* of teachers and students, *advancing* or *withdrawing* students, *promotion* to higher grades, *drills* for learners, *strategies* for teachers, *batteries* of tests, word *attack* skills, attainment *targets*, *reinforcement*, *cohorts*, *campaigns* for achievement in mathematics, and *wars* against illiteracy. The fact that this language seems *natural* to us, that we have all become so accustomed to it, perfectly illustrates the insidious infiltration of militaristic thinking in education." (47)

cans are again tested at least twice more for consistency of content, more of them being bumped off the line in the process. At the end of 12 or 13 years, the cans are sealed up, labels pasted on, and shipped to their appropriate destinations. New cans are moving up the line.

Notice that in this extended metaphor there is no mention of teachers. Viewed this way, other than as content dispensers, teachers are simply there to "humanize" and control what is essentially an industrial process. It is clear from national trends—ranging from classroom standardization and scripting to criteria-based testing strategies and the adoption of technology-based learning—that less and less value is being accorded this humanization. Teachers may be wonderful human beings and have much to offer their charges. I have fond memories of several extraordinary ones, and I'll bet many of you do, too. But from the point of view of education *production*, they are simply a "cost center", not a particular efficient one, and, in the future, perhaps not even a necessary one. As if to prove the point, in some of the Southern states (notably Georgia), school districts are experimenting with the use of teachers without even a college degree or extensive training, and, apparently, without any deleterious effects.

Of course, Holt's metaphor presents a macro view. To bring it down to the level of the child (and to use something a bit more contemporary), a better metaphor for modern public education might be to liken it to transferring files from one computer to another, or perhaps more correctly, unidirectionally from the 'file server' stationed in the front of the room to the 'file recipient' parked in one of those little chairs behind one of those little desks of a type and size never to be seen anywhere else in the real world. To continue the metaphor, if education happens, bits of data move through the pipe to their destination. But as we all remember from our school days, what has moved—if it has moved at all—is simply *information*. It in no way can be construed as knowledge, for to become knowledge, information has to have an action attached to it.

So what is the attached action in the school setting? Dependably, (though still remembering the action of gluing the sugar cubes together), there is only one—test-taking. The education bureaucrats *do* understand this well enough. The future of information-in-action (knowledge) is the ability to dump that information—in much diluted form, of course—on a test, where it becomes pure information again. The theory, or what little that passes for it, is that after the dump takes place, there will be some residual knowledge left over that can be used at some unspecified time for an even more unspecified purpose, but which will, it is believed, make us *more productive citizens* so that "we" (unspecified) *can compete in the global marketplace.*

Now to many teachers, I know this metaphor may seem cruel. Many of them attended teacher training programs and graduate schools of education where they learned all about Dewey, and progressive and "constructivist" approaches to education are all the rage.[2] But nothing can be further from the minds of state and national education bureaucrats who measure results in answers given and facts learned and regurgitated, rather than that loosey-goosey stuff. If there is cruelty in the analogy, responsibility for its infliction does not lie with me. (The fact that teachers stay in the profession at all after witnessing how far the requirements of their classroom are from what they may have learned in graduate school suggests to me that most are either incredibly foolhardy, extraordinarily gullible, or exceptionally courageous. Indeed, they may be all three, and often are!)

We now can come to an expanded understanding of our own experience of public education. It is governed by three administrative principles—to call them *educational theory* would be to give them far more credence than they deserve: children are to be taught a content not of their own choosing, on a timetable not of their own devising, and are to be taught this content through the dumping of data bits. These are lousy principles, and lousy practice, simply because they do not acknowledge our children as those unique and wonderful bits of star-stuff gathered that they truly are.

We all learned how to adapt, one way or another. That was how we survived, and some of us even thrived. In fact, adaptation was probably the lesson more of us internalized than any other. To draw a less than farfetched analogy, there have been studies of the process by which prisoners, when deprived of their freedom, adapt to conditions of confinement. There seem to be three ways: 1) Passivity—one tries to call as little attention to oneself as possible; 2) Slavishness—one does as one is told, as well as possible and as quickly as possible, even learning to anticipate commands, and nothing else; and 3) Mindless rebellion—rebellious acts don't change the

---

2   Constructivist approaches to education are loosely (sometimes *very* loosely) based on the work of the Swiss psychologist Jean Piaget, which suggests that learners actively construct knowledge themselves. Focus is (supposed to be) on the learner in thinking about learning, rather than on the subject/lesson to be taught. Teachers are expected to be companions and guides who stimulate, with a minimal exercise of authority. They are also supposed to be "co-learners". (I've never seen an actual example of this put into practice—if they tried this in high school chemistry, the school district would very likely be sued!)

system, but they force the system to respond to the individual *differently*. The response to rebellion may be to worsen the prisoner's conditions of confinement. But, psychologically, this is a strategy that for the captive may result in increasing one's self-respect.[3]

To those of you who might wish to summarily reject the prison analogy, I ask you only to remember your schoolmates: Alice, who occupied that seat in the back of the room by the closet, praying that she wouldn't be called upon, and who would really have preferred a seat *in* the closet; Alex, the teacher's pet, who the only time he ever got into trouble was when he raised his hand to answer a question before it was asked; and Andrew, who threw erasers, deliberately (but accidentally, of course) fell off his chair at regular intervals, and stabbed Alex with his pen (or whatever else was at hand) on every available occasion. When one systematically denies a class of people their freedom, one shouldn't be surprised when they act as if they are unfree. And none of these three are good ways to go out and meet the world.[4] The very idea that one can educate for freedom or for living in a free society through the exercise of age-based authoritarianism in a compulsory environment of day incarceration (and home monitoring!) is just another example of the Emperor's new clothes. Forget the First, Fourth, and Fifth Amendments, or *habeas corpus*, and just try to get bail!

Do these sound too familiar? No matter. One thing I think I can say with some certainty is that when society operates with these three principles governing its educational systems, children's expectations of learning and of living are lowered so that they learn to expect little out of life other than material gratification. We can argue about whether this is intentional or a byproduct (a good starting point for discussion might be my essay

---

3   The educator Herbert Kohl describes a form of this rebellion or resistance which he calls "not-learning": "Not-learning tends to take place when someone has to deal with unavoidable challenges to her or his personal and family loyalties, integrity, and identity. In such situations, there are forced choices and no apparent middle ground. To agree to learn from a stranger who does not respect your integrity causes a major loss of self. The only alternative is to not-learn and reject their world." *'I Won't Learn from You': And Other Thoughts on Creative Maladjustment.* New York, NY: New Press, 1994.

4   My good friend Jean Reed, author of my all-time favorite homeschooling book *The Home School Sourcebook* (Bridgewater, ME: Brook Farm Books, 2000), gently chides me that I (or, actually, the researchers) left out the example of prisoners of conscience—many Quakers among them—who historically effected positive changes in prison environments through a principled program of nonviolent resistance, including strategic noncooperation and hunger strikes. Would that we would see more of this kind of activity in the public school environment!

The Success *of Public Education,* also included in this volume). But whether intentional or byproduct, this is the real socialization that goes on in school, and the main reason my wife and I have chosen that my kids shouldn't be there!

* * * * *

About four years ago, I took up the violin. Among the other factors that led to this decision, I think one of the main ones was that I grew jealous of my kids. They were growing into exceedingly accomplished musicians: Aliyah as an extraordinary composer, as well as a violinist and oboist, and Meera as an exceptionally gifted pianist and flautist. Among my hopes was that I might become expert enough to play along with them at some future time, though these days that point seems to be receding further and further—they have long since lapped me on the musical track. Still there was all this wonderful western music to explore (I am quite adept, or at least I was, on an Asian Indian instrument called the *veena*), and I wanted to make music rather than just listen to it.

Besides giving freer reign to my love of music, I also wanted to investigate in a rather more conscientious fashion what it is really like to be learning something wholly new. What kind of knowledge would actually be required, or more pointedly, what kind of knowledge would *I* require? What kinds of thought processes would I engage in while this learning was taking place? Could I recognize similar processes in my children's learning? How does learning organize itself? And, if I knew, would it affect the way I think about homeschooling practice, or education generally speaking?

And the very first thing I came to realize is that learning is a magical operation that happens when new information, combined with already accessed and internalized knowledge, forges a new reality. Once learning takes place, one is forever changed. And, unlike information transfer, learning is not linear. I joke sometimes that to map what happens in the learning process is almost an exercise in chaos theory—and our homes (or at least our children's rooms, though my room is hardly any better) are simply outward manifestations of this chaos in action!

This isn't to say that learning happens without structure. In fact, my personal experience—in watching myself learn and in witnessing my children do the same—suggests that learning requires structure. But it is structure *in the mind*, what the anthropologist Gregory Bateson calls "the pattern that connects", the mental architecture that allows us to engage and make sense of the world around us. This has virtually nothing to do with the structure of curricula (and, as we shall see, it may be antithetical to it), which is where school-based curricula and many of those used by home-schoolers (notably *The Well-Trained Mind*) can go radically wrong. Of course, little damage will have been done through their use, provided only that parents pay clear heed to what Frank Smith calls the child's fundamental "right to ignore anything that doesn't make sense" (to *her*, not to the parents), or which doesn't feed the child's engagement in ordering the chaos of the world *as she sees it*.

What I discovered in my "learning about learning" is that this structure takes the form of what might be thought of as "conversations". These conversations take place with the external world, certainly, but also internally within ourselves, as we seek order in the chaos of information pressing down upon us. For adults (or at least for me), these conversations—and I have been able (with the help of Aliyah, who spends an enormous amount of time thinking about thinking) to identify five of them—take place simultaneously; they are like meetings of my homeschool group! I suspect that the seeds of each these conversations exist within children from the earliest age, and they have their own ebbs and flows, points at which one only touches the surface, and others where they become really deep. But as children develop, different conversations come to center stage, engaging them most fully in putting together, for themselves, *a structure that makes sense*.

Aliyah took up the violin before she was two, an experience I write about at length in *And the Skylark Sings with Me*. So, combined with my own learning experience, it should not come as any surprise that I am going to use many musical examples as I examine the five conversations. But as I describe them, I hope you will be able to see how they apply to other arenas in your children's learning experiences, always from the point of view of the child's inner life.

These five conversations are:

- the conversation with nature and the natural order;
- . the conversation with the past and with history
- the conversation with the present and the world of convention and, especially, social convention;
- the conversation with the future;
- the conversation with Oneself (note the capital "O").

I am convinced that these conversations, taken together, represent the individual and unique, yet fundamentally human, need to search for truth, not as a machine-like apparatus registering facts, but in the mastery of material and spiritual life.

1. The Conversation with Nature and the Natural Order

My own religious frame of reference suggests to me that God's handprints are writ large upon the world, and we are all but children learning to read them. But one has no need of any religious point of view to see that children before age seven or so put most of their entire being into trying to make sense of how the natural world, and their bodies—which are part of the natural order—work. For without this understanding and this self-mastery—this structure of the mind—it is difficult to make any further sense of the world around them.

Between the ages of eight and nine, Aliyah took to playing her violin down at the local farmer's market, at street fairs, and various festivals in the area. She'd put down her violin case and, over time, with the nickels, dimes, quarters, and dollar bills collected, she earned enough to enroll in a telescope-making course, purchase a new violin and a folkharp, and go on a wolf-tracking expedition in Idaho. She was just as appreciative when the local vegetable seller would pay her in cabbages for attracting people to her stand, or when a polished rock would appear in the violin case.

Occasionally a three- or four- or five-year-old, often tugging on mom's sleeve, would stop and stare open-mouthed at the musicmaking. Aliyah learned that it was fun to invite the child to give the violin—in this case, a genuine imitation copy of a fake Stradivarius, made in Germany—a try. She'd hand the violin to the little boy and he'd tentatively, and with arms and hands much too small, hold it up somewhere against his chest or shoulder, hands often totally on the wrong side or on the wrong part of the violin, trying to find the right place so that the violin wouldn't drop to the ground. He would try various hand positions, until things would calm down once the right hand reached out for the end of the scroll, and by pushing the violin against his body, gravity would be denied, and the violin would finally be secure!

And then Aliyah would hand him the bow. Most likely he'd grab it right in the middle, and start sawing away over the top of the fingerboard. Strange squeals and scrapings would result.

But, now, and I have seen this on several occasions, it might get interesting. If lucky, mom would be distracted by the lettuces and cucumbers, or a rack of scarves. And the little boy, if he had been observant, would by trial and error try to figure out where to put the fingers of the lefthand in order to vary the pitch. He would thus begin to recapitulate the experiments of Pythagoras, the 6th Century B.C. Greek philosopher, who figured out, with the aid of monochord (an ancient one-stringed instrument), at what point one would have to shorten the length of a vibrating string in order to produce octaves, fifths, fourths, and thirds. In other words, he would start exploring the mathematical physics involved in sound production.

Both of my daughters read music before they could read English fluently. I wouldn't assert that this was either a good or bad idea, only that it was *their* idea. That was where they were led. It facilitated their ability to produce the sounds they wanted to bring pleasure to their own ears. They also learned to do fractions before two-place addition, although they didn't know it—reading whole notes, half-notes, quarter-notes, eighth-notes, and dotted notes (which increases the value of any note by 50%). So much for "scope and sequence". Actually, musical note-reading is quite a sophisticated concept, beyond the mathematics involved. It entails dividing up an interval of time into its respective relative parts, seeing this representation of time as well as of pitch on paper, and then reproducing it in sound. Four-year-olds do this. Five-year-olds do this. Six-year-olds do this.

Music reading or no, what I am asserting is that children's early knowledge quests are driven by the need to understand and master the knowledge necessary to *converse* effectively with the natural world (in this case, the world of sound), and with their natural selves. We have all seen this in the sandbox, where children, left to their own devices, will create worlds in miniature. They come to an understanding of three states of matter (the fourth—*the jello state*—is, they learn, reserved to the kitchen table). They learn all about evaporation and absorption and erosion, and the action of sun, rain, and wind. They master Newton's three laws of motion here and on their tricycles and bicycles and, if actually taught their names, will remember them and identify the actions of these laws in their play.

Because the kids are so caught up in learning about the natural world does not mean that the world of library research is closed to them, even before they learn to read. For her Halloween costume following her third birthday, Aliyah informed us that she wanted to be a penguin. But not just any penguin—an *Emperor* Penguin (she'd seen a picture in a book.) She wanted to know what sound an Emperor Penguin makes. This was hardly knowledge I had at my fingertips. She listened as I called the reference librarian at the local library, who said she would get back to me within a day. Several hours later, the phone rang.

"Hello," I said.

"Ga-ga-ga-GAAAHHH!" came out of the receiver.

"Could you repeat that?" I asked, handing the phone to Aliyah.

"Ga-ga-ga-GAAAHHH!"

Aliyah was certainly the most authentic Emperor Penguin in the neighborhood. At the same time, she watched her ignorant parents go on a fruitful information search about the natural world, the lessons of which I'm sure stuck with her for a long time.

Einstein once said that more than 90% of the physics anyone will ever learn is learned before the age of three. Given free reign, the child's conversation with nature and the natural world forms the ground upon which all future conversations are yet to be built.

2. The Conversation with the Past and with History

It is the age of dinosaurs.

If we have children that are old enough, we all remember *that age*. It could have been six, or seven, or eight, and seems to make its first appearance in the car, or at least that's how we remember it. All those questions! "Why are clouds sometimes shaped like ships, and other times like animals?" "How did the stars get to the sky?" "How do the tulip bulbs know when to sprout?" "What makes an elbow work?"

It may begin with a bunch of questions having to do with the natural or physical world (suggesting continuing engagement with the first conversation) but they seem to move further. "What did you do for fun before I was here?" "Where did you live before you and daddy lived in our house?" "Was grandma able to walk before she broke her hip?" "Were you alive when there were brontosauri?"

And then they begin to progress to a third type of question. "How did people cook before they had electric (or gas) stoves?" "Who invented bicycles?" "Where did eyeglasses come from?" "What was life like before (check one): TV; automobiles; running water?"

You answer many of the questions. You do your own research. And then you think it would be useful to offer to help her look up the answers to the less personal questions at the library, or talk to grandma for some of the more personal ones over the telephone. But you quickly discover that more often than not, your daughter doesn't seem particularly interested in the answers, though she'll take in the new information and sometimes draw upon it when the appropriate occasion warrants.

What she is really learning through all these questions is something different entirely, for she is interested in *your responses*, if not the answers. She is seeking to find out the limits of your knowledge, the sources of it, and how it was acquired. You think she is just looking for information, and she is, but more importantly, she is peeling away at the levels of your mind like an archaeologist, mapping your knowledge storehouses. For now she has discovered that you *don't* know everything, and further, that there is time and experience that predate you, and she will have to find other knowledge resources to draw upon.

So begins the conversation with the past and with history. The budding violinist, for example, may ask what the hair on her bow is made of, and find out that the best is made of bleached Siberian horse(tail) hair. She may discover that, prior to metal strings, violin strings were generally made of sheep gut (*not* cat gut—'catgut' is an anglicization of Catigny, a town in northern France mostly destroyed during World War I, from which the highest quality *sheep-gut* violin strings came. No violin strings were ever made of the innards of felines, or at least I haven't discovered any.) But now how was it revealed that the desired sound was to be made by drawing bleached Siberian horsetail hair across sheep guts stretched over very strangely shaped and fabricated pieces of wood? This is truly a history question!

Or an eight- or nine-year-old child might ask why her violin is shaped the way it is. You (or preferably the violin teacher) might find yourselves explaining that in 17th Century Europe there were two families of stringed instruments competing for supremacy—the viols and the violins. The English (personified by Henry Purcell) selected the viols, and lost, and composers after Bach no longer wrote for them. The violins, championed by the Court of Louis XIV (the "Sun King") were victorious, as people chose to copy French fashion in things musical and artistic. Except for the bass viols. While nominally similar in shape, a bass instrument with its current range fabricated like a violin (rather than as a viol) would have to be 16 feet tall, and people haven't grown *that much* taller since the 17th Century!

Or, she might ask, "who wrote this music they make me play?" "Who wrote 'Twinkle Star'?" (Mozart.) "How about Bach's 'Minuet in G'?" Trick question. The answer, we now know, is one Christian Petzold. Bach, with his almost two dozen children by two consecutive wives, couldn't quite afford their upkeep, so he took in boarders, usually music students. He kept a little book in which visitors and boarders (and his kids) could write little musical ditties, and for his second wife Anna's birthday, he put them all together into a book called *The Anna Magdalena Notebook*, which contains said Minuet. More history, and the kids, once they have tuned into this conversation, love it!

Kids ages 7-10 develop a keen interest in how things came to be the way they are. In this conversation with the past, they begin to become conscious of their own development agewise, and begin to understand that adults change in age and capacity as well. They begin to understand death, and generations, and the fact that the artifacts of their lives, and that of their parents, may reflect a past of which they have no direct knowledge. Reading now becomes a useful tool for opening up conversations with history unavailable to them in any other way. This conversation becomes richer and richer as it becomes interwoven into the fabric of their experience.

Of course, there is a past of which children are aware, and which can be used in helping them acquire a more confident sense of themselves, and that is their own development. Parents often make it a practice to mark the kids' growth in height on a wall so the children can see it for themselves, and some may even graph their weight. But the same can be done with knowledge development. Set aside a day to sit down with your child, preferably with a big cake, and write down (without trying to correct them) all the things she says she knows about the world. It can simply be random facts, or organized into subject headings: history, nature, mathematics, music, family relationships, etc. Take the list and stick it in an envelope, which you agree to open on that same day a year later. When the envelope is opened, she (and you!) will be amazed at how much has been learned in a year, and how wide-ranging learning has been, regardless of whether it has been formally taught or not. The child's view of herself will now be significantly expanded, and she will look forward with gusto to the next episode in her educational adventures.

3. The Conversation with the Present and the World of Social Convention

Round about ages 9, 10, or 11, if the capacity for inquiry hasn't already been shut down by the world around them, the questions begin anew. Again the questions (and hence the conversations) will have changed. They will still often begin with "why", but instead of "Why is the sky blue?" (nature), or "Why is my saxophone shaped the way it is?" (history), one is more likely to hear questions like "Why does Dad have to wear a tie to work?" or (on a visit to London) "Why do the English use their forks differently (especially when they eat peas)?" Or, to use a musical example again, "Why, when I go to a concert, do the cellos all sit in the front on the right side, so I can never see the flute and oboe players? After all, cellos are louder."

From the earliest age, our kids learn conventions—often unspoken agreements about the way things work in the world—and social conventions—the unwritten "rules of the road" governing their behavior. They learn these at a fantastic rate, so fast, in fact, if we don't look carefully, we don't even see them.

Think back on your early school experiences, for example. The real socialization that takes place in schools is effected through the learning of social conventions. Teachers, like lawyers, spend six hours each day asking questions for which they already know the answers. (Imagine being in a workplace 200 days a year, and having your boss, hour after hour, going from desk to desk asking questions for which she already knew the answer. Yet, we have been socialized into accepting this as appropriate behavior in the school environment.) Children are to line up in size places, but size only measured vertically, never horizontally. Children are told again and again how important cooperation is, only to be told that to do so when something important called a test comes along, it's called *cheating*. I probably would never have learned what cheating was (or at least not until much later) if I hadn't been taught it in school at such a young age.

Of course, wherever learning takes place, be it in or out of school, there are the conventions of the lesson itself. How exactly does one behave? In a music lesson, does one just sit quietly, absorbing what the teacher says? Does one ask a lot of questions? Does one copy what the teacher does, or pay more attention to what she says? Is there room for disagreement? Is conversation expected? What are the applicable conventions?

There are even more basic social and artistic conventions surrounding public performances. Without an understanding of them, one can easily be left at sea, and the experience quite uncomfortable, so much so, that individuals who choose to attend once—be it a Shakespeare play or an Italian opera—may never return. (In fact, many of us received 'inoculations' against them in our school experiences.)

I like to use the example of a visiting friend from India. If we go to a rock concert together, he learns readily that the proper time to express appreciation is, well, anytime he wants, really. Then I might take him to a classical music concert featuring Beethoven's Fifth Symphony. "Da-da-da DAAAH; Da-da-da DAAAH," etc. After the first movement, there will be fits of coughing, bouts of sneezing, a torrent of nose-blowing, and a great rustle of seat-wiggling. No applause. My friend might turn to me, somewhat bewildered, and ask, "Didn't they like it?" By convention, in the late 20th/early 21st Century, audiences don't clap between movements. In the 19th Century, they would not only clap, but occasionally demand the repeat of a movement even before the symphony was over. And in the early 20th Century, particularly *avant garde* symphonic or ballet performances might result in riots in the streets, as actually happened during the premiere of Stravinsky and Diaghilev's *The Rite of Spring* in Paris in May 1913.

The strong reaction to *The Rite of Spring* was precipitated by the breaking of musical and dance conventions and the inability of audiences to immediately come to terms with them. Keep in mind, though, that for a 10-year-old, *all* of the artistic conventions may be new, and if the experience is to be a success, preparation beforehand is a must. Otherwise they can be bewildering (as they can be for adults).

In my experience, the western art form with the largest number of conventions that must be understood before true enjoyment can happen is Italian opera. Consider, for example, going to the opera house to see Donizetti's four-act *Lucia di Lammermoor*. It has absolutely magnificent music, but perhaps one of the stupidest plots, based on the Sir Walter Scott novel *The Bride of Lammermoor*.

There are some obvious conventions. All dialogue will take place in Italian, and all of it will be sung. If a character is standing downstage and singing at the top of his lungs, in certain instances it must be assumed that the characters located at another part of the stage can't hear him. Conversations among characters are interrupted by 4-6 minutes of individuals singing lines of poetry. At one point, six characters stand upstage, all singing different words at the same time, all oblivious of each other, but the words fitting the music perfectly! Translations of the Italian flash across an electronic board above the stage, although during the sextet, the board is, frankly, hopeless!

There are various Enricos, Arturos, Raimondos, and Edgardos who run around on stage. But most people go to the opera to hear the famous 'mad scene' in the third act. What sets it up is very simple: Lucia has to marry the wrong guy. The opera chorus stands on both sides of the stage singing some version of "oh, happy day, there's going to be a wedding, we will eat and drink and be merry, etc., etc.", all in Italian of course. And then, down a staircase, center stage, comes Lucia, dressed in white for her wedding, carrying a bloody knife! The chorus recoils in horror. Lucia sings her first aria, accompanied by a glass harmonica (nothing like a "mouth harmonica", but an instrument perfected by Benjamin Franklin[5]), the song being about how she has just made the "supreme sacrifice" (she murdered the wannabe undesirable hubbie upstairs).

Now after the first aria (there being two), the music stops, and people clap wildly. (You can do that here, but not after the first movement of a symphony. Go figure!) "Brava, diva, brava" might be heard from the balconies. (In Italy, in earlier times, there might also have been a convention of throwing overripe tomatoes if audience members hadn't liked what they'd heard.) If the applause goes on long enough, Lucia might step out of character and bow to the left and right, then step back into character and sing her second aria, even more mad than the first, in which she says she believes she is now already in heaven. With her last high "C"s still ringing, she falls down dead on the stage (in one performance I saw, she actually stabs herself with the already bloody knife), and the curtain falls.

But there is a problem. This is a four-act opera named *Lucia di Lammermoor*, and this was only the third act, and Lucia is dead.[6] The tenor has to commit suicide on her tomb in the next act. As there can be no waiting to salute the soprano's performance, Lucia is resurrected from the dead, and steps in front of the curtain, still in her (perhaps bloody) bridal costume, to accept the applause of her fans. Little flower girls will bring her bouquets from the wings, and she might blow kisses to the crowd. But not for too long, as lover-boy must meet his fate.

Conventions have their own histories, though they may be long forgotten by the time your child meets up with them. Spelling (especially English spelling) is among the most interesting of our academic conventions, because thousands of words have intriguing spelling histories, including Noah Webster's successful initiative to banish the "u" from "color", and his unsuccessful battle against silent "e"s. But by age 10-12, the conversation for the child has changed. What she is likely to be interested in is not the history of spelling, but how to ensure her spelling usage is *conventional*, and "fits in". From experience, I have learned that a child may learn more

---

5   See www.finkenbeiner.com/gh.html. The glass harmonica was accused of causing evils such as nervous disorder, domestic squabbles, premature deliveries, fatal disorders, and convulsions in animals. The instrument was even banned from a German town by police for ruining public health and disturbing public order (a child even died during a concert). Having disappeared from the world of music for more than a century, it seems to have been rediscovered and has regained a limited popularity since 1982.

6   Sometimes it is simply presented as the first of two scenes in a final third act.

spelling in three weeks as a ten-year-old than she is likely to in six months when she is seven or eight.

At around age ten, children may also become acutely concerned with what they perceive to be injustice or unfairness, either within conventions themselves or in the violation of them. Different bed times, neighborhood rules or community curfews, or even the receipt of different gifts by siblings based on chronological age may seem like personal affronts. They may decide that our convention of meat-eating is unjust, or the laboratory testing of animals, or the application of capital punishment. Sometimes (and with the help of adults) they will act upon their new-found convictions in concert. I enjoyed reading recently of a class of Massachusetts schoolchildren who became upset that a highway sign displayed a Pilgrim's hat with an arrow going through it, reflecting a conventional attitude and stereotypical depiction of Native Americans. They didn't stop protesting until the signs were removed.

Again, we are confronted with a different set of "why" questions, and "because" becomes an even less acceptable answer (if it ever was!). The world becomes a more uncomfortable place when its conventions (as seen in the attitudes and conduct of the surrounding adults) seem to fly in the face of one's emerging sense of justice. It should not seem surprising then when pre-adolescents seek solace, it is often in the company of their equally discomforted peers.

There is nothing wrong with learning conventions. In fact, the thousands of conventions we develop socially are the grease that allows our daily lives to glide smoothly. And despite the fact that we are often told that the pre-teen or early teen years are a time of rebellion, pre-adolescents tend to be extremely conventional, but governed by the conventions of their peers—who are also questioning—but with whom they want to fit in. They may develop their own conventions—of clothing, hairstyle, musical likes and dislikes, or even speech—to set themselves off from the conventions of their elders which they have not come to appreciate—but they are conventional nonetheless.

Of course we want our children to function appropriately in society. They need to learn to share, to respect each other and to respect differences, to cooperate freely, to make decisions democratically, to use their gifts and talents for community benefit. But the reason to help our children understand the world of social convention is so that they will learn when it is appropriate, even imperative, to resist social and institutional pressures as warranted. This is not something they are likely to be taught in middle school.

This is also the time to engage our children in conversation with the heroes of our planet, those who throughout history have broken with social convention and have put the welfare of others above their own personal comfort. And it is also the time to help children begin to internalize a set of principles, formerly simply understood as a set of external rewards and consequences, as ethical touchstones for them to remember when faced with their own set of moral decisions.

4. The Conversation with the Future

In some sense, the conversation with the future is the foundation conversation, the one which, alongside the conversation with nature, is the first in which the child engages. The acute watching and listening, the constant trial-and-error experimentation, the in-built, relentless impulse to expand one's horizons, this "original seeking" about which I have written earlier, all of which lies at the basis of learning, is what makes it possible to make order out of what might otherwise seem like a chaotic world.

I've already intimated that it is this conversation with the future that is most underdeveloped in the school environment, which both retards and warps educational efforts. For the future of what is learned there, children quickly come to understand, is the information dump.

Let's examine for a moment why a child might decide to play the violin, or any instrument for that matter, at all. (Now my wife comments at this point that there are a few who did so to escape another class!) It might be that she has heard her Uncle Bill perform at the county fair, and wants to be like him. Or maybe she has seen Itzhak Perlman on *Sesame Street* and wants to play like him. Or perhaps there is an older sibling whom she wishes to emulate. Or she has heard a particular Irish fiddle tune and would like to be able to play it in her step dance class. Or perhaps there is a group of friends who are forming a grunge band in a garage down the street, and she'd like to be able to join in. Or maybe, just maybe, and probably less commonly than one might expect, she just wants to be able to pleasure her own ear.

Note that all of these reasons to play the violin are far off in the future (for me personally, they still seem terribly distant!). They have nothing to do with instant or tangible gratification—gold stars or words of praise or success at playing that awful B-flat scale. They have everything to do with a child's imagined image of self, of possibilities and potentialities as yet unrealized, in fact, quite far from being realized, but which serve as the impetus and the prize for those years of learning ahead.

This conversation, still in its attenuated early form, has everything to do with self-esteem and sense of self-worth. It is not the self-esteem that comes from having done better than your neighbor on last month's math quiz, but the self-esteem that comes with knowing that the world is one's oyster, waiting to be fully discovered, explored, and, finally, occupied.

But with the great turning that children experience in their early teens, this conversation with the future comes to the forefront of their consciousness. They are now fully aware that mortality means that their parents are not going to be around forever, and in our culture, not around them as they make decisions about who they are and are to become for very much longer. And peers no longer provide the necessary nourishment, as they are in exactly the same position.

So (as I write at greater length in "Flow II—The Teenage Edition" later in this volume), this is a time when youth do best when provided with mentors, apprenticeships, and opportunities for growth *outside the immediate family*. Mentors provide models and reflect a future of which the child only has an inkling may be open to her with the requisite effort. Somewhat paradoxically, mentors furnish the absolutely necessary model for autonomy and for the young teen's newly emerging sense of freedom and personal power.

In our culture, youth often desperately need our help in finding mentors. Our school paradigm seems to be based on hiding our children away from the adult world as long as possible, but it doesn't work. If youth do not find healthy mentors who can enter into their learning conversations, they will make up for it by trying on other *adult* futures and fixations— namely, sex, alcohol and drugs, and violence. Or, equally destructive in the long run, they may simply fail to engage in this conversation at all until well into adulthood, which simply becomes an extended adolescence during which individuals fail to take responsibility for their own decisions and life choices.

When children begin to seek to have these conversations *early* (if there ever really is such a thing), we often think of it as cute or quaint. Yet, when I talk with my happiest, most self-fulfilled friends, it seems often that they knew what they wanted to be (or at least the fields of human endeavor in which they wished to engage) from a very early age. My older daughter Aliyah (now 15), informed us in no certain terms at age 7 that she *was* a composer, even before taking a single composition lesson. Several mentors later, she now seems well on her way, and is insulted when someone asks what she wants to be when she grows up and refuses to acknowledge that she is a composer *now*.

Shortly after the publication of *And the Skylark Sings with Me*, I was invited to speak to a homeschooling group in a small town. Five minutes before I was to begin, an eight-year-old girl, small for her age, approached me.

"Mr. Albert, Mr. Albert," she said excitedly, "I'm so glad to be here. I'm so happy to be here. I convinced my mother to let me come."

"That's wonderful," I said, bending down slightly to shake her hand, "I'm glad you are here, and I thank you for the welcome. But why did you want to come to see me?"

"Because," she replied with some assurance, "I wanted to meet the famous author."

"Well, dear," I started, somewhat non-plussed by her answer, "I'm really happy that you're here, and I have to tell you that I'm very proud of my new book, but in no way would I be considered a famous author."

"Oh," she said, looking at me somewhat pensively for a moment, and then seeming to gather a new burst of confidence, "Well, that's okay. *I* will be."

And she handed me a shoebox. Inside the shoebox there must have been two or three hundred pieces of paper, closely written scrawls in pencil and pen, pictures of houses and horses and dogs and boats—this must have been her first novel. I suspect she wanted me to read the whole thing in the five minutes before my talk, and I'm not quite sure how I extricated myself from the situation. But of one thing I am clear: the little girl was shopping for mentors!

Engaging in a conversation with futures at ages 12-15, however, should not be confused with having to choose one. There are many futures, and they are to be tried on like so many hats. It should not be surprising to hear a young teen say that she wants to be a judge and a composer (as my older one does), or a photographer and a personal counselor (as one sometimes hears from my younger one), and it really is very healthy, especially when they can learn the demands that must be met in becoming either. It should be noted, too, that in this day and age, the person who chooses a single career path and stays in it for life is the exception rather than the rule, and the person who does so without any sustaining outside interests may turn out to be a dull boy indeed. Be that as it may, these conversations can provide the impetus for both academic learning and, with a range of successful relationships with accomplished adults outside of their own parents, the development of self-confidence. And what is self-confidence, really, but the self-knowledge to recognize that one is ready to tackle the unknown and whatever the future may bring?

5. The Conversation with Oneself

This bring me to the last conversation. I call this the conversation with Oneself, to stress the intimation that one may have that the self is larger than one's own individual ego. If you are of a religious frame of mind, you may of think of it as a conversation with God or the Divine, or, as I like to think of it, with the Inward Teacher.

We could call this the *meta-conversation*, though I would suggest it is implicit in all the others. Or perhaps we can think of it as the meeting point of the other four. For a musician, it would be the place where self-expression, musicianship, knowledge, understanding, creativity, ethics, yes, and even worship come together to make the young person feel secure in her universe—recognizing her own uniqueness and yet at the same time her bonds with others and with the natural world, and, maybe, that which lies beyond.

If we've been lucky in life, we've had those moments, and when we have them, we crave little else. It is the same conversation, perhaps we could say the "romance" that a scientist might have after working for ten years and finally discovering the DNA pattern of the segmented worm. This is what makes him a scientist. Or what happens to an auto mechanic who has not been able to figure out a problem for three days, and then it comes to her, as if in a day-dream, and the car is fixed in 15 minutes. And this is what makes her an auto mechanic. Or the experience of the poet writing a poem while lying under a tree and listening to the hush of falling leaves, and the verse makes its presence known. Or the mathematician dreaming of the interplay of vector lines in the fourth dimension; or that which the amateur musician experiences while singing to herself in the garden as the late afternoon fades away. I am pleased to note that I sometimes experience this conversation while writing.

It is an experience of utter aloneness, yet a sense of being rapt and cared for, of being at one with oneself and the universe. It speaks to us and yet it is we who are speaking. It comes out of silence, one might call it a disciplined emptiness, and yet it is always there, waiting to be accessed and acknowledged, although the child perhaps only catches fleeting glimpses of it at particular points in the voyage of self-discovery. It is a signal that we are truly growing into ourselves, and recognizing, to use the term coined by Thomas Merton, "the hidden wholeness".

It is the end of education, and its beginning.

It doesn't happen in high school hallways.

Let no one suggest that this or any of the other conversations takes place only through music. You have certainly witnessed them in the sand-box, in children learning to dress themselves or tie their shoes, in the discovery that there are letters on signs affixed to parking meters, in the beginnings of mathematical understanding. But if there is a single message I am trying to get across, it is this: a narrow focus on homeschooling technique or upon information gathering and dumping, taken by itself, is a deadening force, as it lends itself to monologue rather than conversation. Regardless of the techniques we decide to employ in our home-schooling practice, I urge us all to listen to, respect, and nurture the conversations—the inner life of our children—as they are the keys to the houses of wisdom.

I began this essay by humorously reflecting upon my public school education in New York City. I now live on the opposite side of the continent, next to the other puddle. When I moved to my current state, I was almost physically taken aback when I saw all these people walking around with big purple "W"s on their tee-shirts and sweatpants and caps, and on the back windows of automobiles. While I would eventually remind myself that I was in "W"ashington State, I couldn't get out of my mind the visceral question: where did all these graduates of Williams College come from?

I graduated from Williams, a fine liberal arts college in the Berkshire mountainlets (Aliyah insists that I not claim full mountain status for them) back in what I now consider to be the "dark ages". The college color was purple, and the school mascot was a purple cow, quite appropriate as the members of the bovine species probably approach freezing to death almost every winter. To this day, Williams holds up as the symbol of the ideal education the image of its 19th Century President Mark Hopkins sitting on one end of a log and the student on the other, and nothing in-between.[7] Brrrrh! I hope they were both wearing long underwear.

Mark Hopkins became President of Williams in 1836 at the age of 34, and remained at the College until his death in 1887. Since I opened this essay with a quotation from the inaugural address of President Simmons of Brown University, I think it appropriate to close with one from the inau-

---

7   The image was first used by President James Garfield, a Williams graduate.

gural address of Hopkins 165 years earlier, which continues to inspire my own educational thinking:

> We are to regard the mind, not as a piece of iron to be laid upon the anvil and hammered into any shape, nor as a block of marble in which we are to find the statue by removing the rubbish, nor as a receptacle into which knowledge may be poured; but as a flame that is to be fed, as an active being that must be strengthened to think and to feel—to dare, to do, and to suffer....

And I might add, "to dream."

Life Companions

A mother, an old e-mail friend whom I first met in person at a music festival where she recognized me and the kids from our pictures in my previous book, approached me in the crowded hallway of a large homeschooling conference with a problem.

"It's my son," she said. "He wants to stop playing the violin. I can't get him to practice anymore. And his teacher can't seem to get through either."

I could easily see she was asking for more than sympathy; she wanted an answer. She knew I have two daughters who are committed musicians, and she hoped I would have some magic words, some mystical formula that would cause her son to recommit and reapply himself.

"How old is he now?" I asked, falling into a thoughtful, rabbinical mood that seems to come fairly naturally to me when I am called upon to play Solomon, whom I most definitely am not.

"He's just turned 13."

"And how long has he been playing?"

"Three-and-a-half years, with a little time off after the first."

"Has he experienced different teachers?"

"Yes."

"Has played different types and styles of music?"

"Yes."

"Has he played in a group, with his peers?"

"Yes."

"Can he play reasonably well?"

"Well, yes. He's no Hilary Hahn (the young homeschooled classical virtuoso) or Mark O'Connor, if that's what you mean. But he plays well."

"Have you ever invited him to try another instrument?"

"Yes, but he's just not interested."

"And does he like music?"

"Oh, yes, he enjoys music of several different kinds. He just doesn't want to play anymore."

"I see." Now was the time for the talmudic pronouncement. I would have tugged at my long, gray, wisdom-signifying beard, if I'd had one.

"Go home. Discuss this with your son. Gently suggest that he prepare one piece of music to the best of his ability. Throw a party. Invite his friends and family. Then have a graduation ceremony. Tell him how proud you are that he'd put in so much effort over such a long period of time, and that he loves music. And that he is now capable of making decisions himself about his educational future." (And remember, the graduation is just as much for you as it is for him!)

Had I been thinking more quickly on my feet I would have added, "Give him two gifts: one a symbol of music or a CD of music that he likes, and one related to any new learning enterprise upon which he is now or soon to be embarked. And tell him how much you love him. Thirteen-year-olds need to hear it, even when they give you that 'Mom, I'm too old for this' look."

* * * * *

Most homeschooling parents I know have a knack for keeping the kids busy—whether it be with flute lessons or tap dance classes, robotics clubs or wilderness tracking workshops, horseback riding or watercolors, gymnastics or clogging. Indeed, if your family is like mine, you spend an inordinate amount of time in the car, as you juggle the three kids ("three" is like the Biblical number "40", and can stand for any number above one) between fencing practice and guide-dog training.

Of course, many of us will claim that the decision to play the accordion (Heaven forbid!) or take up competitive ballroom dancing was "theirs", not ours. Perhaps, but in most cases we as parents made the decision to "expose" our kids to the possibility, knowing full well (or maybe less well than we might have imagined, in hindsight) the potential impacts upon our pocketbooks, the shape of our transportation (anyone out there with an 11-year-old double bass player?), or our weekend schedules! (I do so love the word "expose"—isn't that what we did with ours when the neighbor's daughter came down with chickenpox?) And after screening the possibilities, didn't we also provide the subtle or sometimes not-so-subtle cues as to what might be acceptable to pursue?

As parents, we each come with our own, sometimes strange, histories. Both my kids turned into musicians, perhaps partially in reaction to my desire as a seven-year-old to play the saxophone, only to be given just the mouthpiece until I got to fifth grade. That wasn't going to happen to my kids! (Although both kids know that I now absolutely hate saxophones, and, I have to add, accordions, though the latter dislike may be due to my having to listen to my friend Arthur (the future heart surgeon) interminably butcher "The Lady of Spain". I don't know if the two activities—

surgery and accordion playing—were in any way related, but I do know that the Lady seemed on life-support, and was fading fast.)

Now the entire family must suffer through my crude attempts to play Bach or Transylvanian folk music on my new violin (made from wood from the Rodopi Mountains—get out your atlases!), an instrument I had never even touched until age 39. (Lately, sometimes, I can even get away with leaving the music room door slightly ajar! Ah, small victories...) So we, subtly or not-so-subtly, encourage our kids to engage in activities that we enjoyed in our own youth, or maybe just the opposite, in activities which we feel in retrospect were unjustly denied to us. Gosh, this gets awfully complicated!

What is this all about, really? Few of our sons and daughters are going to grow up to be professional steeplechase riders, ballroom dancers, or woodcarvers, and there are precious few chairs in the big orchestras. And no, it is unlikely that country tap-dancing, fencing, or even accordion playing leads to higher SAT scores, other than the kids learn how to expend concentrated energy in mastering a particular skill, which might in turn be transferable to other fields of human endeavor. (I wish I could take one of those standardized tests at age 55, with those having high enough scores being allowed to retire early!)

I like to think of what I am doing as assisting my children in equipping themselves with life companions. This should not be confused with making them "well-rounded", a strange notion that originated in upper class Victorian households where people had extra time on their hands. Of course, many of us, as we get older, do tend to become "well-rounded", but in the literal rather than metaphorical sense of the term. Unless we have an independent source of wealth or unexpected windfall (my royalties from writing this book hardly qualify), most of us spend a goodly chunk of our day at our jobs; dealing with the needs and maintenance of our families and the education of our children; addressing our material requirements for clean and presentable clothing and at least marginally nutritious food (make sure everyone takes their vitamins!); fighting the entropy law of messy homes; keeping up on our church or other spiritual commitments if we have any; and maybe, if we are fortunate, maintaining one or at most two hobbies. (Don't you hate it when somebody suggests there is a book you just *have to read*?) That's about as well-rounded as we are ever likely to get.

But these life companions are important. As adults, who we are as individuals and as communities is very much determined by the companions we bring along with us. Perhaps I'm stretching the point a bit, but don't the life companions we've acquired along the way help define who we are and who we become, as they help us *recreate* ourselves anew?

And, knowing I am in danger of becoming overly sentimental here, do I want to be remembered by my children every time they balance their checkbooks (which probably won't exist in ten years anyway) for nagging them about counting and recounting the decimal places? No, the legacy we leave to our children can be in some way measured by the quality of the life companions with which we've helped equip them. If we've done our jobs successfully, these life companions will bring joy and color to the path our kids must ultimately choose for themselves, and will help expand their notion of what it means to be truly, and fully, human. Providing our kids with life companions is simply another way of granting them an opportunity to *make friends with themselves*, no mean objective, given that they're going to be spending a lifetime together.

Even if it means playing the accordion.

The Oxford Secret

So long as a man rides his hobbyhorse peaceably and quietly along the king's highway, and neither compels you or me to get up behind him—pray, sir, what have either you or I to do with it?
—Lawrence Sterne, *Tristram Shandy*

When homeschooling parents or conference organizers peruse my resumé, eyes widen when they come upon my Oxford University degrees. They sit on the page like something especially consequential, and the accompanying assumption seems to be that I must be unusually smart, and/or I must have learned something really important. What exists of my hard-won humility—constantly being reinforced by my children—does not allow me to comment on the first. You, dear reader, will have to be the ultimate judge, and I hope you will be kind. Perhaps it is because of the significant failings in my intelligence that it has taken me almost 30 years to figure out the second.

But I have been pushed to do so by homeschoolers because of the recent upsurge in interest in "classical" (actually, neo-Victorian) education. Since it is assumed that I am the beneficiary of such an education in its purest form, it would seem I should be an excellent position to comment on its utility in "training the mind".

Through the good graces of a fellowship awarded by my alma mater in the United States—Williams College—(and barely enough to subsist on, I might add, but that's another story), I was able to attend Worcester College, Oxford to "read for" a combination second B.A./M.A. degree in English Language and Literature. (The Oxford M.A., by the way, confers upon me—non-attorney that I am—the right to use an "Esq." after my name, and—swordsman that I am not—to wear a silver dress sword by my left side.) The first time someone at Oxford asked me what I was "reading", I, not comprehending the question properly, replied "Ken Kesey" (author of *One Flew Over the Cuckoo's Nest* and a leading figure in the psychedelic movement) and had him in stitches! I doubt it has changed too much since then—it used to be joked at with some pride that Cambridge University was 50 years behind the times, but that Oxford had yet to make it into the 20th Century. It has now, or so I'm told, with at least some of the mindless assessment fever that has gripped much of higher education since. Perhaps the secret of Oxford's attraction for Americans—and especially American homeschoolers—is its enduring (and somewhat endearing) commitment to the antiquated and quaint.

The quality of instruction I experienced could best be described as distinctly haphazard. Lectures (for which attendance was never required, and most people didn't attend them) ranged from the competent and thorough to absent-minded and abysmal, never reaching the occasionally sublime I had previously experienced. Seminars were pure exercises in one-up-manship, when they weren't simply occasions for afternoon alcohol consumption.

The supposed heart of the Oxford educational miracle was the tutorial, the rigorous and exciting exchange of ideas between the budding intellect and an experienced, caring, and well-matched mature one. Problem was that it only sometimes and, for some, never, happened. Tutors might have become elected fellows at the respective colleges in their early 20s, and may only occasionally have opened a book since. As in American universities, there was some respect paid to academic publishing (even if much of it turned out to be turgid drivel). But just as prominent was a genteel fellowship of the proudly unpublished, some of whose members cared more about the quality of the port in the college wine cellar (read the opening pages of Evelyn Waugh's droll novel *Decline and Fall* for an excellent and accurate portrayal), or about the herbaceous border planned for the western side of the Main Quad.[1] With rare exceptions, the opportunity to choose one's own tutor was non-existent.

There was no extended independent study or undergraduate research. One did have to learn to write with some facility in order to survive. Two 3,000-word papers a week were not uncommon. But the papers were never finished, and no research skills were required. Rather, they were to be used as the basis for an exchange of views with the tutor, and, sometimes, one or two other students. Oral discourse was at the core of education—one learned to argue one's point, deflect criticism, defend oneself, and conduct oneself by turns in an arch or eminently agreeable manner over numerous cups of tea with biscuits (to which we Revolutionary upstarts apply the appellation "cookies"), or afternoon sherry. I *did* learn to write and, I imagine, to conduct business in either a courteous or cutthroat manner, and this was the extent of my "well-trained mind". There were no exams, except at the end of the first year and at the end of the final year, and no grades until

---

1   The 2001 Edition of my *Worcester College Record* fastidiously reports that the western side of the Main Quad "will adopt a symmetrical architectural scheme, pivoting around specimens of *Yucca gloriosa* and *Euphorbia mellifera*, with Summer use of *Nicotiana silvestris* and *Canna*."

then (and even then there would only be one) or any kind of independent assessment. One "sat schools" (took final exams) at the end of one's time, with all candidates asked the same questions—one received a grade, and that was the end of that!

But now here is the Oxford secret, and it is not the one might have expected to discover. The students who attend Oxford, like those at elite, private American colleges and universities, are the athletes of the academic world. They enter as accomplished young men and women, perhaps compulsively so, as their education has often been designed to impress university admissions officers. But once they get to Oxford, they study only one subject for three or four years (certainly no "self-designed majors" or any other such colonial licentiousness!) and rare would be the opportunity to change mid-course.[2]

There were no courses in drama, acting, playwriting, or stage design. Other than for the few specialists, there were no courses in music, either history, appreciation, or applied. No instruction in choral singing. No journalism. No creative writing. Certainly no "speech communications". No art history. No archaeological field trips. No business management. No foreign languages outside of one's specialty area.

The list could go on. So for what is Oxford University internationally renowned? Poets and essayists. Journalists. Actors. Playwrights. Stage designers. Linguists. Art museum curators. Choral singers and conductors. Music critics. Archaeologists. Business executives. Statesmen.

At least while I was there, Oxford University was the last and greatest bastion of amateurs and dilettantes on the planet. Everyone at Oxford understood that *amateurism*—in the best sense of the term—was what the experience was supposed to be all about, and where the bulk of "education" was to take place.

There were clubs for linguists. There were clubs for debaters (the largest and oldest in the world is, I believe, the Oxford Union, with its own endowment, and which has produced a major share of England's Prime Ministers, and at which current Prime Ministers are in the habit of making major addresses). There were poetry societies with their own magazines, and competing newspapers. There were societies for the study of Roman antiquities, and for the propagation of raw-food diets. There were chamber music and

---

2   The student of Greek would get a little Latin in "Artes Humaniore" (as the Classics program is called, though now, astonishing, one can study classical civilizations at Oxford without either Latin or Greek!), but that is the extent of breadth. When I was at Oxford, required study in the School of English ended with 1791; Modern History ended in 1689, the year of the "Glorious Revolution" (everything written about events post-1689 was considered "journalism".)

singing circles of virtually every possible description, and groups for the play-ing of Scottish bagpipes and Armenian duduks (you can look that one up). Each college had its own theatrical society (and some for film-making as well), creches for English actors such as Sir Richard Burton (son of a Welsh coal miner); the more adventuresome might be found on the stage of the Oxford Repertory Theatre. There were clubs promoting business start-ups, exploring new frontiers in genetic engineering, or for collecting Greek coins. Almost none of these was supported by the University itself.

Perhaps the quintessential Oxford graduate was the other Sir Richard (Francis) Burton (1821-1896)—explorer, linguist, scholar, soldier, anthro-pologist, prolific and gifted writer, who discovered (for Europeans) the source of the Nile, and translated both *The Arabian Nights* and the *Kama Sutra*. Of course, one shouldn't ignore Cecil Rhodes, W.H. Auden, or T.E. Lawrence.[3] There were T.S. Eliot, C.S. Lewis, J.R. Tolkien, and Margaret Thatcher, who "read" Chemistry, and succeeded Sir Edward Heath as Prime Minister. Upon being unceremoniously dispatched as Prime Minister in 1974 (though still serving in Parliament for the next 26 years), Heath, son of a carpenter who had come up to Oxford as an organ scholar, spent much of the next two decades of his life conducting virtually every major symphony orchestra in the world, and organizing and directing European youth symphonies.

So what is the basis for this Oxford secret (other than the fact that through the centuries, the vast majority of matriculates at Oxford were homeschooled)? Well, it starts with an acknowledgment that for the vast majority of people, the most important part of their education may not come from formal study at all, but from the pursuit of passions, the devel-opment of talents, the cultivation of hobbies, and the nurturing of rela-tionships with peers possessing similar interests. And it requires a further acknowledgment that this cultivation requires time, and will not stand to be hemmed in by curricula, whatever their quality.

It continues with an understanding that most people do not end up in careers directly related to the subjects they study formally, and that, fur-thermore, they often make careers out of what had been "mere avocations". And for those who do end up in jobs related to their studies, the quality of

---

3 "Lawrence of Arabia" began his career in the Middle East by taking a "walking tour" of Syria in one of the breaks from his Oxford studies, conducted archaeological surveys for the British Museum, helped develop a Pan-Arab consciousness among Middle Eastern peoples, and returned to Oxford as an absent-minded research fellow, translated Homer's *Odyssey*, and finally died in a motorcycle accident.

their life is often highly colored, perhaps even determined by idiosyncratic interests (Sterne's "hobbyhorses") developed early in life, but allowed to grow to a full flowering (such as Winston Churchill's well-known penchant for oil painting).[4] The Oxford secret gives the lie to the idea that the "well-rounded" individual is a result of the formal study of many disparate subjects, or even that a well-rounded individual is necessarily a happy one. Above all else, the Oxford secret is embodied in the witticism of one of its favorite sons, the 18th Century historian and Oxford dropout Edward Gibbon (*Decline and Fall of the Roman Empire*) that, "The power of instruction is seldom of much efficacy except in those happy dispositions where it is almost superfluous."

So there it is, complete with directions for homeschoolers: consciously create and cultivate the free disposition to learn, and education will virtually take care of itself. Plant, add water and fertilizer, expose to direct sunlight (of which there seemed precious little during my days in England), and watch them grow!

Oh, and P.S.—While I was at Oxford I even planned my own excursion to the northwestern frontier of Afghanistan—English reader that I was—but never managed to put together the funds necessary to accomplish it. Ten years later, I did manage to get myself to south India, learned to play a south Indian musical instrument (called the *veena*), and was invited to play for the south Indian "Pope of Vedanta" and 5,000 people gathered for a religious ritual. I think I planned all these excursions in search of myself. I'm still seeking....

---

4   Churchill, it should be acknowledged, was not an Oxford man. See the wonderful book *Winston Churchill: His Life as a Painter* by his daughter Mary Soames (Boston, MA: Houghton-Mifflin Co., 1990).

FLOW I—
"Don't Worry, Be Happy"

On my trip to New York last year (actually undertaken for the purpose of completing this book), I took Meera along. Meera, just turned 11, had a week off from gymnastics (we know who really controls the schedule in our house), and was pleased to accompany me, among other reasons so that she could go clothing shopping with Grandma.

"No *boring museums*," she made me promise. Now to be fair to Meera, she had on a previous visit spent three hours at the American Museum of Natural History. We had all experienced a highly disappointing (and over-priced) show at the Hayden Planetarium, and on my last book tour of the Northeast, had traipsed around New England art museums with us so that her sister could satisfy her own appetite for Gauguin.

"No boring museums," I promised. "I have something better planned. Steinway & Sons."

"Will they let me play?" asked Meera, already concerned about the fact that Grandma doesn't have a piano.

"Don't know," I replied in all honesty, "though I expect that after they hear you, they aren't likely to object."

The day for our excursion into Manhattan arrives. Grandma drives us to the bus station, and then it is an hour-and-a-half trip on a combination of bus and subway. To keep Meera occupied, we decide to count the number of blonde people we see. Where we live, dark hair is somewhat of an anomaly. But here we are in New York City—the Great Melting Pot—and the bus traveling down Union Turnpike passes Orthodox Jewish Chinese restaurants, Puerto Rican bodegas, Sicilian pizzerias, halal beef butchers, Ukrainian taxicab services, Korean hairstylists, Greek gyros stands, Malaysian nail parlors, Pakistani cloth bazaars, Indian vegetarian sweet shops, and Italian groceries. The variety of alternative health care options is equally astounding. A veritable world geography lesson. The skin tones, hairstyles, and clothing choices of the people on the bus and train seem to match the ethnicity indications of the shop signs. We count seven blondes during the trip in, five of which we think are dye jobs.

We make our way to Steinway & Sons, middle of the block on 57th Street, between 6th and 7th Avenues, on the north side. We ring the bell, and we go in through the gilded double doors into Steinway Hall. Inside, it feels like an old-style bank lobby, but with a huge piano standing in the center with the company logo stenciled in gold on the side. Five dark turn-of-the-century oak desks are arranged in a semi-circle, with extremely well-dressed women behind each one. There is a massive crystal chandelier hanging from the domed 25-foot ceiling, and walls papered, I think, in sea-green velvet. It is, surprisingly, silent.

We are invited to sign the guest book. We note that the previous visitors were from Italy and South Korea. We ask whether we can go in, and the receptionist points us to a long corridor. No salesperson is assigned. I guess maybe that is a good thing, as we walk down the corridor, lined with upright pianos, including that owned by John Lennon at the time of his death. Photographs of famous pianists grace the walls, with quotations touting their love of Steinways. Meera isn't interested in the photographs.

Off to the right, there is a set of curtained double doors. We step in. It is a room containing a few overstuffed, plush brocade couches (from the 1920s? furniture is definitely *not* my area of expertise!), paintings of Rachmaninov, and wall-to-wall grand pianos.

"Can I play one?" asks Meera, looking a little unnerved by the museum-like hush that seems to envelope the entire floor.

"Sure," say I, unsettled by the lack of any human contact or, for that matter, anyone else looking at the pianos. "That's what this place is for."

She sits down at a piano finished in stunning "Serpentine Rosewood". (By the time I leave, I will know everything there is to know—garbage brain that I am—about all of the Steinway models and finishes, where they are made, how Steinways differ from other makers' instruments, and how much they cost, which is totally irrelevant, as we will never be able afford any of them. Meera is entirely uninterested in this information, except for prices—the first piano she has sat down to costs more than what we paid for our house.)

She plays the opening chords of Beethoven's *Pathetique Sonata* (Opus 13). Her teacher has been on vacation for the past six weeks, and told Meera to go a couple of pages ahead. After her last recital, Paul had assigned her a different Beethoven sonata, one from Opus 2. "Sounds like Haydn," Meera whines at me in a very loud voice, after sight-reading the first couple of pages so that I could hear three rooms away, where I am sitting on my favorite beat-up, Salvation-Army-issue, coffee-stained recliner in the family room. Haydn, for Meera, has become a synonym for "boring".

"Yes," I explain to her, "Early in his career, Beethoven was a student of Haydn's in Vienna, and so his early works sound similar." Meera is getting fidgety. "But Beethoven's music changed as he got older. Take a look at this," I say, opening Volume 1 of our collection of the complete Beethoven sonatas to the *Pathetique*. I am now relying on my 30-year-old college-music-appreciation-class lore that has stood me in good stead with daughter number one (I myself can't play a note), but most of which Meera finds less than captivating.

She begins to play it, and is captured by the high drama of the thing. When Paul turns up at her lesson the following week, he asks whether she had been working on her Beethoven. "Boring," she says, "but I like this one," opening the book to Opus 13.

"Oh, that might be too hard for you," says Paul, maybe grimacing just a little. The wrong thing to say if he wants her to swear off it. Maybe he didn't want her to—I don't know. At any rate, she plays through the first five pages. "I like the trills," she says, repeating them, "I figured out how to do them by listening to Alfred Brendel."

While Paul was on vacation, Meera asked me to get other recordings of the *Pathetique* from the library. I brought home Rudolf Serkin and Vladimir Ashkenazy (two old favorites of mine from twenty-five years earlier.) "So, how'd you find them," I inquire several evenings later.

"This one," Meera says, pointing to the Serkin (who was considered a towering figure among 20th Century pianists), "doesn't have any rhythm."

I am pretty shocked by her response, so I put on the recording. Sure enough, Meera is correct. Serkin plays the *Pathetique* almost free-form. It is next to impossible to find a steady beat.

"And the other one?" I ask.

"It's okay," she says. "He's very romantic. Sometimes it is very loud, and sometimes very soft. But he never slows down or speeds up. One-Two-Three-Four. Boring." (I sometimes think nonchalant use of this term must be endemic among world-weary 11-year-olds.) I try to explain *portamento*, the borrowing of time from one measure to elongate the next one, and the idea that the borrowing must always be repaid, and the original tempo restored, just like in the Alfred Brendel recording. She listens to me politely (I don't know if the concept has sunk in), and then goes back to playing, in perfect rhythmic imitation of Brendel. Meanwhile, in the time that Paul has been gone and she away in gymnastics camp for a week, Meera has finished learning the entire first movement of the *Pathetique* by heart.

Back to Steinway Hall: the first thing we notice is that the Serpentine Rosewood is in tune! We have a decent, refurbished 1923 Baldwin-Ellington upright, costing $1,100, in our house, and in need of retuning, as Meera reminds us weekly. Must take care of that when we get back. *All* of the Steinways are in tune! I wonder whether the strings from all of the pianos resonate when someone plays on one, amplifying the tone beyond anything that might be experienced once one gets the piano home. She accelerates into the *Allegro di molto et con brio* section. Two hands without a face reach into the room and pull the double doors closed. I guess we are okay.

"Well?" I ask as she gets to the repeat.

Meera smiles, and moves on to another piano and then another. There are four rooms like this, each with even larger numbers of grand pianos, maybe 150 in all. In the third room, there is a couple in their late 50s, admiring a six-footer with ebonized finish. But neither sits down to play. The husband wanders off, but the wife remains behind, looking longingly at what must be her favorite. Meera places herself on the piano bench, and starts playing Chopin's B *Minor Mazurka*, Opus 33 No. 4, with its exquisite cross-handed passages. And the piano *sings!* The woman looks on with wonder, and whispers conspiratorially to Meera, who doesn't stop playing the whole while, "Now when my husband appears by the door, you stop and get up quickly, and I'll sit down, and maybe he'll think it was me."

Meera is concentrating hard. This is not an easy piece of music. Paul has directed her to do a little sight-reading every day, and one day she pulled this out of an old book lodged in the piano bench, and she was hooked. We try hard not to tell her that this is supposed to be difficult.

Meera finishes the *Mazurka*, and starts off on some Grieg. "You should go visit Carnegie Hall down the street," the woman says, husband having returned, but the ruse not having been pulled off. She turns to me. "Perhaps someday she'll even be playing there. Does she have a card?" A salesman comes in, ignores us, but starts up a conversation with the couple. They must look more like prospects. I interrupt, very politely, and ask whether we can visit the famous basement, where all the Steinway soloists come to choose their pianos for concert appearances. "Sorry," he responds in a wholly friendly manner, "there is somebody down there this morning," leaving us wondering as to who, though the sign outside the Steinway building says that John Browning and Alicia de Larrocha are in town.

And now we are in the fourth and last room, the biggest of them all. Meera sits down behind a nine-foot concert grand (a Steinway "D"), the largest Steinway makes, beneath pictures of Artur Rubinstein and Vladimir Horowitz, and here comes the *Pathetique* again. I can see her confidence growing, as the sounds roll out of the top and into the wood-paneled hall. I have never seen her fingers move so fast, nor her expressiveness be so complete. This time, salespeople have gathered behind her and just outside in the hallway. I snap several quick pictures from behind, Meera dwarfed by this huge, black, single-winged machine.

Everyone applauds when she finishes. A salesperson takes a picture of the two of us. No one even suggests that we might consider purchasing a piano. I have the thought that it is very gracious of them to have sized us up. We walk toward the exit. This time Meera is reading the photographs, and notices a CD by Alfred Brendel. Yes, he plays a Steinway.

On our way to a picnic with friends in Central Park, we stop at a famous sheet-music shop across from Carnegie Hall. Meera wants *The Goldberg Variations*, which she heard on Grandma's car radio yesterday. Also some ballet music. I purchase a piano reduction of Khachaturian's "Sabre Dance", fast and fiery, the way Meera likes her music best these days. And a setting of Vivaldi's "Spring" from *The Four Seasons*, arranged for unaccompanied flute by the philosopher Jean Jacques Rousseau in 1775 (Meera is an accomplished flautist as well, though it has never replaced the piano in her affections.) I try to tell her a little bit about Rousseau. Meera is not the least bit intrigued by this tidbit, but she had asked me for the Vivaldi several weeks ago, so the shopping trip is a success.

The picnic has come to an end, and I ask her what she would like to do next.

"The carousel in Central Park?"

"Kid stuff," she replies with a look of disdain.

"How about the Central Park Zoo?"

"I don't like to see caged animals, especially in New York." (?)

"The Museum of Modern Art?"

"NO MUSEUMS!"

"Saint Patrick's Cathedral?"

"That's like a museum!"

"So, what will it be?"

"Can we go back to Steinway?"

Off we go. The place is still virtually empty. The salespeople don't seem particular surprised to see us again. Between a "Sunburst Mahogany" and a "Chippendale Walnut", Meera finds a shiny, restored, black Hamburg-made seven-footer (a "B").

"THIS is the perfect piano," she says, polishing off a Prokofiev *Tarantella* and going on to Brahms' *Waltz in A*. (And I can hear it, too—for the first hour, they all seemed to sound alike, and then like a lotus bursting forth, their differences became apparent, even to me, in a rainbow of tone colors.)

"How much is it?" she asks slyly.

I look at the price tag—$51,000.

She laughs. "I have $200 in birthday money," she giggles.

This time a salesperson takes us down to the basement. Meera gets to play on Piano #117 (all of Steinway's 300 touring concert grands have a number on them, so the soloists—maybe it is Vladimir Ashkenazy's!—get to order theirs up by number). The salesperson also shows Meera her collection of piano keys signed by the famous soloists of our time. "Maybe someday you'll get to sign one, too," she says.

And a final swing through the big room. This time, Meera plays eight bars of the *Pathetique* on each of the 40 pianos, standing up, moving her way from piano to piano, and ending with the climax at the nine-footer, Vladimir H. and Artur still staring down from the walls.

We have tickets for Alfred Brendel in Seattle next April. Meanwhile, Meera has already asked when we can take another trip to New York so she can visit Steinway & Sons again.

* * * * *

"No profit grows where is no pleasure ta'en,
In brief, sir, study what you most affect."
—William Shakespeare,
The Taming of the Shrew, Act I, Scene 1

I am convinced that the single most important book for homeschooling families published in the last decade is not the one you are holding, and it is not even a work about homeschooling. It is called *Flow: The Psychology of Optimal Experience*[1] by the behavioral psychologist Mihaly Csikszentmihalyi (*Me-high Chick-sent-me-high*). I knew him at the University of Chicago almost 30 years ago (I'm sure he's now long forgotten me), though he now teaches at the Claremont Graduate University in California.

Csikszentmihalyi, unlike many who spend their lives in academia, has a knack for asking the really big questions, and for more than 35 years, he has been asking what I would regard to be one of the biggest: "What is the source of human happiness?" One might think this would be a good question for educators to ponder, though I've never heard it broached in public education circles. But as parents, I think we can all agree that we would like our children to be happy—both as children and as adults—and so, if only on those grounds, Csikszentmihalyi's lifework should command at least some consideration.

---

1   Csikszentmihalyi, Mihalyi. *Flow: The Psychology of Optimal Experience*. New York, NY: HarperCollins, 1991.

Csikszentmihalyi had at his disposal the tools of behavioral psychology. Whether that was an advantage or disadvantage must be left to the reader to decide. His approach to the larger question of what is the source of human happiness is to explore the more concrete question, "When do people feel most happy." "If we can begin to find an answer to it," writes Csikszentmihalyi, "perhaps we shall eventually be able to order life so that happiness will play a larger part in it."

Csikszentmihalyi began his research by seeking to understand how people feel when they most enjoy themselves. He started with "experts"—artists, athletes, musicians, chess champions, and surgeons—those who he believed seemed to spend their time in the type of activities they preferred. In studying them, he discovered that the optimal experience of these experts was a state he called *flow*, in which people become so involved in an activity that nothing else seems to matter, and that the experience itself is so enjoyable that individuals will seek opportunities to perform these activities even at great cost.

Beginning with this model, Csikszentmihalyi sent colleagues and graduates students to the far corners of the earth to interview thousands of people, from the highlands of Thailand to assembly lines in Chicago, from the slums of Calcutta to the offices of Fortune 500 executives. He discovered optimal experiences were described in the same way by men and women, young and old, from among every culture and religious persuasion. Later, he equipped subjects with electronic paging devices. The pagers would be activated at random intervals eight times a day, and at those moments people would be asked to write down what they were feeling and thinking. Still later, he even equipped subjects—who could range from Navaho shepherds to clothing workers in Peru to secretaries in Cleveland—with mobile phones. His students would call them up at all hours of the day and night, ask them whether they were "happy" and, if so, would try to ascertain why.

What Csikszentmihalyi discovered is that happiness is not something that regularly just happens spontaneously. It is not the result of good fortune or random chance, nor is it something money can buy or power command. It is not, generally speaking, about wealth or possessions, religion, employment status, intelligence, being thin, fine food, good sex, or enough sleep. It does not depend on outside events, but rather on how we approach them in our lives. "Happiness," maintains Csikszentmihalyi, "is a condition that must be prepared for, cultivated, and defended privately by each person. People who learn to control inner experience will be able to determine the quality of their lives."

Why this stress upon inner experience? Because it is obvious that there is so much in the fabric of our lives that we cannot control. We cannot choose our parents, or the historical period or culture into which we are born; we can't do much about our looks or our height (and maybe not too much about our weight either!). There are certain limits beyond which we cannot expand the range of our natural intelligence. Science has made some inroads, but our longevity seems to have at least some boundaries, and there is only so much we can do to improve or preserve our health.

This is not to say some modicum of food, clothing, shelter, and the environmental requirements for health is not necessary. On the contrary, security in having these needs met, at basic levels, is essential if individuals are to be free to pursue the optimal state of inner experience. But these levels are very basic. One of Csikszentmihalyi's colleagues, Richard Logan, who has studied accounts of individuals faced with difficult experiences—war-time imprisonment or concentration camps are two examples—finds that they survived by finding ways to turn the bleak objective conditions into subjectively controllable experience. First, they paid close attention to the most minute details of their environment, finding within them hidden opportunities for action that matched what little freedom they had to act under the circumstances. They then set goals appropriate to the situation and closely monitored their own progress. And when they reached their goals, they set new and increasingly complex challenges for themselves.[2]

What is this state of flow? The optimal state of inner experience, states Csikszentmihalyi, is one in which there is order in consciousness. Flow occurs when attention is freely invested to achieve an individual's goals, with no disorder to straighten out, no threat to the self against which to defend. According to Csikszentmihalyi, individuals who achieve control over psychic energy in this way and invest in consciously chosen goals grow into more complex, increasingly extraordinary, *happy* human beings. Those who attain it develop a stronger, more confident self, because more of their psychic energy has been invested successfully in goals they have chosen to pursue themselves.

Certain kinds of goals are more likely to produce flow than others. Flow happens when the level of challenge, self-chosen, is not so easy as to become boring (a la Meera's Haydn), yet not so difficult as to render the individual frustrated or feeling hopeless. Rather, the level of challenge is optimal when it leads to greater skill development and, in turn, invites yet greater challenges, in an upward spiral of competence, confidence, and complexity.

---

2   Logan, Richard D. *Alone: A Fascinating Study of Those Who Have Survived Long, Solitary Ordeals*. Mechanicsburg, PA: Stackpole Books, 1993.

From his more than three decades of research, Csikszentmihalyi has gleaned eight components necessary to produce the flow experience:

1. *We confront (or set for ourselves) a challenging task that requires skill and that we have a chance of completing.* Obviously, if one lacks the appropriate skills, the activity itself is not challenging, but meaningless. Consider playing chess: if one doesn't understand the rules, no enjoyment is likely to come from the activity. But simply learning the rules isn't enough either: one must have the opportunity to play. A similar analogy might be found in learning a foreign language. Without a goal—if it be, say Latin, reading Cicero in the original—there is no flow likely to be created in memorizing the irregular declension of feminine plurals.

    One can learn to control the level of challenge necessary to produce flow—neither too high nor too low—and the good teachers and mentors do just that, until the individual is able to do so for themselves. The best example I have ever encountered is Meera's experience of the sub-elite divisions of competitive gymnastics. Children are not grouped by chronological age, but by their coaches' considered judgment of the next set of challenges appropriate for the competitor. The gymnasts are presented with challenges that are not too difficult for them to perform provided they put in the necessary time, energy, and effort. If they were too difficult, the experience would be simply frustrating. Nor are they too easy—for if they were, the gymnast would quickly become bored. And the experience of learning and then competing is a dynamic one—as new skills are acquired, the bar continues to be raised. As the gymnasts become more adept, they are provided with more opportunities to set their own challenges (often based upon watching others with superior skill and experience), until the only frontier left to conquer is oneself.

2. *We are allowed and able to concentrate on what we are doing.* If we are interrupted from pursuing the activity on the basis of chronological time or someone else's timetable, rather than based upon a particular endpoint or self-selected stopping point in the challenge, the activity can fail to produce flow.

3. *The task has clear goals.* Remember, it's just a task. The goal in playing "Twinkle Star" is to play "Twinkle Star" well, not to solo

with the New York Philharmonic. The goal might not even be that big, it could be that by the end of the hour, one can play the second variation on "Twinkle Star" without getting one's fingers tangled. Empowering small experiences—goals set and goals met—pave the way for larger ones later.

4. *The activity provides immediate feedback.* Climbing a mountain, reading a book, playing a game of tennis, solving a mathematics or crossword puzzle, or sailing solo across the ocean all have these two qualities in common: clear goals and immediate feedback. In each case, the goal is self-chosen, and also in each case, one knows precisely where one stands along the way. One might not actually accomplish the goal—the mountaintop might never be reached—but the well-defined, self-chosen goal and feedback along the journey are essential to the flow experience.

5. *One can act with a deep but effortless involvement that removes awareness about the worries and frustrations of everyday life.* Indeed, this is precisely the experience one has in reading a good book, or, I am told, running a marathon. One might forget the momentary movements of the stock market and their effects on one's retirement fund ten years away, how a date is going to go on Friday, or, for a competitive runner, the aches and pains that have developed over the past two weeks as a result of jet lag, strange hotels, unpredictable food, and interruptions in training.

6. *One can exercise a sense of control over actions.* Csikszentmihalyi points out that during the flow experience, one might relinquish the sense of worry about losing control that is typical in many situations of everyday life. The soprano forgets how much she has fretted over the high "C" in practice, and simply takes control of the recital. If well prepared, she feels in control of the entire situation, and "plays" the audience as much as she performs the music. The writer who is totally wrapped up in the story being created while he brings all the resources of his art to bear, feels strong and powerful as he puts word to page, even while courting the disaster of a misplaced phrase, or the precipice of a description out-of-kilter. The rock-climber knows that a misstep can mean disaster, yet feels totally in charge and in control as she makes the final ascent.

7. *One's concern for the self disappears, yet paradoxically the sense of self emerges stronger after the flow experience is over.* The mathematician poring over a problem is not likely to think much about her appearance. The high-wire acrobat working without a net has no fear of falling as she pours all of her powers of concentration into the next set of stunts. Rock climbers describe their time hanging from sheer cliffs as being akin to Zen meditation. The concern with self is sloughed off, providing, for the climber, a sense of union with the mountain itself. The listener is transported by music into realms unknown, but does not remember that he is wearing the white shirt, jacket and tie he has outfitted himself with to attend the concert, while the violinist is extremely aware of every movement of her fingers, even as she too takes the same journey. And the new self that returns from the experience is a changed one.

8. *The sense of time duration is altered, as hours pass by in minutes, and minutes can stretch out to seem like hours.* The split-second turn of the ballet dancer feels like it takes place in extremely slow motion, the hours spent by the scientist in the lab seem like minutes, and we are freed from the tyranny of time. And there is nothing but ourselves to call us back.

Flow activities provide a sense of discovery, reports Csikszentmihalyi, a creative feeling for the individual of being transported into a new reality. It pushes people to higher levels of performance, and higher levels of consciousness. The self becomes more complex as a result of experiencing flow. Paradoxically, it is when we act freely, for the sake of action itself rather than for ulterior motives, that we learn to become more than what we were. Of course, we don't plot it out that way, for flow activities have their own intrinsic rewards.

Look at the list carefully: It is precisely the *opposite* of what normally happens in a high school classroom or middle school hallway.

* * * * *

"A man is rich in proportion to the number of things which he can afford to let alone."

—Henry David Thoreau, *Walden*

It would be hard to overestimate the scope of the challenge posed by Csikszentmihalyi's flow concept. Within our modern society, the flow experience is recognized—for its existence could hardly be denied. But positive regard for the flow experience is reserved for those activities considered non-essential—music, art, sport, dance, rock-climbing. And even in these areas, we are more likely to be effusive in praise for those who are able to earn a living in these pursuits, even as we, passive as we have become, look somewhat askance at those—especially adults—who pursue them as avocations. Indeed, the position of the artist in contemporary culture in particular is especially vulnerable, for it is really only the "successful" (read: marketable) artist whose individuality is respected; if her works do not sell, she is more likely to be viewed as a social misfit who makes us feel uncomfortable. Surely she should go out and get a *real* job!

But what if people were taught, beginning at an early age, to seek flow in *all* the activities of daily living? What if we were validated for seeking flow in work, in conversation, and (to raise the most radical of possibilities) in education?

I wouldn't hold my breath. There is little money in it. Flow is in direct competition with our contemporary cult of consumption. The latter is singularly focused on creating needs by training individuals to focus on their deficits—real or imagined—and then to teach us that these deficits can only be remedied through the production and consumption of material goods—preferably new ones, and ones that will only ameliorate the deficit for a short period of time, thus precipitating a spiral of consumption. Flow, in contrast, is a state of consciousness whereby we feel strong, alert, in control, unself-conscious of time or emotional problems, and experience at least a hint of a feeling of transcendence. Does this sound like a time when we are likely to be swayed by the blandishments of soap commercials?

And so, understanding the threat—even if oblivious to the term— the bread and circuses and the technics of contemporary culture are effectively designed to prevent individuals from seeking flow, even down to the mindless provision of effortless variety, from the 500 cable channels with precious little worth watching [(other than my two favorites: the trials for the Canadian Olympic Curling Team (can anyone tell me why the teams aren't co-ed?), and Altoids International Strong Women's auto-pull, both on ESPN 2)], to the creation of TV "personalities" who then themselves become the subject of television "news" shows. (If you are among the few odd ones who manage to pick this book up ten years after publication, I would like to ask you: "What do you remember about Darva and Rick?" If you do remember, try to contact me and we can form a 'ten years after' fan club!) A prerequisite of flow is the ability to screen out unnecessary stimulation so that one can listen, really listen, to ourselves and determine our challenges for ourselves. But to modern post-industrial culture, silence—perhaps more than anything else—is the greatest enemy.

Let me be clear: this is *not* a conspiracy. It doesn't have to be. There are no Lex Luthors in this Metropolis. Rather, every salesman for every product knows that, in competition with other salesmen, he has to sell in order to survive, and for his family to prosper. The officers of every corporation producing goods and services know that they must, in competition with other corporations, sell their wares and realize the largest possible income from them in order to meet their fiduciary responsibilities and survive the competition. They do not have to conspire with each other for the marketplace to have the effect of drowning out virtually all non-commercial activity. On the contrary, all they have to do is *compete* with each other, each individually figuring out how to create a feeling of deficiency in the potential consumer that only their Kryptonite can remedy, and thus collectively training the market (us!) to pay attention to little else. (If you want to see the outward manifestations of the newly developed ubiquity of the market, consider the relative absence of commercial messages that might have been found in the average home, say, 85 years ago.)

Educational institutions are "anti-flow training establishments". Consider my local middle school: the experience proffered is designed to prevent the flow experience. Children are made to feel out of control, very self-conscious, dependent rather than strong, very conscious of time (the 48-minute bell will ensure that), passive, and with challenges never set by themselves or for themselves. If there is "dead" time, it must be because the teacher is unprepared. Children *learn*, more than any other content that they will ever take in, that the environment that produces these feelings of inadequacy or, alternatively, happiness that is entirely conditional on the approval of others, is the way things are supposed to be. It is virtually the way education is defined. This is socialization taking place, and is, I assert, a socialization that often leads to a lack of happiness in adulthood, or a belief that happiness can only be gained or purchased from something outside ourselves.

And here there is a conspiracy. For the very institution, filled with dedicated and caring teachers investing their time to try to ensure that Johnny can read—is designed to manufacture unhappiness. Schools—especially the "good" ones—prey upon our (at least partially biologically based) concern for our children's future and co-opt parents into believing that their children are a collection of deficits—defined by standardized evaluative tools developed and institutionalized to key in *only* on our children's deficits and never on their strengths and certainly not on their passions. And, if they had a way, this would be remedied by extending the school's educational enterprise into the home. No attention is paid to the reality that there may be a far greater learning enterprise taking place outside of the confines of the public school, and that the educational magic of flow may be produced in climbing trees, hitting a baseball, or just reading a book for fun, without being quizzed on it the next day.[3]

As homeschooling parents, I think we can all agree that we want our children to acquire the skills necessary to navigate their voyage into adulthood. What the theory of flow calls into question is whether the acquisition of skills and tools must come at the cost of the assertion of independence, self-discovery, and self-knowledge—precisely what the voyage is supposed to be all about!—and which, if Csikszentmihalyi is correct, also lead to higher levels of performance. Is it really necessary to sacrifice what it truly means to learn on the altar of "education"?

* * * * *

"The best preparation for a meaningful future life is a meaningful present."

—William Ayers

One of the obvious results of deficit thinking is that it causes us to be unduly fixated upon the future. We have grown accustomed to the ads that promise our dish-pan hands will regain their soft suppleness suitable for that future romantic moment if we only use the correct dishwashing detergent, or utilizing just the perfect hair coloring will result in our attracting Mr. Right, so that we may be swept off our feet into a future of stain-free carpets, adjustable beds, and odor-free cat litter.

We grow up believing, because we are trained to believe it, that what counts most in our lives is that which will occur in the future. The Protestant ethic described so aptly by the sociologist Max Weber more than a century ago—that hard work pays off in future reward and is a sure sign of ultimate salvation—runs very deep. Our religions tell us that a life of well-born suffering in the here and now will result in a heavenly reward.

---

3   For a fuller analysis of how public education, an instrument of the state, has managed to invade the privacy of our homes (without a search warrant), see Kralovec, Etta and Buell, John, *The End of Homework: How Homework Disrupts Families, Overburdens Children, and Limits Learning.* Boston, MA: Beacon Press, 2000. The book also contains an excellent summary of the research, which fails to show any significant link between homework and academic achievement, except that rooted in economic and social class differences.

We teach our children that if they learn good habits now, they will be better off as adults. (And we are driven by an implicit concern we often don't want to share: if we fail to teach good habits now, or if the kids aren't reading up to "grade level" at five years and eight months, they will end up as a result as drug-addicted, homeless criminals, and it all be *our* fault!) Teachers assure pupils that boring classes will benefit them later, when they are out looking for employment. At our jobs, we work hard and believe that, with patience, it will pay off in promotions, higher incomes, and a large monthly retirement check. (Try telling that these days to a former Enron or WorldCom employee, or those of any of dozens of large American corporations.)

But surely there may be some truth to be realized here. It is sometimes necessary to strive for external goals (hey, I'm trying to finish this book!), and to postpone immediate gratification. And immediate gratification can easily give way to wanton and ultimately empty hedonism.

But the problem arises when we are so brainwashed into believing that all that really matters are rewards to be found in the future, we have difficulty deriving active pleasure in the present. I would emphasize the word "active" here, for in active engagement of our skills, our senses, our whole being, we renew ourselves, becoming more of the persons we truly are, or were meant to be. By focusing on the future to the denial of the present, we stand to forfeit our chances of contentment.

And if the flow theory is correct, we may be forfeiting our future as well. For what we are talking about here are habits of mind, and when you get to be my age, let me tell you, you will have learned that habits of mind are first and foremost *habits*, and often immensely difficult to change.

* * * * *

My long-suffering mother ("Hi, Mom"), whom I love dearly, had a funny habit. When talking about her wonderful son (*moi!* of course) and his sterling successes in school (and there were many), friends would ask her what I was going to be when I grew up. "Oh, I don't know," she'd reply, somewhat tentatively, "Just as long as he's happy."

It was the *wrong* answer in her social set, and she knew it. It would have been best to be able to say a doctor (but from an early age, I hated the sight of blood, and was appalled when my chemistry set called for the use of "yur-eye-nee"). A lawyer or an engineer might have been acceptable. But "happy"? What kind of social standing might accrue—to either her or me—from "happy"?

Now doctors and lawyers and engineers can, of course, be happy people. Or so I am told. (I don't know too many though, either in aggregate or among the subset of happy ones.) And in families without inherited wealth or family businesses, the professions do pretty much ensure freedom from want, no mean consideration, though in such an economically prosperous society, certainly freedom from want should not be a controlling one. (Incidentally, there is a raft of research that indicates that the more people focus on financial and materialist goals, the *lower* their perceived sense of well-being. This has been confirmed by research in both "developed" and "less developed" nations. As one researcher observed when looking at correlates between objective measures of material affluence and subjective measures of happiness, "There appear to be many risks to poverty but few benefits to wealth when it comes to well-being.")

So "as long as he's happy?" Happy now? Or happy in a future a long ways away? Both? In educational circles, happiness is at best an afterthought. You'll never find the word among the other high-sounding words in the mission statements of the local public school district. Nor even among the elite private schools (where they are more likely to talk about "moral character" or the "creation of intellectual capital"). I have never heard "happy" included in the vocabulary of school administrators. Certainly, preparing their charges for happiness was never a part of the training of any schoolteacher I've ever met. Happiness is not among any state's "mandated learning goals". You will find nary a course about "happiness creation" in a state-financed teacher training college.

To be fair to my mother, she (like all mothers) really did want me to be happy. Her recipe for happiness was no different from that of millions of other parents: the kids should be able to get good jobs and spouses (not necessarily in that order or in the plural), drive nice cars, and buy nice houses, not get into any trouble, rise in the social strata, and breed absolutely perfect grandchildren. The schools play an important role in maintaining social stratification, and perpetuating themselves as institutions by claiming to cater to this recipe. (After all, Lake Woebegone fans, all kids must end up above average.) Not to be overly brutal about it, but in large measure, children (often, but not always) get the schools their parents deserve.

My mother still wants me to be happy, but her life experience has caused even her to question the recipe. Still, and in the context of her having raised me in the 50s and 60s, the idea that there are other specific, concrete ways to educate for happiness would never have crossed her mind. No blame intended.

We no longer have such an excuse.

So where does the theory of flow suggest that the curriculum of happiness begin? It's quite simple to state, really, but difficult in execution. Individuals, beginning in childhood, must *learn* not to be puppets jerked around by external controls, whether well-meaning or otherwise, which violate their own emerging sense of themselves. ("Sorry, Mom, even by their mothers.") The goal is not "to determine in what manner the working unit (sic!) may be made to return the largest dividend upon the material investment of time, energy, and money" as William Bagley, a major theorist of public education, put it in 1911. Nor is it to turn out "well-trained minds" conversant with all the diverse strands that make up western civilization. Nor is it to increase the store of intellectual capital. The curriculum of happiness demands that we educate for freedom, pure and simple.

The curriculum of happiness dictates that we assist our children in gradually freeing themselves from reliance upon societal rewards and substituting those under their own control. Indeed, isn't the whole point of skill-building to free up potentialities and possibilities so they can be enjoyed? If our children do not learn the intrinsic *pleasure* that can come from mastering increasingly complex, self-chosen tasks, how will they know that such enjoyments even exist? Many of them, sadly, never will.

"The most important step in emancipating oneself from social controls," says Csikszentmihalyi, "is the ability to find rewards in the events of each moment. If a person learns to enjoy and find meaning in the ongoing stream of experience, in the process of living itself, the burden of social controls automatically falls from one's shoulders.... Instead of forever straining for the tantalizing prize dangling just out of reach, one begins to harvest the genuine rewards of living." But, as I've already suggested, dear reader, habits of mind are dearly bought. And, in working with children, the point is to avoid creating poor habits of mind in the first place. For, as the philosopher Aristotle said, "In short, the habits we form in childhood make no small difference, but rather they make *all* the difference."

* * * * *

Habits of mind may be dearly bought. But, for better or worse, flow can be packaged and sold like any other commodity.

Not only can be, but has. The best (or at least the most highly paid) child and behavioral psychologists, as if there was ever any doubt, do not work for your local school district. You can find them at the corporate headquarters of McDonald's, Burger King, and Tricon Global Restaurants (Pizza Hut, Taco Bell, and KFC). (The psychologist Louis Cheskin is responsible today for the ubiquitous golden arches at McDonald's, as he persuaded the company that they had great Freudian significance in the subconscious mind of consumers. According to Cheskin, the golden arches resembled a pair of large breasts: "Mother McDonald's breasts."[4]) For purposes related to flow, you can find these psychologists at Nintendo.

I don't intend here to discuss the relative merits of allowing your children to watch television, videos, or spend time at the computer. Suffice it to say that passively watching "Survivor II" (similar in many ways to a child's experience in the classroom), actively choosing to learn about a subject of one's choice on the Discovery Channel, typing away in a chat room, and playing a computer game are each vastly different experiences, regardless of one's age.

But if you have one of those children who has become addicted to Nintendo (or any of the myriad of computer games or "PlayStation" activities), you should know that the reason is game design, in which behavioral psychologists have played a heavy hand. From the flow perspective, it is absolutely brilliant. What the games do is continually adjust the level of challenge. When the computer "learns" the player has mastered specific skills and is in danger of becoming bored, it adjusts the difficulty of the game upward, creating new challenges. When the computer recognizes that the player is having difficulty meeting the challenges, the game is dumbed down just enough to relieve the frustration that the player may be experiencing. And what is the result? The player feels alert, in control, unselfconscious, and unconscious of time or emotional difficulties (and also unconscious of competing requirements, a dynamic that can drive parents nuts when they are trying to get the dear boy to come to dinner or clean his room!)

But every computer game has its limits, also built in by design. For if the single game was totally satisfying, in perpetuity, the company would never be able to sell another one! Planned developmental obsolescence. I have spoken with literally dozens of parents concerned about their children's computer or "PlayStation" addiction, but I have yet to meet a child who carries this addiction into early adulthood. (But when I do, I expect she will be a millionaire game designer before the age of 23!) Nonetheless, if you as a parent decide that you must intervene, you need to know what it is you are up against, and that is the transformation of flow into a commodity that can be bought and sold.

---

4   See Schlosser, Eric, *Fast Food Nation: The Dark Side of the All-American Meal.* Boston, MA: Houghton-Mifflin, 2001.

Once we are clear about goals—to produce aware and alive human beings who can order their own consciousness, and direct their own search for meaning in freedom, regardless of external circumstances—we can then focus more clearly on what it might take to nurture them. If we do our jobs well, our children are not likely to opt often for pre-packaged flow when they can have the full meal deal.

The key point is to put this nurturance of flow at the center of our homeschooling efforts, rather than on the periphery. I've never much liked the word "homeschooling". In our family, so little of it actually happens at "home", and it bears only the slightest relationship to what schooling in our society has come to represent. What we attempt is "family-centered, child-directed learning", and a key being that while the "learning" is direct-ed *by* the child, it is not only *for* the child, but for all of us. Perhaps we should call it "optimizing the family experience".

The flow theory does not deny that certain activities are repetitive, or difficult, or inherently dull. Rather it postulates that what is important is an attitude toward the knowledge quest, one that relies neither upon pun-ishment nor reward, but upon the intrinsic value realized in carrying out a learning activity. This can be accomplished when the child has learned to set reasonable goals for herself, and achieves a state of happiness in work-ing toward them. As I suggested earlier (in "Original Seeking and the Voyage of Self-Discovery"), this attitude toward learning does come natu-rally from the earliest age (remember your child's learning to walk?) But given the powerful forces that would block its full development, it is our responsibility to ensure that such an attitude toward the knowledge and competency quest is nurtured and cultivated.

Csikszentmihalyi suggests that there are five central characteristics of family contexts that promote the kinds of optimal experience that the cre-ation of flow demands:

1. *Clarity*: Children know what their parents expect of them, and feedback in the family interaction is unambiguous. Similarly, children know what they can expect of their parents—it is a two-way street, not characterized by disorder. There is no threat to the self that requires the raising of defenses, by either child or parent.

2. *Centering*: Children perceive that parents are interested in what they are doing in the present, and in their concrete feelings and

experiences, rather than whether they will be getting into the right college or obtaining a well-paying job in some far-off future.

3. *Choice.* Children feel they have a variety of possibilities from which to choose, including the breaking of parental rules or expectations—provided they are prepared to face the consequences. The famous Polish-Jewish educator Janusz Korczak included in his "Rights of a Child", "The child has the right to a *lie,* a *deception,* a *theft* (but not to lie, deceive, or steal)"[5], for there is no other way to learn what the limits of freedom really mean than through its exercise. Perhaps the most important part of the curriculum of freedom is to learn where responsibility comes into the equation. Regardless of what school administrators like to suggest, there is no such thing as responsibility without freedom, and the choice whether or not, and in what manner, to exercise it.

4. *Commitment.* Children feel enough commitment from their parents, enough trust that they feel comfortable setting aside any shield or defenses and can become unself-consciously involved in whatever interests them. This is especially important when the child chooses to pursue her own passions, rather than where parents or others perceive her to have the greatest "gifts".

5. *Challenge.* Parents are dedicated to providing increasingly complex opportunities for action for their children. And they do it today! for who knows what tomorrow may bring?

Taken together, these five elements, according to Csikszentmihalyi, provide the ideal context for finding enjoyment in life. Children who grow up in such environments will generally have a better chance to order their lives and consciousness to make flow possible. And, no surprise here, children who learn to order their lives and consciousness early to make flow possible are more likely to become happy, successful, and creative adults.[6]

* * * * *

---

5 See Betty Jean Lifton's extraordinary book *The King of Children: A Biography of Janusz Korczak.* New York, NY: Farrar, Straus & Giroux, 1988.

6 Csikszentmihalyi has written another book on this subject. *Creativity: Flow and the Psychology of Discovery and Invention.* New York, NY: HarperCollins, 1997.

> *The music in my heart I bore*
> *Long after it was heard no more.*
> —William Wordsworth,
> *The Solitary Reaper*

Eric Clapton's *Tears in Heaven* ("Would you know my name/If I saw you in heaven?") is rolling in from the living room. I purchased the sheet music for it (together with a piano version of *In My Life* by the Beatles and Chopin's *Military Polonaise in A Major*) after Meera asked to hear James Galway's flute version on the car stereo. Good opportunity to get her to reflect on the evils of drug use (Clapton, the blues guitar wizard, is a recovering heroin addict and alcoholic, and the song is an elegiac tribute to his four-year-old son who died in 1990 after he fell out the window of his estranged wife's 49th-floor Manhattan apartment). A teachable moment: it made an impression, and Meera will remember it, and the fragility of human life, every time she plays the song. I hope I haven't ruined it for her.

Upon our return from New York City, Paul the piano teacher abruptly fired himself. "It's not that I don't like teaching Meera; it's just that there are others who are more likely to be effective in getting her where she wants to go." (Don't we all wish we would have had public school teachers who would have let themselves go for similar reasons?)

Paul's resignation didn't really come as a complete surprise. We knew that while he was an excellent pianist, Paul had to relearn all the pieces Meera was working on to keep up with her, and since his other students hadn't come nearly that far along, it added significantly to his workload. He did us a great favor by choosing not to just hang around, and, as an additional bonus, he found another teacher, a university instructor and performer with whom, as it turned out, we happened to be already peripherally acquainted, living not too far from our home.

Meera is now beginning to prepare for her first solo recital (a debut as it were) to take place next May. We've got the hall, a large local church, complete with...no, it's a Baldwin. Meera is going to perform as a joint benefit for the scholarship fund of her student orchestra and the local animal shelter where she volunteers. A readymade audience. At this point, she seems wholly unconcerned about the hour-plus music she will have to learn by then (sure to have some Bach, Mozart, Beethoven, Chopin, Brahms, and Albeniz, the current fave), and more concerned with whether she can get a new fancy dress for the event (sleeveless, in midnight blue, she insists) (yes), have her hair done (yes), and her nails done up (we'll see), and whether we will print fancy invitations (no).

Meera at piano recital, May 2002. photo by Bob Iyall

This recital business, though highly recommended and supported by her piano teachers both old and new, is our idea, not Meera's. But we are doing it for the opposite reason than might be assumed. While both my wife and I hope and expect music will be part of Meera's life forever, we doubt she will decide to become a concert pianist. Performing for others is not what gives her the greatest thrill—it is *not* what she lives for. And I'm not sure I would wish that for her, as the life of a concert soloist, I'm told, can be very lonely, and Meera is an extraordinarily sociable person. Of course, things could very well change (they always do!).

So we put forward the recital idea (over some initial hesitancy on her part) so that she could actually experience what musical preparation for such a performance might be like, be part of the planning for the event, and experience the agony and ecstasy of actual concertizing. Regardless of how well she does, Mom and Dad will have their chests puffed out.

But that's not the point: at the end of this experience, Meera will have significantly more information about whether this is a path she truly wants to pursue. We expect she won't, but that will not mean an end to lessons. At least she will have known what that path might have been like for her, and to have made at least a semi-informed decision regarding whether that was a direction she wants to take, at least for now. A goal may not be to become a concert pianist, but to master Beethoven's *Appassionata* or a Rachmaninov Prelude. But even that will not be a goal, really, at least for us. Our goal for Meera will be for her to know, deep down, that she can take on learning challenges in ways that are energizing, self-directed, and ultimately, self-satisfying. In short, she will have experienced that learning, at a high order of complexity, can produce flow.

Now this has turned out to be an expensive lesson, to be sure. Over the decade, bills for Meera's piano lessons will have run well into the thousands, and if we add on the cost of a grand piano (which we can barely afford, and the royalties from this book are not likely to help much!), will run well into the five digits. It certainly won't be a Steinway! Luck of the draw—we drew musicians (and they drew us!). Will it have been worth it? I think so. People spend tens of thousands of dollars to send their kids to college where they can flounder around trying to "find themselves". If our homeschooling efforts are successful, that's just not going to be an issue for our kids. This has little to do with career choices. They may later choose to be single-mindedly focused on a calling throughout their lifetimes (increasingly rare these days), or they may find fulfillment in a multiplicity of choices.

But my kids' ability to create flow for themselves will have put them in what I consider to be an enviable position—*they will never have to be bored*. They will have learned that they are able to control their inner experience, and enhance it as they choose with a high-level investment of psychic energy. Beyond the easy reach of the engines of a social economy run amok, they will never have to depend on the production and consumption of goods and services to find happiness, self-esteem, or meaning in their world.

"Will it work?" one might be tempted to ask. And there is only one meaningful answer: "Already has."

I get a free concert every night.

* * * * *

> *What we call the beginning is often the end.*
> *And to make an end is to make a beginning.*
> *The end is where we start from.*
>   —T.S. Eliot, "Little Giddings",
>   from *Four Quartets*

The following *¡*Kung? Bushman tale was told at the memorial service for

Colin Turnbull, one of the leading anthropologists of the 20th Century:

> One day, a Bushman child drinking from a clear waterhole saw in the shimmering surface the reflection of a beautiful bird. It was the most beautiful bird, in this land of birds, the most beautiful thing he had ever seen. But looking upward, he couldn't find the bird, and knew that it had already gone off.
>
> The boy decided he had to follow and find the bird, so he set off. He sought after it, through his childhood, and his adolescence, and on into adulthood. Far from being criticized for abandoning his adult role as a hunter, the young man was recognized by his fellow tribe members for contributing to society by pushing both his faith that the bird actually existed, and his belief that he could find it, to the limits. He had, in fact, become a true hunter.
>
> The man's quest continued through adulthood, with him now always being one step behind his quarry. Village after village told him the bird had just left, heading north. In his old age, the hunter reaches the lower slopes of the highest mountain, and is informed that the bird has been seen high up on the snowy summit. With the last of his strength, the old man—whose quest began as the vision of a child—climbs laboriously up the mountainside. Nowhere does he see any trace of the great bird he devoted his life to finding.
>
> Finally, he reaches the top, and he knows that his quest is over, for there in the equatorial snow and ice, all his strength is gone, and there is no bird, nothing but emptiness. He lies down to wait for the end, recalling the vision of his childhood, content with a life well spent, for he has been lucky enough to find beauty once, and in his heart he has never lost it.
>
> He closes his eyes for the last time and as he stretches out his arms in a final gesture, his hand upturned, down from the sky came a solitary feather that settled in one hand. The hand closes slowly, then holds this feather as tightly in death as the vision of beauty had been held during his lifetime.
>
> "That," says the Bushman, "was a life well lived."

* * * * *

If you are visiting New York City (or even if you live there!), Steinway Hall, 109 West 57th Street, New York, NY 10010; 212 246-1100, is open for visitors. No appointments are needed, but you might call first to check on their hours. In addition, on 57th and 58th Streets, there are other piano stores showcasing virtually every piano brand on the market. On Steinway's website (www.steinway.com), there is an on-line tour of the factory in Long Island City. The factory itself is, I'm told, open for tours on select days. Call 1-800-366-1853.

Carnegie Hall, 881 7th Avenue, New York, NY 10019; 212 903-9600, is right down the street, and also offers tours. For kids not ready for full-scale concerts, there are shorter, low-priced family concerts ($5!), and for the 3-6-year-old set, in the fall and spring there are "CarnegieKids" programs with music and storytelling. Check it out at www.carnegiehall.org.

The area is also filled with famous violin shops, some of which are right in the Carnegie Hall high-rise. I especially recommend a visit to Saint Cyr Violins, #915 at the Carnegie Hall address above (212 262-1827; www.eviolin.com). For $5, you can purchase a cake of very fine French-made Millant-Deroux violin rosin, and then your budding violinist can say her rosin comes from Carnegie Hall! (20 bucks will get you the premium stuff in a beautiful cylindrical boxwood box.)

Joseph Patelson Music House (www.patelson.com), the place for sheet music, is just around the corner at 160 West 56th Street, New York, NY 10019; 212 582-5840.

Testing, 1-2-3

Out of the blue one summer morning, younger daughter Meera (ten years old at the time) asked me whether she could take a test again.

Thinking she might be referring to a strength-and-agility test from her gymnastics club, I took another swig of my morning drug of choice (I only drink 'instant') and probed, "What kind of test?"

"You know, Dad, where they ask all kinds of questions and I get to fill in the little boxes with a pencil."

"Oh, one of those," I replied, remembering our last foray into the strange world of academic testing. "Why would you want to do that?" I asked, seriously interested in the answer.

"Because the questions are so funny, and the answers always turn out to be even funnier!"

* * * * *

> The weeping child could not be heard,
> The weeping parents wept in vain;
> They strip'd him to his little shirt,
> And bound him in an iron chain;
>
> And burn'd him in a holy place,
> Where many had been burn'd before:
> The weeping parents wept in vain,
> Are such things done on Albion's shore?
> —William Blake, "A Little Boy Lost",
> from *Songs of Experience*

Funny and funnier. In this era of "burned-at-the stakes" testing, I can handle her characterization. Here in Washington State, children receiving "home-based instruction" (a legal term; "homeschooling" remains undefined, and much disputed, territory) are required either to undergo an annual assessment by a "certificated person currently working in the field of education" (I think that could mean me, but I'm not sure) or take a standardized test from a list approved by the State Board of Education. We don't have to report the results to anyone because these evaluative tools are supposed to be used by us parents to ensure our children are making "reasonable progress" and to "remediate any deficiencies". We've always gone the testing route, as the less painful alternative.

We've taught our kids strategies for taking tests. From day one, we've made it clear that we don't particularly believe they measure much of anything except their test-taking abilities, but sometimes, if you do well, "they" (whoever "they" are) give you stuff (fun summer programs and the like). And some other folks somewhere else at some time might believe the results mean something, so why disappoint them?

For us, the tests come in two varieties. With the ones aimed at determining whether the kids get stuff, we don't expect to see either the questions or the "correct" answers, and we can deal with that. But for those that claim to be telling us something either about our children or the education they are receiving, we want to see, not jut their test scores, but, more importantly, the questions, the answers the testmakers presume to be correct, and the answers provided by our kids. We won't allow our kids to take any other kind. I'm surprised when I find parents—whether their children are homeschooled or receiving public or private school educations—who don't insist on the same basic right. *They're our kids*, and information submitted by them to the test manufacturers or the education politboros— especially in this era of "burned-at-the-stakes testing"—first and foremost belongs to *us*.

* * * * *

So I decided to go back and review what Meera found so funny from the "social studies" portion of her fourth grade UmpTeeDeeUmp Achievement Test, which is used in 39 different states. And I'm sure glad her educational future didn't depend on it. Thirty-five questions, but I focused on only 10 of them. "Uh-oh," I thought, when I saw the sample question:

To say the Pledge of Allegiance, you stand with your right hand—

    A.   *raised in the air.*
    B.   *over your heart.*
    C.   *down by your side.*
    D.   *pointing toward the flag.*

Now this one is really problematical for us. First of all, Meera hasn't ever been to school (or at least at the time of the day they'd do the Pledge). She has seen and heard the Pledge at gymnastics meets. But as Friends, we don't "pledge" to the flag, and we've taught her why. We have a major Testimony against oaths, not only because of the Biblical injunction—which is very clear and unambiguous—but because to swear at some times and not others is to imply one is lying the rest of the time, and we try to teach our children to be truthful. We also have qualms about idolatry—we don't worship symbols, nor even allow them (even pictures, usually) in our Meetinghouses, no less flags. We question nationalism in all its forms. And, finally, "with liberty and justice for all"? I'll let others decide whether the Pledge is truly an exercise in honesty. So much for being a religious and cultural minority.

Things already didn't look too good for Meera. Then came the *real* questions:

> *What should the boys do if a girl wants to join their soccer team?*
>
> A.   *Tell her she can't join because she's a girl.*
> B.   *Let her join but not let her play.*
> C.   *Let her try out for the team.*
> D.   *Tell her to join a girl's team.*

Are they looking for "C"? The only problem is that various soccer leagues, football leagues, wrestling teams, little league teams, *school* teams, etc. are still not co-ed. Why should the boys be expected to make these decisions when the adults aren't clear? Can the boys "let" or "tell" her *anything* that makes any difference? And what should the boys do if a gay or atheist youth wants to join their Boy Scout troop?

Next:

> *One of the duties of United States citizens is to—*
>
> A.   *read the newspaper.*
> B.   *work every day.*
> C.   *attend a church or temple.*
> D.   *pay taxes.*

How many non-working adults do you know (or working poor for that matter) who pay federal taxes?

> *Abraham Lincoln is famous for trying to—*
>
> A.   *Have everyone treated equally.*
> B.   *Get people to move north during the Civil War.*
> C.   *Make the Republican Party larger.*
> D.   *Grow more cotton in the South.*

The testmakers are probably fishing for "A". Only problem is that it isn't true. Lincoln was a firm believer in African-American inferiority, and both acted and wrote accordingly. (Frederick Douglass wrote about this at length after meeting him.) Lincoln had been a backer of plans to resettle African-Americans in Liberia, as he believed they couldn't adapt to life in the U.S., and shouldn't be treated as if they could.[1] So much for equal treatment. A good man, a great man, but do we do the kids a favor by dumbing him down, especially when there were other men and women of his time and earlier who *did* believe in treating everyone equally?

Start with the Quaker-born Prudence Crandall, who established the first private integrated female academy and, in 1833, the first academy for African-American women, in Canterbury, Connecticut. You can visit the Prudence Crandall Museum in Canterbury, a national historical landmark (www.ohwy.com/ct/p/prucramu.htm). In 1995, the Connecticut General Assembly declared her "Connecticut's State Heroine". There is an excellent young adult novelistic treatment of her experience—*Prudence Crandall: Woman of Courage* by Elizabeth Yates (Honesdale, PA: Boyds Mills Press, 1996), in which the story is told of how Crandall was subjected to imprisonment because "she wouldn't yield her belief that all are equal in the eyes of God." Meera was well familiar with the work of Crandall before she met up with this test question regarding Lincoln. And the Republican Party did grow *much* larger, and that's why they nominated him! But okay, maybe I'm reaching....

---

1   In the first Lincoln-Douglas Debate (Ottawa, Illinois, August 21, 1858), the future President said the following:

> "I will say here, while upon this subject, that I have no purpose, directly or indirectly to interfere with the institution of slavery in the States where it exists. I believe I have no lawful right to do so, and I have no inclination to do so. I have no purpose to introduce political and social equality between the white and the black races. There is a physical difference between the two, which, in my judgment, will probably forever forbid their living together upon the footing of perfect equality, and inasmuch as it becomes a necessity that there must be difference, I, as well as Judge Douglas, am in favor of the race to which I belong having the superior position."

Lest one think Lincoln's opinion evolved in these matters, look to his Presidential Inaugural Address of 1861, where he quoted his own statements of 1858: "I have no purpose, directly or indirectly, to interfere with the institution of slavery in the states where it exists. I believe I have no lawful right to do so, and *I have no inclination to do so*." (my italics) But here he went further, and argued that the Constitution protected slavery in perpetuity, that the Fugitive Slave Laws and the Dred Scott Decision were both in keeping with the Constitution, and that he would take all necessary measures to enforce their provisions. Lincoln acted upon this belief, and never did free the slaves remaining in the northern states.

People communicate in all of these ways except—

A.   *riding a bicycle.*
B.   *talking with a friend.*
C.   *reading aloud.*
D.   *singing in a choir.*

Meera got this one wrong, I guess. She says she sometimes reads aloud to herself, so that's not communication, and she notes you can't have a conversation when you're reading aloud or singing in a choir, but you can while on a bicycle. And, she adds, when she gets on her bicycle, she always goes to see her friends.

I like this next one:

Most of America's customs have come from—

A.   *books.*
B.   *immigrants.*
C.   *television shows.*
D.   *songs.*

Can anyone doubt that the only correct answer, at least as it governs our consumption habits and customs, is "C"?

Each of these fills a basic human need except—

A.   *construction.*
B.   *agriculture.*
C.   *cotton cloth production.*
D.   *entertainment.*

Anyone want to hazard a guess as to what the testmakers think the proper answer is? I know that when we go to visit our family in India, we come back with heaps of cotton clothes, the one luxury we allow ourselves. I guess cotton is still used for dishtowels, but basic human need?

The next one is cute:

People who take out a loan are—

A.   *earning something.*
B.   *buying something.*
C.   *borrowing something.*
D.   *selling something.*

Now Meera put "B"—"Why would you take out a loan unless you were buying something?" she asked seriously, looking rather quizzical. Now all adults know the correct answer is "A"—one *can't* take out a loan unless one is earning something. Benjamin Franklin, citing Shakespeare ("Never a borrower nor a lender be"), argued against taking out loans because to do so would be to *sell* one's good name, and one might not be able to buy it back!

If an empty lot in the community needs cleaning, whose office should be called?

A.   *The mayor's.*
B.   *The fire chief's.*
C.   *The police chief's.*
D.   *The county judge's.*

Okay, you New Yorkers, how many of you interrupted former Mayor Rudy during one of his steamy affairs to get him to clean out the rats that had taken over the lot on the corner where the dope pushers congregate? In Washington State, one is supposed to call the local public health department. I know, because I worked for the State Board of Health for almost ten years, and that's where I was supposed to direct all such calls.

Young children are probably having the most fun when they are—

A.   *crawling.*
B.   *napping.*
C.   *eating.*
D.   *giggling.*

I don't claim to have a Ph.D. in child development, but I do know that what we think of as an infant's "giggling" can be an automatic reflex. But if you've spent any amount of time around 18-month-olds lately, have you watched what happens when they're eating?

Who would probably not take part in planning a school bake sale?

A.   *Custodians*
B.   *Parents.*
C.   *Teachers.*
D.   *Students.*

Bake sales? I'm clear I don't know the correct answer to this question, so I can hardly expect that Meera will. We'll have to call grandma, a 30-year New York City schoolteacher, and see what she thinks. I know the custodians would have to set up the lunchroom and do the cleanup, but I'm sure the teachers would never involve themselves in such an activity, at least not where I live. Huh? The kids might buy things at the bake sale, but planning?....

Mind you, there were only 35 questions on this test. If the test was administered at the local school, its funding future might be burning at the stake, and, if your child was enrolled in school, her future as well.

Now I know there are parents, including homeschooling parents, who believe that standardized tests, even when not a measure of children's abilities or achievement, are useful in ensuring that their kids' education has met some rational minimal standards. Fair enough. After reading these actual test questions, from a test used in 39 states, will someone please tell me what these standards really are?

Is it *fun*, or just *funnier*?

Glad we're homeschooling.

* * * * *

"Dad, they did it again," whined Aliyah, looking up from the page I had just printed from the Internet.

"Again" was the operative word, as this was the "Third International Math and Science Study—*Repeat*" (TIMSS-R). It was all over the news media at the end of the previous millennium (December 5, 2000) and, as with the prior TIMSS report, was being used by the President, the U.S. Department of Education, and leaders in the public education community to shill for more money.

Funded with tens of millions of dollars from the National Center for Education Statistics (NCES) and the National Science Foundation (NSF), the TIMSS was billed as "the largest, most comprehensive, and rigorous assessment of its kind ever undertaken." It was undertaken as "the result of the need in the American education community for reliable and timely data on the mathematics and science achievement of our students compared to that of students in other countries."

NCES/NSF created a TIMSS-R Technical Review Panel (TRP) to serve as the U.S. steering committee for the exercise, including 19 leading (and, I'm sure, extremely well-paid, wined and dined) experts in mathematics and science education, and international comparative studies. The TRP was co-chaired by Dr. Margaret ("Midge") Cozzens, University of Colorado-Denver, and Dr. Susan Furhrman, University of Pennsylvania, said to be two of the nation's foremost scholars and leaders in education. Members included professors from the California Institute of Technology, the Universities of Michigan, Washington, Georgia, and California-Los Angeles, Michigan State University, representatives of the American Association for the Advancement of Science, and the National Academy of Sciences, and, of course, our favorite representatives from the Hudson Institute (those are the same folks who deny the existence of global warming) and the national Business Roundtable. TIMSS-R was co-directed by Drs. Ina V.S. Mullis and Michael O. Martin of the International Study Center, Lynch School of Education, at Boston College.

TIMSS-R was administered to eighth graders in 38 countries, including more than 9,000 of them in 221 U.S. schools. "Each nation," notes the explanation to be found on the TIMSS-R website, was "thoroughly trained in data collection and scoring procedures specifically designed for this purpose....The TIMSS Study Center then continues to monitor the work of the NRCs (National Resource Centers) and their staff for scoring reliability."

When results are issued from TIMSS studies, NCES shares a few test questions with the public. I guess the purpose is to increase public confidence in the results and provide newspapers with some sidebar copy. This is one of the three questions (each test consists of 80 questions) they chose to publish:

In a quadrilateral, each of the two angles has a measure of 115 degrees. If the measure of a third angle is 70 degrees, what is the measure of the remaining angle?

A.　*60 degrees*
B.　*70 degrees*
C.　*130 degrees*
D.　*140 degrees*
E.　*None of the above*

There you have it, folks. Eighth graders have been informed, unequivocally, that quadrilaterals have only two angles. And so this is obviously a trick question.

As a result, only 19% of U.S. eighth graders answered it correctly, but 40% of international students [who probably had the question properly translated (or actually reworded) to make it clear that there are more than two angles in a quadrilateral] got it right. How many U.S. students put "E" as their answer? What is totally amazing to me is that NCES, probably with the consent of our wined-and-dined leading experts, chose this as the one question they wanted us all to see. What did the others look like?

Anyhow, on this comprehensive and rigorous assessment, U.S. eighth graders ranked below 14 other nations, including both Slovenia and Slovakia, Malaysia, Bulgaria, and Latvia—nice places to visit, I'm sure (I've even been to two of them), but hardly countries with booming economies or happy, healthy citizens as a result of their advanced eighth-grade knowledge of quadrilaterals. (Interestingly enough, U.S. eighth graders ranked ahead of the English, who would have read the same nonsense in the original.)

As I had done previously when a report of the earlier TIMSS study, costing tens of millions of dollars more, contained a similar improbability (as I wrote about in *And the Skylark Sings with Me*), I conducted another (unfunded) scientific experiment. I wrote to the co-chairs of the TRP, to NCES and NSF, to the TIMSS-R Co-Directors, to the Secretary of Education, and to the President, enclosing copies of the question, and suggesting the danger with coming to conclusions and making policy decisions based upon suspect data derived from questions poorly formulated to begin with. The scientific hypothesis was that, as in my previous experiment, I would never receive a response from any of them. And I didn't.

But policy would be made, indeed. "It is imperative the United States once again take stock of its position internationally in mathematics and science education," sounded the alarm of the Secretary of Education. The President proposed $60 million for the Department of Education and the National Science Foundation "to implement an Action Strategy to support local efforts to put in place the rigorous courses and effective teaching that will build a strong foundation in the middle school years." They also decided that U.S. assessments of education (SATs, ACTs, APs, etc.) need to be more rigorous (too many U.S. students, they intimated—especially, I would add, racial minorities who are in poorly funded schools, often with no advanced math or science courses, and badly paid teachers in broken-down buildings, but now successfully headed for college—are doing *too well* on SATs—see www.ed.gov/inits/TIMSS/overview.html). So Clinton proposed an initiative to "Raise Standards and Measure Student Performance with a Voluntary National Test at 8th Grade." President Bush withdrew the Clinton proposal and convinced Congress to pass his own, for testing every year!

On April 5, 2001, the "Benchmarking Study" related to TIMSS-R was released. To no one's great surprise, public school students from the school districts with the highest per capita parental income (like Naperville, Illinois, where they have rock-climbing walls, 60 exercise machines, and as many treadmills to use in middle-school PE) scored better than those in all countries tested except Singapore, Taiwan, and South Korea. Those from school districts with the lowest per capita parental income among students attending (Chicago, Rochester, New York, Jersey City, and Miami-Dade County, Florida) ranked with children in Tunisia, Macedonia, Turkey, and Jordan. Did we really need a multi-million dollar test to find this out?

Oh, one last thing: an independent analysis of eighth grade TIMSS scores *by country* indicates an increase of 40 points (the U.S. scored 515) for every one percent *decrease* in Gross Domestic Product spending on education.

Glad we're homeschooling.

$$* * * * *$$

> *"The more important that any quantitative social indicator becomes in social decision-making, the more likely it will be to distort and corrupt the social process it is intended to monitor."*
> —Social science variant
> of the Heisenberg Uncertainty Principle[2]

"Okay, Mr. Know-It-All Homeschooling Author, now you've gone completely over the top. We want to make sure our kids—whether at home or in school—are learning something, right? and how will we be able to tell unless we test them? The new tests—those required in the schools for movement from grade to grade and for high school graduation, will prevent 'social promotion', and make sure that teachers are really teaching. Scoring well on tests will lead to feelings of success, while doing poorly will lead others to increased efforts to learn. (Can't lose either way, can we?) It will level the playing field between schools (and between schools and homeschoolers), and provide an equal opportunity for all students to demonstrate their knowledge. And if they want to require them of homeschool-

---

2   The Heisenberg Uncertainty Principle, as it is used in physics, is a lot more exciting than this stuff! Check out www.aip.org/history/heisenberg/—especially the story about Heisenberg's doctorate!

ers, too, that's acceptable to me, because we know our kids are going to do just fine, thank you."

I didn't actually receive this note, but I could easily imagine one. At bottom is the assumption that the standardized tests truly measure something useful, perhaps a semblance of knowledge or some surrogate for it that is transferable, and that can be utilized in another setting. This is what all those stories in the local newspaper are about, yes?

This is perhaps the best that could be hoped for, but the evidence is to the contrary. In a rather exhaustive study published in 2002, two educational "psychometricians", Drs. Audrey Amrein and David Berliner at Arizona State University, examined high-stakes testing programs in 18 states to see whether and how they actually were affecting student learning.[3] The scores on the high-stakes tests themselves were not analyzed for evidence of learning, as previous research had proven rather conclusively that such scores could be easily manipulated through test-preparation programs and strategies, narrow curricula focus, or exclusion of (low-scoring) students, etc. Rather, the researchers asked whether the high-stakes programs resulted in higher scores on other independent measures of academic achievement—SAT, ACT, NAEP (National Assessment of Educational Progress), or Advanced Placement tests—covering similar material, but which might be used in other contexts such as university admissions.

The results? In all but one analysis of the 18 states, student learning was either found to be indeterminate, remained at the same level it was before the policy was implemented, or actually *declined* when high-stakes testing policies were instituted. This is even putting aside the documented unintended consequences of such policies: increased drop-out rates; teachers' and schools' cheating on exams; teachers' defections from the profession; the minimum content of the tests becoming the maximum that is taught; fewer poor and minority students taking tests required for college admission; and the banishment of all non-tested subjects (music, art, etc.) from the school. All of these, of course, could be predicted by the social science variant of the Heisenberg Uncertainty Principle.

I don't mean to suggest educational policy for the nation. The nation's education movers and shakers haven't asked for my opinions and aren't likely to. I haven't been invited to lunch with Susan or Midge recently, let alone dinner. And there is little profit to be made in any thing I have to

---

3   Amrein, Audrey L. and Berliner, David C. "High Stakes Testing, Uncertainty, and Student Learning," *Education Policy Analysis Archives*, 10 (18), March 28, 2002. For the full text, see http://epaa.asu.edu/epaa/v10n18/.

say on this subject in any case (hope my publisher isn't listening...).

But you can be sure that when the testocrats knock on your home-schooling door, it won't have anything to do with improving the education of your children. It is simply not in their nature. When they come, treat it as you would any other attempted alien abduction. Be prepared!

Beans!

I believe that school makes complete fools of our young men, because they see and hear nothing of ordinary life there.
— Petronius (~27-66 A.D.), *Satyricon*

The first science project I can remember undertaking was in fourth grade. There we were at Public School #131 AND 3/4 in New York City, in the middle of winter, and we were all going to grow beans. This was very exciting for me, as I never ate beans cooked from scratch at home, only those that came out of a can, much like those that we ate with hotdog pieces in school lunches. We each soaked our little blood-red (non-irradiated) kidney bean and wrapped it in moist tissue paper, and waited. Within a couple of days, the bean skins cracked, and the white flesh began to firm up. And then on that special day, the little cotyledon began to show. Then the roots sprouted, all creamy and virile. The mystery of life itself! Had they been inside the whole time? No one bothered to explain.

And then another special day came, and we cut the bottoms off empty milk cartons, filled the bottoms with moist dirt (I don't remember hearing the word "soil" until I went to college), pushed our little fecund beans down a bit into the squishy medium, placed the carton bottoms with our names scrawled hastily on the sides in brown crayon on the windowsill, and again we waited. Stalks emerged, poking tentatively at first, as if it was a struggle, and then with assurance—"Here we are," they announced themselves. Green stalks, and then a first branch, and another, and another, and then a leaf, first all curled and then opening like a baseball glove.

And then, one by one, as if on predetermined signal, at four or five or at most six inches tall, they all died. One after another, with no warning, they drooped and then keeled over, lifeless. And one day, we arrived back in our classroom, and the cartons had disappeared. Gone without a trace, and without comment. Perhaps because of a taboo, as among some native tribes, one can't speak of the dead. I can't remember them ever being spoken of again.

And so that was our science lesson. We had proven conclusively, without exception, and with scientific certainly, that one cannot grow beans from a bean. To paraphrase the fishing captain in *Jaws*, "thirty-two went into the carton bottoms and thirty-two died," and I expect that in the 40 years of Mrs. Bonein's teaching career, not a single bean was ever produced in the fourth grade. This left quite an impression.

Later in that same year, still in Mrs. Bonein's class, we made bean paintings. We took little white, navy, pinto, and kidney beans, red and yellow lentils, split and blackeyed peas—I being unfamiliar with all of them— and pasted them with our Elmer's to a 14-inch plywood square, and then brushed them with slow-drying, sweet-smelling, cancer-inducing shellac. I was very proud of my painting—it was a house!—and for several decades thereafter my mother still had it on the shelf over the kitchen sink.

Of course, I did learn something about agriculture in those days. Every Saturday morning, I'd get up at 6:00 a.m. and watch episodes of *The Modern Farmer* on TV. For me, it must have resembled what folks in other countries experience when they see a "Voice of America" film or, now that I think of it, a Soviet realism highlight reel. There would be amber fields of grain (on my black-and-white ten-inch television screen), with six or eight industrious combines doing whatever it is industrious combines do while winding their industrious ways across the rolling prairies of Iowa or Indiana or New Jersey or some such place (I wouldn't have known the difference); row after row of happy chickens (boy, were we innocent!) triumphantly laying their eggs which rolled victoriously down onto long conveyor belts, packed into cartons by cheery-eyed matrons in white hair nets and shipped on refrigerated trucks to the four corners of this great and bounteous land. Tobacco leaves waving like flags in the American breeze, hops ("what are hops?" I wanted to know) covering hillsides; self-satisfied pigs enjoying the midday sun, never suspecting their fate but ultimately contributing to the national purpose; row upon row of huge, contented cows ("thank you, Carnation") plugged into gleaming steel milkers and sending their (strontium-90-laced) products to our nation's tables to strains of patriotic hymns. No mention of foot-and-mouth disease. I asked my mother why we never had alfalfa for dinner. (I don't remember her response, but I suspect she didn't know what alfalfa was either. I would be in my mid-20s before either she or I would see an alfalfa sprout, and now every time I see one, the memory of my question makes me giggle.)

There is a kind of cultural literacy that is not covered in the "not-so core knowledge" sequence, and it is a quality of knowledge without which our children grow up fitted for bread, circuses, *Who Wants to Be a Millionaire*, the E.D. Hirsch masquerade ball, and little else. It is basic knowledge for it is the foundation of all things material and cultural, and that is, where and how we as individuals and as a community come to meet our food, clothing, shelter, water, and energy needs, both on a biological and social basis. Roman citizens may have been well-equipped with "core knowledge" (after all, they all spoke fluent Latin), but the fall of the Roman Empire came about at least partially because of these same citizens' fundamental ignorance and hence inability to make wise choices about how as a civilization they organized themselves to meet their basic needs.

Our children need to know where their food comes from, how it is grown, what's in it, who grows it, how it is packaged and how it is transported, and how it is paid for. Ditto for their clothing, shelter, and water. Do they understand that 80% of the energy used in these energy-poor times is expended in transporting the stuffs necessary to meet their basic needs, and in supporting the jobs necessary so that we can pay for them? Do they know what their clothes are made of, and why they are made in Sri Lanka or Bangladesh? Do they understand that up to a fifth of their parents' working time goes, through taxation, to support defense of energy sources in far-off lands, or to produce the weaponry and equipment necessary to do so? Do they know how the water gets to the faucet and what has happened to it along the way? Without this kind of knowledge, aren't we all but strangers in our own land?

But back up a bit: this is much too serious stuff, and it won't fit on a grid of somebody else's lame idea of "what your child needs to know" in the second, fourth, or sixth grade. So (try these out): keep a compost pile, and make sure you have your child observe it. (Later you can do unit studies on the social and political history of waste disposal—it will be a real eye- and nose-opener!) Go out and plant some pole beans, and, if the opportunity arises, learn to appreciate that some of them are going to be pulled into the underworld by your neighbors the moles. Or better: join a community garden, and let your children experience diversity, both in gardeners and in gardening practices. Research: seeds, planting seasons, fertilizers. Set aside some of your tomatoes and bring them down to the local soup kitchen. Investigate why it is that some people go hungry in the land of plenty.

Explore local waterways, and map them. Sewers, too—see where you end up. Visit the local wastewater treatment plant. (Your kids may be shocked to learn they use the same water again and again.)

You might suggest to the kids that you all make up stories together of what life would be like without highways or electricity, both the good and the bad. Figure out together what might be the result if all your food and clothing had to come from within 50 miles of your home. Perform an experiment: try living for one week on only locally grown produce—plan meals and cook them together. Encourage questions about values: how much is variety worth to us, in terms of more crowded highways, higher energy costs, increased working time? Don't worry: there are no right answers.

Not much into the gardening thing yourself? (I'm not—I find it totally nerve-wracking—but that's an essay for another time and another book.) Well, there's still hope. Next year, join a community supported agriculture (CSA) group. This is basically a subscription to a local farm, where, in exchange for a weekly or monthly fee, the farmer supplies your produce needs. There are no middlemen involved, and risks are shared. You may pay less than you would in your local multinational, energy-sucking supermarket, you'll get terrific, often pesticide-free produce, and you'll be doing the environment a favor. And often you'll have the opportunity to get outside with the kids and pick! (For a list of CSAs in all 50 states, try www.nal.usda.gov/afsic/csa/.)

And so back to the beans: the little blood-red kidneys are perhaps, for me, a metaphor for what happened in Mrs. Bonein's classroom. We watched, we monitored, we measured, we treated them all alike. We wrapped them in tissue paper. We set them on an overheated windowsill. And then they were swept away without ever experiencing the freedom to see the noontime sun.

Until next year's set of beans....

* * * * *

P.S. If there is anyone out there besides me who remembers *The Modern Farmer*, I'd love to hear from you!

Buy Nothing!

Novermber is a good month for homeschoolers to learn how to be frugal consumers. Of course, the shopping lessons, at least in our family, occur year round, but November has a holiday specifically devoted to this purpose, so we try to take advantage.

There is neither a domesticated fowl nor a funny-hatted man with silver buckles on his shoes associated with this holiday. It is not Thanksgiving. In fact, it is a holiday without a name. I write of course of the day after Thanksgiving

On the evening of Thanksgiving Day, after the turkey has hit the soup, we gather up all the hundreds of pages of ads for the "After Thanksgiving Day Sale". Now in our homeschooling family, as Quakers, we don't celebrate a traditional gift-giving Christmas, so some of the heat is off. But the sales are good, I'm told (though I've often suspected that the stores just mark up all the prices on their winter goods and then take 40% off so that the prices are pretty much the same). We then decide what we "need" or "want". There's usually one or at most two items to be found in each of six or seven different stores, the stores of course being scattered in various and sundry parts of the city.

My daughters and I arise at 6 a.m.—this is a special homeschooling outing! I having pressed upon them how important it is to arrive early, and having convinced them of the compelling superiority of each particular item in the store that is our destination. We arrive at the first store a little before 7. Stand in line. Purchase item. Then on to the next store, and the next. We are relentlessly efficient. Sometimes we have to choose among colors, or designs, or whatnot. But no tomfoolery—we know how to do this. We stick to the list. We don't browse. We don't look at socks in the store where we buy jackets, or ties where we get bedspreads. We don't get distracted by trinkets, sale signs, Santa Clauses, or handbills. We refuse to be distracted. By 11 a.m., we are home, like homeschooled big game hunters, having bagged our limit.

By 11:30, after surveying our cache over a second cup of coffee, nausea begins to set in. I have convinced myself, and started to convince most of the rest of the family (my wife, having conscientiously abstained, doesn't need much convincing), that at least half the things we purchased we really don't need, or they aren't particularly nice, or they aren't any better than the same item we saw in the local thrift shop for ten percent of the price we paid, and I don't like sleeping under a blanket made by exploited women in Bangladesh or watching my younger daughter run around in athletic shoes fabricated in unventilated sweatshops in Indonesia (has anyone found a good alternative for these?). And so my holiday will turn into a weekend of returns! How do I communicate all of my thoughts and feelings about these issues to my two daughters as part of our homeschooling experience?

There is no question that I (like many Americans) suffer from a very particular neurotic 'thought disorder', and I am now in recovery. Teaching our children to become knowledgeable consumers is important, even an essential part of our homeschooling efforts. But, to me, liberating my children by providing alternatives to America's religion of consumption (for which public education serves as a prime training ground) and helping them understand the non-material basis for a truly satisfying life is central to my family's homeschooling efforts.

And now I've gotten some help. The day has been given an appropriate name—"International Buy Nothing Day"! Check it out at http://adbusters.org/campaigns/bnd/. Started about seven years ago by a Canadian magazine named Adbusters. BND, as it is now affectionately known, was celebrated last year in more than 30 countries, including France, Japan, Panama, Israel, South Korea, Canada, Brazil, and the United States. Billed as a "global carnival of life in the face of consumer conformity", BND has gone so far as to produce radio and television spots to get their message across, though in most cases the spots have been rejected by network executives ["Contrary to the function of advertising itself and against our ethics (sic)," said one] only to make their appearance on the evening news. On the BND website, you can download "Christmas Gift Exemption Vouchers" to give to friends and family, templates for buttons and tee shirts, and a full range of posters and press releases. A celebration is likely coming to a town or city near you. Your rebellious (or just socially conscious) homeschooled teen or pre-teen will love it!

Not quite ready for Buy Nothing Day? Well, then connect up with the Center for a New American Dream's "Kids and Commercialism Campaign". You can find them online at newdream.org/campaign/kids/index.html. Download their excellent brochure, "Tips for Parenting in a Commercial Culture". There is a website for kids full of fun, non-commercial play ideas, advice from responsible consumption gurus, essay contests, and links to dozens of groups who will keep you better informed as you gird up your loins, take up your battle axe, and stand ready to defend your homeschooling hearth and kin against the next advertising onslaught.

Holidays are an important part of our lives as homeschoolers. We can, if we choose, use our holidays to reconnect ourselves with friends, with nature, and with our playful, creative sides, with our spirituality, and help rebuild communities that extend far beyond the confines of the shopping mall parking lots. And, if we're really smart, we can do that with our children every day. For me, that's what homeschooling is all about.

Make a poster with your kids emblazoned "More Fun, Less Stuff!" Try it out as a homeschooling family slogan (you could even write a family jingle!), and hang it in a prominent place. Next time you feel the urge to shop coming on, look at the poster, and you'll know it's time to clean out the garage. "Hey, this could spell the end of civilization as we know it," says my friend Anthony (I think he was referring to responsible consumerism, not to the new era of uncluttered garages across America).

Who said homeschooling is not a subversive idea…?

Social Studies—
The Courage of Our Questions

I—A Curriculum on a Plate

"If they can get you asking the wrong questions, they don't have to worry about the answers."
—Thomas Pynchon, *Gravity's Rainbow*

Since Aliyah (now 15) turned seven, we have helped prepare and serve dinner at our local soup kitchen once a month. It is not a big commitment, and was never meant to be. Two hours a month, after all, is not a lot of time even in our family's busy schedule, though the fact that our stint always falls on the first Monday means that Meera can't join us during gymnastics season.

The commitment seems even smaller due to the fact that, objectively speaking, we probably aren't even needed. A retired couple, as part of their religious commitment, purchases all the food for this meal out of their own pockets, and prepares the food themselves. The first Monday of the month is always meatloaf night, and everyone in the little community of the soup kitchen knows it. The kids and I (and Ellen, when she can make it) vie for the opportunity to roll the cart with the milk pitchers on it out to the tables, dish up the potatoes or the salad (Meera gets a special kick out of handing out dessert), or bus a few dishes left behind. I enjoy wearing an old lime-green gingham smock with frills on the sides and pockets down the front, but in reality, if they were organized well, those on the receiving end of the food could just as well dish it out themselves (though the health department would have a fit), and when we are shorthanded, they do.

What I like to believe is important is our actual presence, a dependable and continuing one, month after month, year after year. The regulars all know us, by sight if not by name, and have watched my kids grow up. We are, in our own little way, bridges to the larger community that currently does not require the soup kitchen's services, and may even resent that we provide them. Perhaps the best gift we give is in our smiles, our friendly greetings, and our recognition of people who often walk around in our community unseen, or as simply "those people who take up the good seats in the library" and are "bad for business." The soup kitchen also provides some little things: a lost-and-found, a phone for local calls, a couple of showers, a computer for sending e-mails or preparing resumés, a locked room for folks' somewhat limited possessions, a mailing address, and, for some, just a place to sit down.

"Important" is too strong a word. As noted, the soup kitchen could do fine without us, though of course every little bit helps. It is clearly more significant to me (and, I hope, to my family) than it is to the people we ostensibly serve. It reminds me of my web of connection to the community around me, and even to the idiosyncrasies of people who otherwise remain faceless.

I insist that we eat with those we serve. I've broken bread (or at least eaten meatloaf) with a former college professor who was an encyclopedia of knowledge when it came to Thomas Paine (he'd even written an opera based on Paine's life, or so he told me); a minister who had lost his faith (and his congregation); a woman who had been an account executive for a major semi-conductor manufacturer but who succumbed to panic attacks every time she had to make a phone call (and who slept in gas station restrooms, as she couldn't sleep in a room with other people); more women who had been beaten or sexually abused by husbands, lovers (what a misnomer!), brothers, fathers, or uncles than I care to remember; a bedraggled Japanese man, unfailingly polite, who bows slightly to me when I put potatoes on his plate and then says "thank you very much"—in Hebrew!; a man who thought his greatest service to humanity was in being a vehicle for society's charitable instincts (I wasn't about to debate the point); and another young man, unfailingly cheerful and helpful in the kitchen, who believed that the only way to assist the poor is to be one of them. Then there are the more than occasional Josephs, Marys, and Jesus', down on their luck, fleeing an old place, and seeking a new future and a new way to get on with life. By spending just two hours a month or so at the soup kitchen, I have become much more fascinated by the individual differences among the folks I see here than by their common penury. And I learned a lesson in that as well.

I didn't choose this particular activity with homeschooling in mind. But I did want my kids to become engaged in service to their community from the earliest possible age, and I wanted it to be in providing something to which they could easily relate. Food well fits the bill.

Perhaps the most salient feature of this particular choice is its regularity. It is not something special we do once a year, or as the spirit moves. Yes, it is true we have one family Christmas tradition. Since as Friends we don't celebrate Christmas (or any other holiday for that matter) as a religious observance, the afternoon of Christmas Day is reserved for the kids to play carols (violin and flute) through the wards of the local hospital. The patients, when they are alert, are appreciative, the staff generally more so, but most grateful are the families of the patients, who silently bemoan not being at home celebrating as they should be, and then deem themselves somewhat guilty for feeling that way. I've often been called upon to explain that just because we don't celebrate a particular holiday shouldn't disqualify us from helping other people do so.

But the regularity of the soup kitchen carries a different lesson for our children, and for us as well. And that is that service to the community should carry no special aura about it. It is not *an extra*. It is just something that should be expected of us, without any special acknowledgment or recognition attached to it. Too often, community service is celebrated by our local schools, newspapers, or churches, as if to say it is something peculiar, newsworthy, in a word, *optional*. Perhaps instead we should publish the names of those who *haven't* done their bit lately, rather as we do those of deadbeat dads.

All right, I'll get off my high horse. Over time, the kids learned to personalize what we do. Call it profiling, if you will. When there is a young child there with her mom, Aliyah will scrounge in the cooler to see if she can come up with a special treat, like a day-old muffin or a piece of cake or a strawberry-banana yogurt, and ask the mother whether she needs some extra milk to take out with her. Or if they've noticed there is an old woman who had barely gimped her way to the front of the line to get her meal, they'll go out to her table to see whether they can get her seconds, rather than her having to get up again. The point is to learn to *pay attention to the particulars*, and to act upon them to the best of our abilities. I suspect my kids are more likely to carry an ethic of service into their adult lives because they have joined me in doing so, and have seen in action where I place value, a more powerful lesson than preaching at them, whatever my oratorical powers. Only time will tell.

In the meantime, they ask questions. Usually simple questions in form, but often extraordinarily difficult to answer. This, I guess, is the stuff of "social studies". Now, granted, the social studies I remember from my public school days did everything but answer questions I or anyone else might have had about the way the world works. I remember learning about dead Egyptians and the order of the Presidents. (Do you think kids in Italy have to learn the order of the 78 Prime Ministers since Garibaldi? Will this make them better Italians?) And I learned where the number of stars and stripes came from. But no one dared explain why one candy bar cost more than another, or how money worked, or why money was even necessary at all to satisfy a sweet tooth. (For years, Meera used to bait us by stating emphatically that we should abolish money, to see, I think, how many paragraphs of long-winded explanation we would feel it necessary to demonstrate how difficult this would be. By the time we were finished, she would have long since lost interest, or would be found smiling at us slyly. Anarchist!) Why was it that only adults had money and kids didn't? And how did it happen that some kids got free lunches and others didn't? Didn't they think we noticed? I learned over time to keep these questions to myself until, finally, I stopped having them. Perhaps what the schools foisted on us should have been called "anti-social studies" for their ability to mislead us and obfuscate what was really important in our daily lives.

But my kids kept on having these questions, and it was harder for me to escape.

"Why, after all the food is almost gone, do those men in dirty clothes always come in? They're always late."

"They just got here from work. They are day laborers, and they work on buildings and stuff."

"Well, why don't they go home for dinner?"

"Maybe they don't have a home to go to."

"Why not? They work."

"Yes, they work hard, but their wages aren't high enough for them to afford a place to live, or if they aren't homeless or living in the shelter, they live in a motel where cooking isn't permitted."

"But they have to pay for the motel, right?"

"Yes, but they don't have enough money for a deposit that would make it possible for them to rent a place where they could cook."

And so on and so forth. I reminded them of something we had seen on our trip to India several years ago. In Mumbai (formerly Bombay), families of construction workers were encamped in huge cement sewer pipes that were waiting to be laid, and taxi drivers, fabulously rich by Indian standards, were living with their entire families in their cabs because the drivers needed to be near their work, and it was too dangerous to leave the cabs unattended on the street. Homelessness could as well be a sign of the wealth of a city as of its poverty. For wealthy cities tend to have higher rents, and needs for a low-wage workforce. Counterintuitive, perhaps, but it explains why we see so many homeless people in the world's richest cities. Social studies.

And why, all of a sudden, were all these old ladies turning up for dinner, especially at the end of the month? It seems, or so I found out from folks who ran the soup kitchen, the city had paid a developer to build low-income senior housing which the city would subsidize for ten years. The ten years ran out, the developer sold the property, and the new owner doubled the rents. Meanwhile, most of the male spouses of the women had died, and, for some, their pensions were buried with them, or survivor benefits were extremely low. The women had virtually no disposable income and no place to move. The senior center offered complete meals for $2.50. At the end of the month, the women had run out of money and couldn't afford them.

Wealth. Poverty. Construction. Economic development. City planning. Gerontology. Demographics. Pension and retirement planning. All rolled into understanding the plight of our neighbors to whom we serve meatloaf once a month. A curriculum on a plate!

And I came to understand, more slowly than I should have perhaps, that there weren't any textbooks produced in America (or probably anywhere else for that matter) that would even begin to address my kids' questions, or an elementary or middle school classroom that would deign to contemplate them. Much of the social studies I encountered (and contemporary textbooks don't seem to have changed much) treats Americans roughly the same way it does dead Egyptians—names and dates and famous people and battles and large monuments. Almost entirely missing are insights about the average person's daily life, or the links between daily living and larger social or economic forces.

None of the Egyptians we ever studied was poor....

II A Question in the Car

Not everything that is faced can be changed. But nothing can be changed until it is faced.

—James Baldwin

Suddenly, while sitting next to me in the front seat of the car as we drove home from gymnastics practice, eight-year-old Meera asked me, "Dad, why are Black people poor?"

I don't remember exactly what I replied, but I'm sure I fumbled the answer. It's likely I began with something like, "Well, they aren't always poor," and then tried to make her aware of the accomplishments of individual people, rather than focusing on race. I probably referred to African-American friends of ours who weren't poor, including the president of our local state college who occasionally attends our Friends Meeting. I may have pointed out that she knew many poor white people, including all those she'd met down at the soup kitchen. And then, knowing that this was not even close to being a sufficient response, I probably mumbled some liberal platitude (being more of that ilk than of the other kind) about limited opportunities, and how we should all work against racism.

All of this in our seven-minute car trip. I'm sure she came away unsatisfied. I came away uncomfortable, and somewhat embarrassed by my limitations. (Ah, the joys of homeschooling!) I could have probed for the limited evidence upon which she based her observation, or plied out of her the reason the question came up, but I expect that would have ultimately resulted in satisfying *my* curiosity rather than *her* inquiry. (Was she worried, given the color of her skin, that *she* would grow up to be poor?) Why can't we answer kids' questions forthrightly without having to subject them to a third degree about why they have them? The Socratic method has its uses, but I've often wondered whether the philosopher's young friends sometimes walked away thinking, "Well, I'm sorry I ever asked!"

Besides, regardless of where Meera's question came from, the observation upon which it was based is generally speaking true, or at least that the differences in wealth are extremely apparent. Now I tend to be a data junkie. (I should probably be careful in using this term, as in my professional work in the substance abuse prevention and treatment field, I deal with real junkies all the time.) Putting aside people actually living in poverty, as Meera would not have run into many of these other than at the soup kitchen or in India, there are clear disparities even among the well-educated U.S. folk of different racial groups we are accustomed to seeing every day.

- In 1999, college-educated whites had average family incomes of $38,700, average net worths of $74,922, and net financial assets (net worth minus equity in owner-occupied housing) of $19,823.
- Similarly educated African-Americans had average family incomes of $29,440 (24% less), net worths of $17,437 (77% lower), and $175 in net financial assets (99% less).[1]

And, perhaps more interesting, African-Americans with the same income are poorer. This is *not* a non-sequitur. In 1999, comparing those earning incomes up to $50,000 a year (and hence eliminating all wealthy people who could distort the averages), African-Americans had average net financial assets of $290, compared with $6,988 for whites (or about one-twentieth.) How could two groups of people—the one African-American and the other white—who have the *same income*, display such disparities in wealth?

This realization made me dissatisfied, too. I now wanted to know more, especially in the particulars, whether Meera did or not. I attended what were considered to be decent elementary and junior high schools; what is often adjudged to be the best public high school in the country; and hold degrees from three major institutions of higher learning. But I felt like I couldn't give a well-articulated answer to a simple question from my eight-year-old. I couldn't just say "go read a book or look it up" either. I don't know of a single book that clearly addresses this question of economic disparity in a comprehensive manner—at any level, certainly no textbook. I do know it would be avoided like the plague in any social studies class I've ever seen. Or at best addressed with little more than the platitudes, like those I used in the car. It's not likely to show up as a question on any of George Bush's standardized tests anytime soon, for to do so would be to admit the obvious—simply, that it is *true*. It is certainly not anything our nation's educational experts believe is worthwhile for our kids to know, or at least to dwell on at any length.

Race has always been an issue of discussion in our household. Meera is ever-so-slightly darker-skinned that the rest of us. "Coffee-colored," I'd declare, she knowing full well of my love of coffee heavily

---

1   This gives new, and even cruel, meaning to the phrase "house rich and cash poor". As will become clear later in this exploration, African-Americans are not "house rich" either.

dosed with skim milk, and hence my proclamation of the shade as the perfect skin hue. Adopted from northern India, Meera is, genetically speaking, Caucasian, related to the peoples of western Europe. Ellen, Aliyah, and I, on the other hand, are Mongol-Semitic (we love filling out government forms), and our claim to the throne of England is at best rather tenuous.

When she was younger, Meera seemed to have come to the conclusion that all non-white people of whatever age—whether African-American, Japanese, Korean, Hispanic, Asian or American Indian— must be adopted. It seemed obvious to her somehow that for all people who were not pinky-gray, this country could not really be their home. Hmm. (Don't let anyone ever tell you that their kids—white or Black— don't notice skin color and how it gets played out around them. They almost always do, even if their parents won't admit it.)

At any rate, I decided to spend what turned out to be the better part of the next six months trying to find out how one might adequately answer the question. (Meera, I'm sure, wasn't waiting with great anticipation.) I soon came to realize that to do so would require a rewrite of every history textbook in America. It's not that the stuff of an answer isn't to be found there, but rather that the material is organized in such a way as to prevent students from figuring it out. I am not expecting any textbook manufacturers to knock on my door any time soon.

The dishes are piling up in the kitchen. There are piles of clothes in the laundry room. I haven't vacuumed the living room floor in a week, and dinner is late.

They'll just have to wait. You will too, dear reader, if you will allow, while I take you on an extended history excursion. Think of it as an intellectual adventure, as you join me on kind of an adult treasure hunt, searching for clues in the past 300 years of American history—most of which was never hinted at in school—all to try to satisfactorily answer Meera's question.

* * * * *

The first realization I came to, I think it was while scrubbing a pot, was that one could not understand why some people are poor until one understands why others are not. It was the English art critic and philosopher John Ruskin who once opined that the value of a shilling in one's pocket only reflects the lack of that same shilling in the next fellow's. It is the obvious secret of modern economic systems that I can enrich myself by employing you to work the same number of hours I do without sharing equally in the profit gained as a result. We can debate as to whether that is a good thing or a necessary one (though I am not sure it is worth the effort), but that this is the way things work seems pretty obvious to me.

The second realization I came to is equally obvious. Wealth is cumulative. Often (though not always) wealth has to do with historical advantages that are maintained and built upon over time. When it comes to businesses, this is easy to see. The little community bank of yesteryear in four generations becomes the multinational financial giant; the single storefront set up by the traveling salesman when he grows tired and settles down becomes a chain of hundreds of department stores; the single hamburger joint on the strip becomes the internationally recognized fast-food behemoth.

It shouldn't surprise us then that this dynamic of wealth accumulating over time and through generations is at work for individuals and families, too. And since in the infancy of our nation European settlers (again, with rare exceptions) came to America with little indeed, it is not very difficult to plot out the advantages that worked and continue to work to the advantage of some, and to the disadvantage of others.

The early wealth of America was, of course, land-based. Indeed, that is why the northern European settlers came. Putting aside the fair question as to who actually should have had legitimate title to the land, wealth was built up over a period of generations, often by dint of very hard labor, mostly timber-felling, land-clearing, and family-based agriculture. Wealth, enhanced by the use of indentured servants and slaves, and also increases in male life expectancy (after the first few catastrophic decades of settlement), could now be passed on through intact extended families. At least this was true for white people.

Looking at the other side of the equation, the first African slaves arrived in Boston in 1638, shortly thereafter in Connecticut and Rhode Island. By 1774, there were 6,500 Black slaves in Connecticut (and probably fewer than ten free people of African descent[2]), many of them working on tobacco plantations. The public school textbooks take pains to point out that Crispus Attucks, a "free" Black man and a seaman, was the first person to die in the Boston Massacre of 1770; what they neglect to point out is that he was *not* a free Black man, but a *fugi-*

---

2   It should be remembered that most anthropologists agree that we are *all* of African descent; the only question is how far back we choose to go!

tive seaman, having escaped from a Massachusetts slaveholder in 1750 and still fearing recapture.

What was not an option among slaves and fugitives was the very thing that fueled the accumulation of wealth among whites. Extended family inheritance among some of the first European settlers freed up capital for small industries and, among other things, for the education of their children for entry into high-paying or high-status professions.

We immediately see the historical disadvantage faced by early African-American inhabitants of North America. The horrors of slavery have been well documented elsewhere.[3] But what I want to focus on here is what the lack of freedom of African-American slaves meant for future wealth creation. Specifically, while slaves certainly labored as hard as everyone else, they were denied:

- the fruits of their own labor, and the right to enjoy them (hence, any incentive to work hard other than fear);
- the right, in most cases, to own land or any other real property;
- the right to maintain and nurture intact nuclear and extended families;
- the right of inheritance;
- the right to and/or opportunity for education; and
- the expectation of extended male life expectancy.

As I did my research—keeping the reference librarian busy in processing interlibrary loans, and hogging our home computer—I watched these six themes get played out repeatedly right up to the end of the 20th Century.[4]

---

3   I heartily recommend the two-volume set *I was Born a Slave: An Anthology of Classic Slave Narratives*, edited by Yuval Taylor (Chicago, IL: Lawrence Hill Books, 1999). These were among the most popular works of American literature in the 19th century.

4   One of the early rationalizations for slavery in North America was its appearance in the Old Testament. Putting aside the fact that it was just that—a rationalization—we should note the fundamental difference in Israelite slavery, which (along with Divine intervention) facilitated their transformation from bondage to what appears to have been a rather prosperous freedom. The ancient Israelites, while in Egypt, owned their own agricultural land and real property in Goshen, which could be inherited; they lived in extended families; they had some form of educated priesthood (the whole Exodus story is built upon the wish of the people to go into the desert to worship); they were allowed to own their own slaves; and male longevity is rather obvious. Recent archaeological evidence suggests that the pyramids and

And I discovered that, barring complete economic serendipity, which I learned about as a child by watching episodes of the *Beverly Hillbillies*, these six characteristics show up again and again as the preconditions for the accumulation of wealth and capital, both for individuals and over generations.

It should be noted that, from earliest colonial times, when African-Americans were not faced with these historical disadvantages, they were quite adept at both wealth and knowledge creation. An excellent example (and an historical figure that homeschoolers should know about for he was, for the most part, self-educated) was Benjamin Banneker (1731-1806). The free-born grandson of an enslaved African prince and a transported English milkmaid who together carved a homestead out of the Maryland wilderness near the shore of Chesapeake Bay, Banneker became a farmer, mathematician, and astronomer, and helped survey the site for the nation's future capital in Washington, D.C. Banneker was best known in his lifetime as the fabricator of the first completely American-made clock, and author of an almanac that outsold Ben Franklin's *Poor Richard's*.[5]

As the family capital of early free settlers grew, new outlets were sought for its use. As in the North there were few natural resources (outside of fur, some little fish and lumber and, later, whale oil) that were heavily sought after in Europe, people naturally turned to industry and trade. But this was far from pure capitalism at work (if such a thing could ever be said to exist). A century's worth of Navigation Acts adopted by the English Parliament either prohibited or highly taxed the manufacture and export of goods by the colonies for sale in England that could otherwise be produced in the mother country.[6]

The Navigation Acts forced the creation of the "Triangle Trade", as we all learned about in school (and promptly forgot—they never did tell us why it was important). Under the Acts, sugar, for example, could only be

---

other public buildings were not built by slaves at all, as the Egyptians had no administrative machinery nor infrastructure to maintain such a large capacity of *forced* labor. Rather, it is suggested, the monuments were built by agriculturalists during the non-tilling or harvesting seasons, with extracted labor being a form of taxation, and during which time the workers were required to maintain themselves.

5   A fine "young adult" account of Banneker's life can be found in Patterson, Lilli, *Benjamin Banneker: Genius of Early America* (Abingdon, PA: Parthenon Press, 1978).

6   This pattern of English protectionism in the service of its own capital interests continued well into the 20th Century, with the deliberate destruction of village-based cloth manufacture throwing a once-prosperous and virtually self-sufficient India into abject poverty.

sold to England. The way around the prohibition on the sale of sugar to other countries lay in the production of rum. Distilled in New England from molasses made from sugar grown on slave plantations in the West Indies and then shipped north, rum could be sold on the Continent, and the funds from the sale used to purchase goods in England to be sold in the colonies or the West Indies. More commonly, rum was exchanged directly for slaves on the east coast of Africa. The slaves were then brought to the West Indies, thus completing the triangle.

The institution of slavery as the basis of wealth creation, of commerce, of banking, was virtually entirely an affair of the *northern* colonies and, later, states. Through the 18th Century, Rhode Island merchants alone controlled between 60-90% of the American trade in African slaves. The slave ships were built and equipped in Newport (often by Quakers, I might add, who made up 75% of Newport's population in 1700); ironworkers wrought the chains; local merchants outfitted the ships; local captains and seamen sailed the waters, guarded and herded (and murdered) the slaves; local and regional capital bankrolled the voyages.

Great fortunes were amassed in this northern slavery-dependent economy. Somewhere in my public school education, I must have missed this! A good illustrative story is the founding of Brown University. While originally conceived of as a Baptist institution of higher learning, funds came from the Quaker merchant Nicholas Brown, Sr. (the University was actually named for his son), on land donated by Nicholas' brother Moses Brown (also a Friend), who made his fortune by establishing the first water-powered cotton mill to process cotton grown and picked by slaves and brought to Rhode Island on brother John's ships. The first Chancellor was the Governor of Rhode Island, the Friend Stephen Hopkins, later to be a signer of the Declaration of Independence. Trading empires were established, merchants and tradesmen profited and passed on their businesses to their sons, educational institutions were inaugurated, all without any benefit accruing to those who made all this possible— the slaves, who were simply commodities.[7]

The point is that the major outlet remaining for capital in the North was the slave trade and its commercial and banking offshoots. In the draft passage on slavery left out of the Declaration of Independence, Thomas Jefferson asserted that the King of England was responsible not only for slavery itself, but also for the continuing trade in human flesh:

---

7   To their credit, Friends were the first group in North America to give up ownership of other human beings, with almost all their slaves freed before the American Revolution, but not before their own fortunes were already well-established.

> he has waged cruel war against human nature itself, violating its most sacred rights of life and liberty in the persons of a distant people who never offended him, captivating and carrying them into slavery in another hemisphere, or to incur miserable death in their transportation hither, this piratical warfare, the opprobrium of infidel powers, is the warfare of the Christian king of Great Britain. [determined to keep open a market where MEN should be bought and sold,] he has prostituted his negative for suppressing every legislative attempt to prohibit or restrain this execrable commerce [determining to keep open a market where MEN should be bought or sold]....

A noble, liberal sentiment, one might think, a credit to Jefferson. Except look what comes next!

> ...and that this assemblage of horrors might want no fact of distinguished die, he is now exciting those very people to rise in arms among us, and to purchase that liberty of which he also obtruded them: thus paying off former crimes committed against the liberties of one people, with crimes which he urges them to commit against the lives of another.

Now, this *is*, after all, the draft of the Declaration of Independence, but Jefferson—he of the "unalienable rights" and governments that derive "their just powers from the consent of the governed"—could not seem to conceive why a people deprived of their liberties would choose, without foreign provocation, to rise up in arms to re-establish them! In fact, Jefferson's major complaint was not so much that the King was the source of the slave trade, but on the contrary, that he, in the person of Lord Dunmore, Governor of Virginia, urged existing slaves to assert their freedom![8] Jefferson's grievance, whatever we may think of it, was accurate. In the years following a 1775 proclamation by the Governor, some 5,000 slaves escaped and were inducted into "Lord Dunmore's Ethiopian Regiment", and were outfitted in uniforms inscribed with the words "Liberty to Slaves". At the conclusion of the Revolutionary War, more than 3,500 of Dunmore's recruits sailed out of Virginia to freedom on British ships.[9]

---

8   See Wills, Gary, *Inventing America: Jefferson's Declaration of Independence*. Garden City, NY: Doubleday & Co., 1978.

9   This is only a little piece of the story. As so many of the American leaders, such as Washington and Jefferson, were slaveholders, many Blacks saw the British opportunity as

The situation in the southern part of what was to become the United States was quite different, in many ways having more in common with the West Indies than with the northern colonies. (In fact, South Carolina was founded by English slave-planter colonists from Barbados.) Their economies were similar to what would have been found in Third World countries in the last century. Imports consisted mainly of slaves and luxury goods for the owners of the plantations, who performed no useful labor themselves. In contrast to the northern colonies and states, exports consisted entirely of raw agricultural commodities, primarily tobacco, indigo, rice, and cotton. Children were sent away to school, if they were to be educated at all.

Wealth was a product of three factors: fertility of the land, the ability to extract wealth at the lowest possible cost in labor, and the prices paid for agricultural commodities in foreign markets (including the newly mechanized, highly efficient, and very profitable weaving mills in the North). Again, in contrast with the North, virtually no industry of any real consequence existed in the southern colonies (and, later, states) until the Civil War. Technology was a double-edged sword: the invention of the cotton gin made it possible to process raw cotton more quickly and with less labor, but it did not enhance acreage yields, and so more acreage might now be

---

their only chance for freedom and joined the British forces in large numbers. The historian J.A. Rogers notes, "5,000 (African-Americans) joined Dunmore at Norfolk; 25,000 fled from their masters in South Carolina, and nearly 7/8s of the slaves in Georgia." Almost 2,000 slaves joined the British forces under General Cornwallis, including numerous slaves from George Washington's plantation. Jefferson declared that Virginia alone lost 30,000; others estimate that as many as 100,000 slaves found their way to the British lines. In the North, a garrison of Blacks known as the "Negro Fort" defeated their masters in a battle in the Bronx, north of New York City. Ex-slave Thomas Johnson claimed to have conducted the detachment which surprised and defeated the Colonials at Monk's Corner in North Carolina in 1780. The British even created a Black cavalry troop in 1782. The Continental Army finally agreed to accept African-American volunteers (both slave and free) when the desertion rate among white soliders reached enormous proportions. Washington wrote Richard Henry Lee on December 20, 1775 that, "We must use the Negroes or run the risk of losing the war…success will depend on which side can arm the Negroes faster." Next time you see one of those TV specials on the American Revolution, make sure to ask yourself where all the Black soldiers (on both sides) are!

Following the end of the war, some 3,500 Black soldiers of "Lord Dunmore's Ethiopian Regiment" were relocated to Nova Scotia. Most eventually intermarried with the European settlers and provided the core of what became the national culture, language, and early leadership of the Province. Many celebrate their descent from the Regiment to this day. Virtually all of the remaining African-American soldiers, however, were returned to slavery at the end of the war. See Rogers, J.A., *Sex and Race: A History of White, Negro, and Indian Miscegenation in the Two Americas: The New World* (Helga Rogers, 1967); also www.ccds.charlotte.nc.us/vaugh/Diversity/lordd.htm.

devoted to cotton production, but at the risk of depressing prices. The main beneficiaries were the cloth industries and merchants of the North, who had the options of maintaining the cost of finished goods, or flooding markets with cheaper ones.

In the meantime, the land itself began to give out. Charles Ball, the African-American author of the longest and most detailed slave narrative of the antebellum South,[10] notes that as he was driven south from Maryland in 1805 (finally to arrive in Georgia, from where he twice escaped), he saw whole areas of Maryland, Virginia, and North Carolina "exhausted and depopulated," with "large old family mansions, of weather-beaten and neglected appearance, standing in the middle of vast fields of many hundred acres, the fences of which have rotted away." He indicates that once-proud tobacco and indigo plantations of 200 slaves were reduced to ruins, with all that was left being the owners and seven or eight slaves. The owners were now in as poor a state as the slaves themselves, until the later were sold for the subsistence of the former, and the owners fled to Kentucky or Alabama to play out the sordid ecological drama again. "I am convinced," Ball writes, "that in nine cases in ten, the hardships and sufferings of the coloured population of lower Virginia is attributable to the poverty and distress of its owners." In short, an economy dependent upon slaveholding could and did leave slave owners destitute, as Jefferson himself—a renowned spendthrift—was so painfully to find out. The third President died a pauper, with huge, unpaid debts for which all but five of his remaining 105 slaves were sold off, even while northern banks and merchants continued to benefit from low agricultural

---

10 Ball, Charles, *Slavery in the United States: A Narrative of the Life and Adventures of Charles Ball, A Black Man...*(1836); reprinted in Taylor, Yuval (ed.), *I was Born a Slave: An Anthology of Classic Slave Narratives—Volume One*, op. cit. During one of the periods in which he was free, Ball fought (on the American side) in the War of 1812. In contrast, African-American slaves saw the British as *liberators* and the War of 1812 as a war of national liberation. In 1813-1814, thousands escaped slavery by making their way to British ships. Ball says they were treated by British naval officers as military deserters. Many enlisted in the British Colonial Marines garrisoned on Tangiers Island, near the eastern shore of Chesapeake Bay. Later, they were brought to the West Indies (most notably to Trinidad), as free men and woman. (This can be found in any standard history of Trinidad.) In one instance, Ball was enlisted to go aboard a British naval vessel as slave owners tried, unsuccessfully, to bargain for the return of their "property". Now try to find *that* in any high school textbook!

prices made possible by slave labor.[11]

After the traffic in foreign slaves was outlawed in 1807, approximately one million slaves from states that produced less cotton (Maryland, Virginia, the Carolinas) were sold or kidnapped to states that produced more (Georgia, Alabama, Mississippi, Louisiana, Texas). As the fertility of the land continued to decline, the value of slaves soared as they were the only mechanism by which more could be gotten out of the land. By 1860, the capital investment in the four million slaves in the South exceeded the value of all other capital worth in the southern states, including the land itself.

The impact on the slaves themselves was devastating. Their enhanced "value" likely increased the rate of their being bought and sold, with even more family disruption, and reinforced the reality that African-American households were to be headed by a female separated from her children's putative father. Parental affection tied to any particular child was a highly risky emotional proposition, as the child was likely to be sold off and never heard from again.[12] As the value of slaves was tied almost exclusively to field labor, and the cotton plantations grew larger, the percentage of slaves possessing any specialized skills likely declined. Laws against the education of slaves were more rigorously enforced, as an educated slave was thought to be more likely to assert his or her liberty. Labor was hard and continuous, nutrition and hygiene poor, and the value attached to the elderly low, all contributing to reduced male life expectancy. All in all, the African-American holocaust, (and it is a travesty to call it anything less than that), left Black Americans, even after being freed, without virtually any of the preconditions for wealth creation—from owning the fruits of their own labor to property ownership; from intact families to inheritances; from the right or opportunity for education to enhanced male life expectancy.

---

11 Jefferson's attitudes toward slavery did not improve with time. In fact, they hardened. By the time of his death in 1829, he had become an ardent advocate of the expansion of slavery into the western territories. By 1822, Jefferson owned 267 salves. During his lifetime, Jefferson freed a total of three slaves (all blood relatives), but sold more than a few into the Deep South to cower his remaining slaves into obedience. See Loewen, James, W. *Lies My Teacher Taught Me: Everything Your American History Textbook Got Wrong*, 140. New York, NY: Touchstone Books, 1996.

12 Of the two-thirds of a million interstate sales made by slave traders in the decades before the Civil War, 25% involved the destruction of a first marriage, and 50% destroyed a nuclear family, many of them separating children under the age of 13 from their parents. Nearly all of them involved the dissolution of a previously existing community. And this only accounts for interstate sales. See Johnson, Walter, *Soul by Soul: Life Inside the Antebellum Slave Market*. Cambridge, MA: Harvard University Press, 1999.

Whew! That was a mouthful! I've got to go pick up Aliyah from her oboe lesson. And what *am* I going to make for dinner?

* * * * *

One of our newly opened local public educational institutions is called the George Washington Bush Middle School. The title is not a reference to either our current President, or his father. But the name "George Washington Bush", which my kids learned early in our discussions of local history, is a big deal in our community, and in our state. The official history has it that Bush, an African-American, in 1845 was among the first settlers of what became the town of Tumwater, in an area called "Bush Prairie". And successful he was, establishing orchards and a sawmill, and heavily responsible for the growth of commerce in what was to become the capital of the state of Washington, Olympia (our home).

Bush's name is dusted off and paraded about during Black History Month or on special "George Washington Bush Prairie Days", with his picture and that of his farm mounted on display in our capital rotunda. We know a little of the story of how he had to struggle to overcome prejudice. From his previous sojourn in Missouri, Bush headed for Oregon. But this was not to be. Laws had just been passed in Oregon forbidding the settlement of Negroes as a way of avoiding the potential controversy as to whether Oregon was to be slave or free territory. The stain of this history remains to this day, as Oregon has a tiny African-American population. Bush then made his way north into what was then known as the Washington Territory. But problems related to the way others viewed his racial identity continued. In 1855, Bush's friends petitioned for a special act of Congress allowing Bush to obtain a deed to his land, as federal law otherwise denied these to African-Americans. Today, politicians incorporate his story in speeches; articles are published in the newspaper, while local schoolkids dress up as hearty settlers seeking a new home as they are taught his life story as an example of overcoming obstacles. It serves as an important parable that wealth creation may be possible by dint of perseverance.

There's only one problem with this story. Historians, including African-American historians, now generally agree that George Washington Bush was *not* an African-American, though they seem somewhat averse to speaking about it publicly. The myth could have been more readily punctured by asking his descendants, many of whom have lived in the Seattle area for the past 100 years, and none of whom has ever been invited to a Black History Month celebration or a George Washington Bush school opening. (There are several Bush schools in the state.)

Or someone could check the records of his parents' marriage. Bush's father Matthew was a free merchant seaman of South Indian origin, and with dark skin, working on British ships in the port of Philadelphia. He was employed by a Quaker named Stevenson, and married an Irish serving girl working in the Stevenson household in Germantown, Pennsylvania. The records exist at Germantown Friends Meeting to this day. At his death, Stevenson left part of his inheritance to the elder Bush, laying the groundwork for son George's future wealth.

Like his father, Bush married a white woman, named Isabella, in Kentucky. The stories of these free, interracial marriages (in a slave state) prior to the Civil War should be of interest in and of themselves. But, at the time, was Bush's marriage even considered interracial? We have no way of knowing.

So my children and I have witnessed the creation of "official history", and it is not a pretty picture. We have communicated with the official city and state historians, and they readily agree with facts that can hardly be questioned. But the reality that the official history denies my Indian-born daughter, and that of all Asian-Americans, a piece of *their* history, or that the true history could add to mutual appreciation and respect among minority communities which are often fragmented, does not seem to sink in.

The importance of the Bush story lies in illustrating how extraordinarily difficult it was for free African-Americans (or even for one assumed to be so) to participate in the new wealth creation opportunities made possible by the opening of the American West. The Gold Rush made many men rich—both those few who discovered gold, but more commonly those who took advantage of the migration in supplying these men with the necessities of life and their trade, or those who created banks that enabled trade in the newly mined natural resources. The lands opened up to settlement formed the foundation of a new self-sufficiency, and the basis of future inheritance and capital creation. Crucially, virtually none of these were available to African-Americans. In a telling exception that proves the rule for people of color, George Washington Bush—African-American or not—had to travel literally from one end of the continent to the other, to a land virtually uninhabited by "civilized" men, to command even his little share.

* * * * *

A biographical interlude:

We are not big genealogy buffs in our family. I actually think genealogy is a great way to introduce the study of history in homeschooling families, once children have become aware (usually around ages 7-10) that the artifacts of their lives have a history, as do they themselves and the people around them.

But in our family, there is simply not much that can be known easily. Records relating to Meera's birthparents (she was abandoned at a Mumbai hospital at birth) are non-existent. As for the other three of us, we are from Eastern European Jewish stock, with ancestors often from towns and villages (and even countries!) that no longer exist. We'd have no way of knowing if our ancestors got to sometime-Poland, give or take a couple of hundred miles, from Spain following the expulsion in 1492 (and hence were originally from North Africa), or if they arrived in an earlier wave from Kazakhstan, or wherever. Cheekbones seem to suggest Mongolian hordes fit in there some place, maybe with a few Cossacks mixed in.

We have our stories nonetheless. My wife's impossible last name ("Sawislak") may originally have had some more "z"s, "y"s, or "c"s in it; the current iteration was created by the immigration office in Galveston, Texas, with half the family getting this unpronounceable appellation (but at least they were able to buy some vowels!), and the other half being more fortunately blessed with "Sawyer".

But it is a story from my half of the family that reminded me of that of George Washington Bush. Seems that my father's father (who died long before I was born) was a Lithuanian Jewish sea trader named "David Klopman." Following World War I, he ended up in Turkey, with a Turkish passport. When he came to Ellis Island, immigration would not allow him into the country, not because he was Jewish, nor Turkish, but because he was "Oriental". However, since he was fluent in many languages, he somehow found his way to Canada, changed his name to "David H. Albert" (with the last name perhaps pronounced in a French manner), and, having no identifiable non-Caucasian characteristics, entered the United States as a French-Canadian. To this day, I own a gold pocketwatch with his new initials (which are my own!) engraved into the back. Now how much of this story is actually true, I'll never know—all the relatives on my father's side of the family are long dead.

The point of this little detour into personal history is to note the centrality of skin color as a marker of how people actually get treated over time. For my grandfather, country of origin, religion, passport, language, or even his name presented no permanent obstacles to eventually finding a way to fit in quite comfortably in American society. For George Washington Bush, no truth about his origins, or a name makeover, or any other factor over which he might have had control was going to affect the way he was treated by custom, tradition, or even law. The pigmentation of his skin determined his treatment. This is not even his "race", genetically speaking, but simply the social construction of race based upon his skin color. One would like to believe this would have been substantially remedied following the Civil War; my research amazed me to the degree that it hasn't been.

* * * * *

Dinner is over. The little white dog has torn up the tv listings in the family room, and is now whining at my door—he wants to go for a walk. The big brown dog is shedding all over the living room carpet, only the carpet is so old it is hard to know where the carpet ends and the dog hair begins. (They are exactly the same color!) Ellen is giving a client a massage. Meera needs help with the second movement of her Mozart sonata. I don't play a note, but it seems if I just sit with her, she concentrates better, and she likes to get it right. And Aliyah is complaining that we've run out of milk!

I'll deal with it all somehow or, as is the case on some days, I won't! Meanwhile, they are amused (I think) seeing me come in with this big heap of books from the library, and the pages from the yellow legal pad spread out all over my desk, and me scribbling away. They know that I think my research is important, and Meera likes the idea that she started it, even if what I'm discovering currently escapes her entirely. They'll be plenty of time for her to understand, even if it is years from now.

I can imagine Meera in a couple of years (all right, probably a half dozen) reading the first part of this essay and remonstrating with me, "Dad, all that stuff was a long time ago. The Civil War ended in 1865, and while attitudes have sometimes been slow to change, shouldn't 150 years have been enough to time to even things out?"

And I'd have to sigh. Attitudes *have* been slow to change, but my focus has not been on attitudes, which can indeed be difficult enough to change, but on the aforementioned six conditions that make the creation of wealth (and hence the end of poverty, given our current economic arrangements) possible. Remember—Meera's original car question was "Why are Black people poor?" not why they are treated badly.

And so my focus has not been upon attitudes, except as they result in actual policies and conditions, though it cannot be ignored that the results of these policies and conditions serve, in turn, to reinforce attitudes. I learned that to focus solely on individually held racial attitudes, without examining how they get played out in the real world, does little to help explain how we ended up where we are today. To have our children learn about the evils of the Ku Klux Klan, for example, without also learning that the attitudes that produced the Klan were very widely shared (after all, D.W. Griffith, in the wildly popular 1915 movie *The Birth of a Nation*, portrayed the Klan as the voice of "virtuous Christianity") and that these attitudes were then translated into policy, does our kids a grave disservice indeed.

Racism is more than prejudice, and more than bigotry. People in groups defined any way one chooses can hold and even express hateful attitudes toward members of other groups. But the difference between prejudice and racism lies in the fact that in the latter, power to control institutional policies is bound up with prejudice to produce benefits for some, deficits for others. This power confers advantages whether or not those who receive the benefits had any part in creating or ensuring them. Racism is a *system* of advantage, not simply a set of personal attitudes. As a person with lighter skin-tones, I have substantial advantages (as shall yet become clearer). I didn't ask for them. It would take a monumental effort on my part to reject them, especially as in the context of contemporary culture, most of the time I don't even notice that I have them! As an individual, George Washington Bush may have loved people with lighter skin (we know he married one) or he could have hated them. In neither case would that attitude have affected his beige-skinned neighbors' ability to own the piece of land next to the one on which he finally settled.

* * * * *

With regard to equality, this word must not be understood to mean that degrees of power and wealth should be exactly the same, but rather that with regard to power, it should be incapable of all violence and never exerted except by virtue of status and the laws; and with regard to wealth, no citizen should be so opulent that he can buy another, and none so poor that he is constrained to sell himself.
—Jean Jacques Rousseau

But Meera's hypothetical followup question seemed like a fair one. If the end of slavery broke the shackles that prevented wealth creation among African-Americans, why the persistent disparity? It is a fair question, I thought, and required another dive into the books. And the answer, it turns out, is a simple one, though it's going to take some more pages to demonstrate: the shackles weren't shattered; they were merely hung in new ways.

The First Freedman's Bureau was created before the end of the Civil War for the purpose, among others, of compensating freed slaves who joined the war effort and marched across Georgia with General Sherman in late 1864/early 1865. The Bureau had authority to set apart for "loyal refugees and freedmen such tracts of land within the insurrectionary states as shall have been abandoned or which the United States shall have acquired by confiscation or sale...." Under the authority of the War

Department, Sherman distributed tracts of up to 40 acres to approximately 40,000 freedmen and ordered the Union Army to lend these freedman animals no longer useful to the military. Hence the origin of the phrase "Forty Acres and a Mule".

However, by 1866, once introduced into Congress, the Freedman's Bureau Act was overwhelmingly defeated. President Andrew Johnson restored all redistributed land to the plantation owners, and vetoed all proposals to provide land to the freedmen.

So the plantation owners suffered the devastation of the war and the loss of their slave "properties", but emerged from Reconstruction with all six characteristic preconditions for the accumulation of wealth and capital relatively intact. Northern capital, already built on the fruits of slave labor, while it experienced its own ups and downs, was now being deployed in newly emerging industrial and financial ventures.

But what of the former slaves? There are important historians such as Rayford Logan who have suggested that the last quarter of the 19th Century, and *not* the slavery era, was the low point in African-American history.[13] Four million former slaves wandered rootlessly around the defeated South, their homes and way of life, poor as it had been, disrupted to a far greater extent than those of their former masters. A new practice arose that continued the practice of slavery well into the 20th Century. (Did you ever read that one in your history books?) This practice was called "peonage" (being a particularly virulent form of sharecropping), or, even worse, "convict peonage".

"Convict peonage" was quite a complex system. A Black man would be arrested for "vagrancy" (another word for unemployment). There was plenty of that already, but it could also be created by a plantation owner simply firing a hired hand, and then having the worker arrested for trespassing or vagrancy for occupying his own house situated on the owner's land. The employee would be ordered to pay a fine, which he couldn't afford, and would be incarcerated. A plantation owner would pay the fine and "hire" the employee until the latter could afford to pay off his debt, which might be never, or at least until the value of his labor declined to the point that he wasn't worth keeping. Peons were charged exorbitantly for their food, clothing, and shelter (which was often minimal), with all

---

13   See Logan, Rayford W. *The Negro in American Life and Thought: The Nadir, 1877-1901.* New York, NY: Collier, 1965. Also recently released, though only on microfiche, are *The Peonage Files of the U.S. Department of Justice, 1901-1945,* a gold mine of material on this system. See www.lexisnexis.com/acadadmic/2upa/Aaas/PeonageDOJ.htm.

records of the debt, of course, kept by the "employer" alone. They would be chained together at night in barrack conditions and guarded, at state expense. If the peon ran away, he would be hunted down with blood-hounds, again at state expense.

One important difference between peonage and slavery is that while slaves represented considerable monetary value for the plantation owner, peons had almost none and therefore could be mistreated, whipped, and even murdered without monetary loss. While convict peonage was out-lawed by the federal government in 1901, enforcement of the law was slow. The first case against peonage in Texas was brought in court in 1927, and convict peonage was still practiced (though rarely) as late as 1960, during the lifetimes of many of the readers of this book! In the areas of the South where convict peonage was not practiced, the system of sharecropping held African-Americans (and some poor white people as well) in bondage to the ground they worked to pay off debts, or in perpetual bondage because their contracts prohibited quitting one employer and hiring on to another with-out the former's knowledge and consent. These were certainly not condi-tions under which Black Americans could engage in wealth creation.[14]

Hundreds of thousands of African-Americans came north, seeking a new life. They had to compete for jobs and other resources in the industri-al cities with the new waves of immigrants, like my grandparents and great-grandparents. Now the new European immigrants had it hard. They had to adapt to a new culture, new language, and new customs. Many were peas-ants who had never lived in cities before. Few had brought any resources with them. They had few marketable skills and, of course, no bargaining power in the marketplace for labor.

So why didn't the new immigrants fare as poorly as African-Americans on the wealth creation front? Well, for one thing it would be a disservice to neglect the great gifts the European immigrants *did* bring with them. Many of the new immigrants came in family, extended family, and/or village/regional groupings. They brought with them traditions of commu-nity assistance. They shared a common language and culture, and many were literate in their own native tongue. They had traditions of inheri-tance, and many brought their children with them. Having arrived here, they were free to own real property, including their own homes, once they could purchase them (often with the assistance of self-help associations).

---

14 It should be noted that a small number of white and Mexican-Americans were held in con-
    vict peonage before the turn of the 20th Century as well. For an excellent firsthand account
    of convict peonage, go to www2.h-net.msu.edu/~hst203/documents/peonage.html.

Ethnic-group-based credit associations facilitated the setting up of small businesses within communities, as they do to this day. In short, though initially without tangible resources, immigrants such as my ancestors within a generation had access to many of the preconditions of wealth and capital accumulation.

African-American males usually came to the cities without their wives or children. They were the last hired and first fired, and usually were restricted to the most menial and dangerous positions on the factory floor. They were paid the least and had the fewest benefits. In many northern cities, their options for home ownership (an absolutely key element in the creation of wealth for most people, as will be discussed below) were severely restricted, even when they could afford it. In many places, public schools were segregated from their very inception. And it is here that the contrasts between race and ethnicity become apparent, because unlike other immigrants, African-Americans shared little in common with each other beyond skin color, a legacy of slavery, and present-day poverty and oppression. They were bound neither by common heritage nor culture, nor former free association. Rarely did they experience the advantages of extended family or kinship groups. And right through the end of the 20th Century, because pensions (and, later, Social Security benefits) were based on wages earned during one's working years, older African-Americans were condemned to poverty. As they could not afford decent health care and were much more likely to be exposed to poor working conditions, life expectancy for African-American males remained much shorter than for white Americans, and surviving females were so much poorer as a result than their white counterparts. Almost needless to say, there was little basis for inheritance among African-American families.

In the 20th Century, tens of thousands of American males escaped poverty by joining the military, sometimes making a career of it. Virtually no African-Americans made careers in the military prior to 1950. So-called "intelligence" testing, the child of the eugenics movement, prevented most African-Americans from entering the military. For those who did get in, the military was segregated, and benefits available to those who did were far from equivalent to those of their white counterparts. When veterans marched on Washington in the 1930s demanding benefits and relief for the nation's veterans, there was nary a Black face among them.

Another avenue for wealth creation was entry into steady white-collar employment in federal, state, or municipal civil services, fire and police departments, and into the professions. But because of systemic discrimination, these had almost a complete absence of African-Americans, even as second generation members of European immigrant communities made their way into them.

* * * * *

We spent a day with other members of my Friends Meeting helping out at the Habitat for Humanity building site. (Check out similar opportunities in your community at www.habitat.org.) Ellen has a real way with hammers (at one point she earned her living as a drywaller). I, on the other hand, am all thumbs, and was soon assigned to rock wall detail. The kids are amused by my shortcoming, and, luckily, there are other Meeting members who are prepared to take them under wing.

We take so much for granted. For years now, I have been raising funds (including using royalties generated by my previous homeschooling book *And the Skylark Sings with Me*) to help my Indian "mother" (non-biological, but we discovered each other about 25 years ago, and that's another story!) purchase cinderblock-making machines so that poor people on the east coast of Tamil Nadu (India's southernmost state) can build their own homes. Without them, they live in "houses" (actually, a euphemism!) made of mud and thatch, with kids often sleeping on the wet floor, the rats eating the roofs, and the huts reduced to rubble during the monsoon season.

Here, we are so far removed from the production of life's necessities—food, clothing, shelter, and fuel—that I sometimes wonder what would happen if their delivery were to be disrupted in a really major fashion. It is my impression that cultural illiteracy in this regard is now epidemic, and that most children grow up far more ignorant about the fundamental ties between material resources and basic economics than previous generations. And it is my suspicion that, ultimately, this illiteracy—in part the result of technology, and part the child of compulsory education—places our entire social order at great peril. Ah, yes, fodder for another research project!

* * * * *

Foreign visitors coming to America have often noted that there is nothing so American as home ownership. It seems to have become an integral part of the American way of life in two distinct historical periods. The early European settlers saw a seemingly "ownerless" land before them (hmm)—there was clearly no one to rent from! and the homesteaders pushing west found another seemingly ownerless country in front of them, and bound up their very lives with the soil. Ownership of one's own home was associated with the ethos of rugged individualism and became the *sina qua non* of the American dream.

But more mundanely, home ownership was and remains for many Americans the key to wealth and capital creation. A home is for most people a leveraged asset. Instead of paying the landlord monthly, the same income is "banked" against a mortgage placed on the asset itself. Rather than an expense, it is a fixed form of savings. For most Americans, their home remains by far their largest financial asset. Secondly, the value of this asset tends to increase even while it provides the critical need for shelter and serves as the center of family life, with, it is hoped, a somewhat limited cost in upkeep. This growing asset can then be passed on in the form of inheritance either in its current form or when sold for cash, enhancing the opportunities of future generations. Finally, as an asset, houses can be leveraged against for other purposes. It is most common for banks to offer loans to small businesses—the bread and butter of wealth creation—leveraged against the value of the home. This entails risk, of course, as many have found out. But such risk is actually no greater than agreeing to pay the landlord on a monthly basis, rather than putting the money into mortgage payments. In other words, the failed small businessperson simply ends up a renter.

In 1900, the African-American home ownership rate (20%) for males ages 20-64 was less than half that of whites (46%). Worse yet, much of this home ownership was in the form of sharecropper shacks in the South, hardly an asset that could be leveraged. In 100 years, while there have been gains in relative terms, and home ownership is more common among both, the percentage-point gap between African-American and white home ownership has not improved. In 2001, 73.8% of white families owned their own homes, compared with 47.6% of Blacks, representing the same 26 percentage-point gap that existed at the dawn of the 20th Century.[15]

There are obvious reasons for the continuing gap. These include continuing differentials in income, based upon lack of access to better-paying jobs, lack of community capital for small business ventures, lack of inheritances, and lower male life expectancy (meaning that a greater portion of the African-American working population would be closer to 20 rather than 64). Discrimination of course played its own role. As late as 1950, the Federal Housing Administration provided subsidies to white mortgage holders who were bound by restrictive covenants to exclude African-Americans from any

---

15 Wolff, Edward N., "Recent Trends in Wealth Ownership 1983-1998, Levy Economics Institute, April 2000; Bureau of Labor Statistics, 4th Quarter, 2001; U.S. Census Bureau.

ownership of real property. In short, African-Americans remained renters and missed out on billions in wealth accumulation from home equity, virtually all of which went into white landlords' pockets, and, later, in some cases, into white-owned business ventures. White folks stand on the shoulders of their ancestors, without denying that some of them might not have been very tall. By comparison, African-Americans, in the best of circumstances, stand on the ground. It isn't that they didn't create wealth—they created a lot if it. But others were the beneficiaries.

* * * * *

World War II represented a time of opportunity for African-Americans, which, however, did not last long. As white servicemen headed off to war, and following a threat on the part of A. Philip Randolph to lead a march of 100,000 African-Americans on Washington, D.C. in 1941, Black Americans were finally allowed an opportunity to work in the war industries. On the eve of World War II, three out of four African-Americans lived in the South, almost nine out of ten below the poverty threshold, and fewer than 5% of Blacks in the southern states could vote. More than 700,000 African-Americans moved north and west to work in the defense plants. In Detroit and several other cities, they were met by race riots among the white population protesting their arrival. But still they came. African-American women, who had earned $3.50 a week as domestic servants in the South, found themselves making $48 a week in aircraft plants in Los Angeles. And by 1947, African-American males earned 54% of what white males earned, a tremendous step forward.[16]

Some 700,000 African-Americans eventually served in uniform during the War, though entirely in segregated units, and at the lowest possible ranks, where they were systematically denied promotions. Secretary of War Stimson justified his denial of field commands for African-Americans by stating, "Leadership is not embedded in the Negro race yet; trying to make them into combat officers would be a disaster."

And now we come into the period of current memory. My parents benefited greatly from the largest welfare program in U.S. history—the G.I. Bill and related veteran's benefits.[17] The overwhelming numbersof beneficiaries

---

16 Comments by Ben Wattenberg, *The First Measured Century*. www.pbs.org/fmc/segments/pro-greg.8.htm.

17 This is not in any way to denigrate the service of World War II veterans. They often fought at great personal sacrifice, especially as they had no expectation of any of the benefits under discussion here.

of these programs were white. As these programs were subsidized by all tax-payers, including those who could not participate in them, they represented a significant wealth transfer from African-Americans to white Americans.

There were many categories of benefits, all of which seem to have been taken advantage of by my parents. In 1950, fewer than half of Americans had finished ninth grade. Through the G.I. Bill, veterans, like my father, were able to obtain college educations at little or no cost, opening up new employment and wealth-creating opportunities. With poorer educations to begin with, African-Americans were then discriminated against in private university admissions nationwide and prohibited entrance to public universities in the South, where the majority of them lived. In other words, they had great difficulties in taking advantage of this feature of the G.I. Bill even if they qualified. The G.I. Bill thus exacerbated the education gap between Black and white Americans.

Other aspects of post-military benefits were also part of the system that assisted white Americans while leaving African-Americans behind. Subsidized mortgage loans available to veterans made home ownership possible, and created opportunities for white developers and white-owned real estate companies in newly created (and virtually all-white) suburbs. African-Americans could not purchase houses in the same tracts.

The racist impacts, even if not the intent, of G.I. benefits were reinforced by other choices in government spending. Federal transportation funds that might have gone to the refurbishing of urban public transportation systems (most African-Americans in the northern states living in cities) went to the building of new highways to, and ring roads around the suburbs. Tens of thousands of new jobs were created in the then lily-white construction trades.

With the exodus of the tax base to the suburbs, cities were (and continue to be) hard-pressed to maintain public education and city services to the remaining residents and businesses. The residents found it difficult to leave, but businesses found no such difficulty and often did, taking with them many of the available wage-earning opportunities. As if to add insult to injury, income tax deductions for mortgage interest paid are, generally speaking, based on the size and value of the house—the more valuable the house, the bigger the deduction. To this day, working African-Americans returning to rented tenement apartments in the inner city every evening, who get no tax deductions for paying rent, are thus afforded the opportunity through their taxes to subsidize white homeowners in wealthy neighborhoods such as Scarsdale, Los Altos Hills, and Shaker Heights, even as they enrich white landlords (and their descendents) with the rent money.

Public policy also demanded that veterans be afforded the opportunity to work, and so a series of tax incentives were created to induce moms to stay home with the kids. The so-called "marriage penalty" in the federal income tax was not created with the intent to penalize, but rather as a "stay-at-home-mom" incentive. However, the benefit was only available to 1) intact nuclear families (extended, female-headed families, consisting, for example, of a mother, a grandmother, and children did not qualify); 2) families in which two adults did not have to work to make ends meet; and 3) families where the husband's income was large enough to take advantage of the tax break. African-American women (like women generally speaking) lost their higher-paying factory jobs, and were now located in the northern states (and with a smaller market for domestic servants), and were unlikely to be able to avail themselves of this incentive. Now that most families with two parents have both of them working, this incentive seems like a penalty, and has come under fierce attack, but not because it was unfair to Black families.

Welfare policies directed at the mostly urban, heavily African-American poor were almost diametrically opposite to governmental policies directed at the overwhelmingly white veterans. Welfare could only be accessed, in many cases, where a potential male wage earner was not present, thus providing an incentive for the splitting up of African-American families, reinforcing a non-nuclear family structure that had been created in the slavery period. These welfare policies were strictly means-tested, and as city tax bases eroded, benefits declined. This is in sharp contract to benefits for predominantly white veterans that were not means-tested, but were universally available to them regardless of income, and did not decline. Instead of new homes, individually owned, that could be a source of pride, public housing confirmed poor urban dwellers as tenement renters. Public health clinics—among the last available sources of health care for the inner-city poor—closed or were severely curtailed, leaving hospital emergency rooms as one of the few remaining options.

So we need to contrast the two welfare programs (and they were both "welfare", whatever we wish to call them): the first rewarded intact nuclear families (including those with inherited wealth) with adult education benefits, access to home ownership and to the suburbs and subsidized mortgages—thus enhanced savings, subsidized transportation, provided better funded schools for children, increased employment opportunities for males, gave incentives for mothers to stay home and care for their children, and was available to all regardless of income. The second penalized intact families, were only available after all other assets were exhausted (effectively penalizing people for earning money), provided no adult education benefits, reinforced lack of opportunity for home ownership and confined recipients to tenements. These programs also ignored transportation infrastructure needs, and (later) forced single mothers away from their children and into the low-wage workforce. It is no wonder that the income gap and, especially, the asset gap between African-Americans and white Americans persisted. As already noted, in 1999 the ratio of net financial assets of the latter to the former—*in the same income brackets*—reached as high as 99 to 1.

* * * * *

What happens to a dream deferred?

Does it dry up
like a raisin in the sun?
And then run?

Does it stink like rotten meat?
Or crust and sugar over –
like a syrupy sweet?

Maybe it just sags
like a heavy load
Or does it just explode?

—Langston Hughes,
"Montage of a Dream Deferred"

And so what does the future hold? Well, for one thing, there is affirmative action…in prison admissions. Beginning in the 1960s, white college students increasingly took to the use of illegal drugs, especially marijuana and hallucinogens. Not surprisingly, penalties for marijuana possession were reduced, and those for hallucinogens set lower than for other drugs. White young adults are able to plea bargain in many cases and stay out of prison (good lawyers help), instead serving shorter sentences in jails or on probation or being diverted out of the criminal justice system altogether. African-American young adults go to prison.

Beginning in the late 1970s, cocaine was used in two different forms: in powdered form by predominantly white Americans, and in crystalline form (known as crack) by African-Americans. In many states penalties for crack cocaine possession are 3-4 times those for powdered cocaine. The result again is that African-Americans go to the state penitentiary,

while whites, if convicted at all, are more likely to go to the county jail
or drug treatment. In 1998, African-Americans constituted 13% of the
nation's drug users, but made up 30% of those arrested for drug use, and
49% of those serving time in state prisons. In Washington State, African-
Americans are less than 4% of the state's population, but represent
almost 40% of the prison population.

The "war on drugs" is actually a war on African-American males.
Blacks account for 62.7% of all drug offenders in state prisons, even though
there are five times as many white drug users as Black ones. Nationally,
African-American men are admitted to state prisons for drug offenses at a
rate, relative to population, 13.4 times greater than whites. In ten states—
Wisconsin, West Virginia, Ohio, New Jersey, Minnesota, Maryland, Maine,
Iowa, Illinois, and North Carolina—the rate was 27-57 times greater. Note
that all but one of these ten are *northern* states. Most of those in state prisons for drug offenses are low-level, nonviolent offenders; 84% of drug
offenders in state prisons had no prior sentence for violent crimes. The
result of these policies is nothing short of devastating. In 1995, one in three
African-American men between the ages of 20-29 was in jail or prison, or
on parole or probation.[18]

This has a direct impact on wealth creation. Many businesses—
even if they do not discriminate on the basis of race—are much less
likely to hire convicted felons. And now federal college benefits may
be denied to those who have a drug offense on their record, a policy
that appears race-neutral but, once again, disproportionately impacts
the futures of African-Americans. Convicted rapists, serial child
molesters, murderers, armed robbers, and savings-and-loan executives
convicted of bilking the public of billions of dollars can access federal higher education benefits; those convicted of selling less than $50
worth of drugs to support their crippling addiction, and for which
there was no treatment available, are effectively barred from further
education.[19] Some 13% of the African-American male population has
lost the right to vote because of felony disenfranchisement laws, many

---

18 Human Rights Watch, *United States—Punishment and Prejudice: Racial Disparities in the War
on Drugs*, Vol. 12 No.2, May 2000. www.hrw.org/reports/2000/usa/Rcedrg00.htm.

19 Even when substance abuse treatment is available to African-Americans, it is dispropor-
tionately likely to be inadequate. In a study published in the August 21, 2002 issues of the
Journal of the American Medical Association, "Changes in Methadone Treatment Practices:
Results from a National Panel Study, 1988-2000" by Drs. Thomas D'Aunno and Harold

having committed exactly the same offenses as white voters, the difference not being the nature of the crime, but whether they were imprisoned for it.[20]

Of course, affirmative action that might provide enhanced opportunities for African-Americans is virtually gone. Voters in Washington State seemed to be so upset that 2.8% of the students at the University of Washington were African-American (only a small portion of whom were admitted through affirmative action), that they banned the practice altogether (as has happened in at least five other states).

Federal welfare legislation enacted under President Clinton now prevents welfare recipients from attending school or college instead of working while receiving benefits. According to the National Coalition for the Homeless, in 2000 nationwide on average an hourly wage of $13.87 was required to afford a two-bedroom apartment, more than twice the minimum wage, this at a time when more than 30% of the workforce (and a significantly higher proportion of African-Americans) works for $8 an hour or less. The Preamble Center for Public Policy (www.preamble.org) has estimated that the odds against a typical welfare recipient's landing a job at such a "housing wage" are approximately 97 to 1. This is not a condition likely to foster an individual's ability to save for further education. According to a U.S. Department of Housing and Urban Development report to Congress dated March 2001, there were 36 affordable rental units for every one hundred low-income families, roughly half of what there was 20 years ago. In my state of Washington, low-wage workers, just the kind we see at our soup kitchen, are crowding into cheap motels up and down the I-5 corridor.[21]

Segregated housing is mirrored in increasingly segregated public education, and huge disparities in educational quality. Recent studies suggest that racial segregation in housing, by itself, is responsible for significant

---

Pollack, it was found African-Americans are far more likely to be prescribed doses of methadone inadequate to deal with heroin addiction. While it is known that adequate dosages are linked to better therapeutic outcomes, African-American patients are then blamed for the failure of treatment.

20 *United States—Punishment and Prejudice,* op.cit.

21 An interesting account of what life might be like for low-wage workers in the U.S. today can be found in Ehrenreich, Barbara, *Nickel and Dimed: On (Not) Getting By in America.* New York, NY: Metropolitan Books, 2001.

gaps in education, employment, and even single parenthood.[22] Since the late 1970s, a growing body of research has documented that race—not income, property values, or other indicators—is the single most significant determinant in the siting of toxic facilities and in permissive environmental enforcement. Three out of every four off-site commercial hazardous waste landfills in the southeastern U.S. are located in African-American communities, even though African-Americans make up only one-fifth of the population. Even if African-Americans own their own homes, their housing values under such conditions are not likely to rise, making the possibility of opportunity creation through inheritance even more unlikely. Residents of communities of color are at much greater risk of environmental health disorders such as eye and skin irritations, chronic headaches, respiratory illnesses, lead poisoning, asthma, certain cancers, and a host of other debilitating diseases.[23] At the same time, they are less likely to receive health care for these conditions. Among the 44 million Americans without health insurance, African-Americans are way overrepresented. As a result, they die sooner from chronic illnesses like AIDS, hypertension, diabetes, cancer, stroke, and heart disease. And when they do have insurance, according to a 2002 Institute of Medicine study commissioned by the U.S. Congress, and even when their income and age are the same, they will likely get poorer quality medical care. "Relative to whites, African-Americans—and in some cases Hispanics—are less likely to receive appropriate cardiac medication or to undergo coronary artery bypass surgery, are less likely to receive hemodialysis and kidney transplantatation, and likely to receive a lower quality of basic clinical services." "Significantly," the report adds, "these differences are associated with greater mortality among African-American patients."[24]

---

22 See Orfield, Gary, *Schools More Separate: Consequences of a Decade of Resegregation.* Cambridge, MA: The Civil Rights Project—Harvard University, 2001 (www.law.harvard.edu/groups/civilrights/publications/resegregation01/schoolsseparate.pdf); and Applied Research Center, *Facing the Consequences: An Examination of Racial Discrimination in U.S. Public Schools.* Oakland, CA: Chardon Press, 2000 (www.arc.org/downloads/ARC_FTC.pdf).

23 See the ongoing environmental justice projects of The Preamble Center (www.preamble.org/OngoingProjects/EEJ&H/eej&hindex.html).

24 Board on Health Sciences Policy, Institute of Medicine, National Academy of Science. *Confronting Racial and Ethnic Disparities in Health Care.* Washington, DC: National Academy Press, 2002 (www.nap.edu/books/030908265X/html/).

If this seems very distant from your experience, or (if you are white) you do not see how you might benefit as a result of these health inequalities, I ask you only to consider the following (as I found myself forced to do). The middle-class African-American male in Washington, DC, with a life expectancy of 62 years, will have paid into Social Security and Medicare for 40 years, without ever receiving a single dime in return. His contributions will instead go to the fund the retirement income and health care needs of (for example) a white woman *who earned the same income* during her working years, but with a life expectancy of more than 80. This is not a new development, but one which has been an impact of Social Security since its inception. In short, even our society's vaunted "safety nets", (and certainly without any intention on the part of elderly white women, who may already be struggling to get by), have been and remain, vehicles for race-based income redistribution.[25]

The combined economic impact of these inequities is immense. Just looking at home ownership, Robert Westley, Professor of Law at Tulane University, estimates that, based solely on discrimination in home mortgage approval rates, the projected number of credit-worthy homebuyers and the median white housing appreciation rate, the current generation of African-Americans will lose about $82 billion in equity due solely to institutional discrimination. This is an underestimate, however. It must be remembered that in all those years, African-Americans will pay that money in rents and will be building equity—just not their own. Rather than increasing their net assets and enhancing the wealth creating opportunities of future generations of African-Americans, these funds end up in the pockets of white rental property owners and investors. Later, the children and then grandchildren of the white owners inherit the assets, which can then be utilized in further wealth creation.

In short, the reason people are poor is simple—they are prevented from having money, and don't have access to the preconditions necessary

---

25 Christopher Murray of the Harvard School of Public Health reports that life expectancy of the Black rural poor living in the South is even lower—below those in India, Bolivia, most of Central Asia, and much of Central and South America. The highest life expectancy in the U.S. is among Asian women in Bergen County, New Jersey—97! See "Surprises in a Study of Life Expectancies," *The New York Times*, December 4, 1997; and www.harvard-magazine.com/issues/mj98/right.lifelines.html. Of course, a substantial portion of the differences in life expectancy among racial groups is accounted for by differentials in infant mortality rates. However, the insults to health—poor environmental living and working conditions—coupled with inequities in health care delivery, result in significant differences in life expectancy even for those age 50 and above.

to create it. They are not prevented from this access by attitudes, but by institutional and systemic policies that spring from those attitudes. And when that is true, it generally means that someone else reaps the benefits.

* * * * *

So there it is—my homeschooling research project, with its origins in a car question. It was a transformative journey, even if based on a query from my daughter that has long since passed its urgency.

That doesn't matter too much in the total scheme of things. What matters is that the way I view the world has changed. I may not like what I see, but I do like the new clarity with which I see it. And I have grown as a result. Isn't that what I want for my kids as they seek out their own learning adventures?

And, as to the results, well, to say they are disquieting is an understatement. The truth of what I have gained from my research flies in the face of what we would all like to believe makes us distinctly American, that success is determined by an individual's hard work, perseverance, creativity, follow-through. These are the lessons we want our children—Black, white, other—to learn. The statistics and the reality behind what I have just written make at least some of us distinctly uncomfortable, or at least it does me.

But I make no apologies. For me, this is a very personal and concrete issue—I have two homeschooled children with two different skin colors. I share Martin Luther King, Jr.'s dream for his four children that they "will one day live in a nation where they will be judged not by the color of their skin but by the content of their character." But to assume that this is the case now would be an exercise in wish-fulfillment, rather than contributing to an understanding of where we are.

So, for me, this is very much a homeschooling issue. My "social studies" plan is to teach the promise of the American dream, rather than its fulfillment. My country—warts and all. My sense is that we are obligated to do so because to neglect it is not only to segment out and ignore a very unique part of our history and culture, as distasteful as it might seem, but also because to ignore the legacy of racism is to ensure that our children remain mystified about how the world around them actually (as opposed to ideally) works. One could ignore a question such as Meera's only so many times before there is an implied answer that this state of affairs is simply the way things are, and brooks no questioning. Been there, done that, and I am sure I can do better.

To my way of thinking, both parenting and homeschooling (and education, properly understood) are audacious acts of faith that the way of the world is neither immutable nor inevitable. With apologies to the dead Egyptians, *we* are history unfolding. Put *that* on a standardized test.

III Embracing the Song of the World

We make our world significant by the courage of our questions and by the depth of our answers.

—Carl Sagan

Following September 11th, our Friends Meeting received a request from the American Friends Service Committee (AFSC). AFSC (www.AFSC.org) is the service arm of American Quakers, and has provided relief and reconstruction assistance around the globe for eight decades, and for which it received the Nobel Peace Prize in 1947. The request, similar to ones that are received and responded to regularly by Friends whenever human catastrophes are in the making, was that each Meeting—starting with the children—take up a collection of blankets—new or in excellent condition—and ship them to several different locations around the U.S., where they would be loaded into containers and flown to help keep thousands of Afghan refugees warm through the long winter. In two months, 75,000 blankets, worth $1.3 million dollars, were collected and shipped. AFSC was appropriately self-congratulatory. Needless to say, we sent a blanket.

There was only one problem. As I went to two local department stories to look for a suitable blanket, I noticed where they were manufactured: Turkey, Macau, Sri Lanka, Bangladesh, China, Pakistan. PAKISTAN! Now I felt obligated to explain this to the kids. In former times, Friends probably would have made their own quilts, knitted shawls and sweaters and warm hats and gloves and mittens, and sent abroad these products of their own hands as labors of love. (To be fair, it should be noted, some few still do.) Now, we go to the local department store. Blankets destined for Afghanistan were fabricated in Pakistan, shipped on huge, oil-guzzling cargo ships, unloaded in American ports, transported in diesel-powered trucks to warehouses across the country, from which they were then distributed to local stores. Friends (like myself) drove our 3,000 pounds of steel and aluminum and plastic made in Japan (with components manufactured in Korea, China, and Indonesia) to the local mall, purchased our blanket, and sent it (along with the others gathered by our Meeting) via UPS trucks (built in Mexico) consuming gasoline and oil products refined in Saudi Arabia, to the proper location, where they were loaded onto airplanes (likely Airbuses, made in France) burning thousands of gallons of jet fuel (and spewing exhausts into the atmosphere). The jets then landed in Pakistan where the blankets were unloaded and shipped to the refugee camps. According to AFSC (they were trying to raise cash as well), there were 15 containers, and the cost of shipping each container from Philadelphia to Pakistan (forget all the other transportation costs) was equivalent to that of educating 80 Afghan children for a whole year. In other words, the blanket program—the recommended channel for my own charitable instincts and those of my children—directly cost 1,200 Afghani children their education.

I know—this makes your head hurt (or at least it does mine!), but there's more. Pakistan is infamous for child labor. In 1996, the esteemed journalist Sydney Schanberg (author of *The Killing Fields*) published an exposé in *Life Magazine* titled "Six Cents an Hour."[1] He went to Pakistan and posed as a soccer ball exporter. He was offered children for $150-$180 who would labor for him as virtual slaves. Children as young as six, Schanberg wrote, are "sold and resold like furniture, branded, beaten, blinded as punishment for wanting to go home, rendered speechless by the trauma of their enslavement." Photos displayed children working in dank sheds, for six cents an hour or less, stitching soccer balls with the familiar Nike swoosh and logos of other transnational athletic equipment companies.[2] It is not unlikely that some of the blankets shipped halfway around the world to be purchased by Americans to be shipped halfway around back again to keep Afghan refugees warm were made by the brothers and sisters of these same children.

Quakers are a somewhat peculiar lot, and we have among our peculiarities as pacifists not only an injunction to "abjure all outward wars and strife" but, to paraphrase the words of the 18th Century Quaker abolitionist John Woolman, "to seek out the seeds of war in our

---

1   Schanberg, Sydney H., "On the playgrounds of America, every kid's goal is to score: In Pakistan, where children stitch soccer balls for six cents an hour, the goal is to survive." *Life Magazine*, June 1996.

2   I have since been delighted to learn of successful efforts by students at Monroe High School in Los Angeles to get the school board to adopt a policy allowing purchase of soccer balls only from countries that enforce a prohibition against child labor. To be fair, under intense pressure, Nike and several other manufacturers are being forced to curb the practice of using child labor, though they only pledge to "abide by all applicable local regulations" (which is why they moved to Pakistan to begin with!). It is clear that without public pressure, it would have been "business as usual."

possessions."[3] This has become a more daunting task as the globe has, through the wonders of modern technology, become a much smaller place. Friend or not, the requirements of living in the contemporary world would seem to require a degree of global understanding by our children that is unprecedented. It's quite a job we have!

Aliyah and I are both opera lovers, though this love hasn't yet rubbed off on Meera. In the final act of the wonderful Puccini opera *La Boheme*, Mimi the impoverished heroine is dying of tuberculosis, and complains that her hands are cold. One of the bohemians, the philosopher Colline (a minor character, and a bass), sings an aria "Vecchia Zimarra" to his old cloak, which he has decided to pawn to purchase Mimi a handwarmer. Translated from the Italian, he sings:

> *Faithful old garment, listen,*
> *I'll rest down here,*
> *you, however, must climb*
> *the sacred mount of piety.*
>
> *My thanks you must receive.*
> *Never has your poor worn back*
> *bowed before the rich and powerful.*
> *Deep in your calm cavernous pockets,*
> *you have protected philosophers and poets.*
>
> *Now that our happy days*
> *have fled, I must bid you farewell,*
> *faithful friend of mine.*
> *Farewell, farewell.*

What I am suggesting is that an important step to helping our children make sense of the world around them is providing the opportunity for the cloak to sing back!

---

3   "Oh! that we who declare against wars, and acknowledge our trust to be in God only, may walk in the light, and therein examine our foundation and motives in holding great estates! May we look upon our treasures, and the furniture of our houses, and the garments in which we array ourselves, and try whether the seeds of war have nourishment in these our possessions, or not." Woolman, John, "A Plea for the Poor", Part X. *The Journal and Major Essays of John Woolman*, edited by Phillips Moulton. Richmond, IN: Friends United Press, 1997.

* * * * *

I hear America singing, the varied carols I hear;
Those of mechanics—each singing his, as it should be, blithe and strong;
The carpenter singing his, as he measures his plank or beam,
The mason singing his, as he makes ready for work, or leaves off work;
The boatman singing what belongs to him in his boat…
                —Walt Whitman, "I Hear America Singing", from
                                                    Leaves of Grass

Whitman got it right, though had he lived in the 21st Century, he would certainly have gone global. Indeed, the real question is how to enable our children to understand that every person they meet, every object and every idea they encounter in their expanding world is singing, and has its own song.

One way to inspire children's interest in history, culture, and the larger social world is to connect them with the (sometimes dissonant) harmonies of economics. No, it doesn't have to wait until high school, and it doesn't have to be the "dismal science". Economics is the song of how people relate to each other through the production, distribution, and consumption of material goods and services. So start with the everyday—say, a bag of jalapeño potato chips (I happen to have a taste for these; Meera hates them!). Where do the potatoes come from? Who grows them, and who harvests them? Where and how are they prepared? What does the equipment look like, and who makes it? What are the bags made of? How does printing work and who prints the bags? What about those peppers? Where are they most commonly used? Why do people in southern climates tend to use more spices? Is there a history to the spice trade? How do the printed bags, jalapeños, and potatoes all turn up at the same place? And how did they get to us? Are they nutritionally any good, relative to what we have to pay for them?

Have the kids draw a flow chart of inputs and outputs. Put the bag of chips in the center and backtrack as to how it came to be. Work back in time and see how many cultures you cross (who raised the first potatoes, and the hot peppers?). When the kids find a geographical spot or historical period that particularly interests them, let them linger. And then do the same thing with outputs. Where does the gasoline that fuels the trucks come from? Who discovered oil? Who owns it? You could take a detour into physics: how does the internal combustion engine work? And, finally, how did you come to buy the chips? Where did your money come from? How did you come to know jalapeño chips existed? How does a supermarket work? Do some math: how much does the average potato chip cost? How does this compare with the price of a whole potato? And you could work backwards again: what cultures saw the origins of modern arithmetic? and where did money originate? Don't be surprised if you end up learning as much as the kids—at its best, that's what homeschooling is all about!

Another way to engage children in similar learning is to have them help you sort the laundry. (Doing laundry really should be among the state's mandated learning objectives.) As you pull pieces out of the dryer (or off the clothesline!) together, look at the label in each piece of clothing to see where it is made, and put push-pins into a world map, hung on the wall for that purpose, for every item. You could get colored flags—one color for socks, one color for trousers, one for shirts, etc., or better, give each family member a color so it can be easily seen what a veritable United Nations each of us carries on our body. This can also lead to wonderful essay assignments, such as "The Story of My Underwear", in which your son can explore what it is made of, where it comes from, and how it ended up (with any luck) in his dresser drawer. Maybe he might even volunteer to write a song! The point is to connect the kids to the tangible, the song of things and of people that are already part of their lives, even when they don't realize it.

* * * * *

When I was in elementary school, I remember learning a little bit about Harriet Tubman, an African-American woman, former slave, who in 19 trips to Maryland, helped 300 African-Americans escape via the Underground Railroad to freedom in the North or (after the passage of the Fugitive Slave Laws) into Canada. I am grateful for having been presented with a Black heroine, and especially the example of one who fought not only for her own freedom but who risked her life for the freedom of others. But I had trouble identifying imaginatively with her. It was not so much because of her color or her gender (though that didn't make it any easier), but, I think, because I couldn't see the parallels with slavery in the contemporary world. (That there are 30 million people held in slavery around the world today didn't cross my radar screen until I was into my 40s!) Tubman was simply presented as part of the celebratory and victorious march of American history.

The name that did not flash by in the celebration as it was presented to me in school was Levi Coffin. Coffin, a Quaker from North Carolina who moved first to Newport, Indiana and then later to Cincinnati, Ohio, was proclaimed in his time the "President of the Underground Railroad", having helped more than 3,300 African-Americans to safety.[4] Coffin and his wife Catharine are believed to have been the models for Simeon and Rachel Halliday, who harbor runaway slaves including Eliza, in Harriet Beecher Stowe's *Uncle Tom's Cabin*. But even when he is mentioned, Coffin is not remembered for what ironically probably has the most contemporary relevance for our children. Coffin moved to Cincinnati to set up a wholesale "Free Produce Store", selling food, clothing, and other items completely free of the taint of slave labor. He made several journeys south to find sources of cotton or sugar not produced by slaves. At one point, Coffin bought a $300 cotton gin in Cincinnati (a huge investment in those days) and had it shipped to Mississippi, relying on it for a continuous supply of free-produced cotton.[5]

The importance of this story for our children is in learning that there are choices that can be made in consumption that go beyond either price, individual taste, or the lure of advertising. One of the publicized advantages of a free-market economy is that consumers have a wide latitude of choices (including not to consume!). But those advantages quickly fade away unless our children learn to make intelligent, informed, ethical decisions about those choices, and to act upon them. The historian James Loewen, author of *Lies My Teacher Taught Me*, emphasizes that the most jarring omission in the teaching of American history today is lack of mention

---

4   Levi Coffin appears in neither of the two best history books often used by homeschoolers—Joy Hakim's *A History of US* (Oxford, UK: Oxford University Press, 1999) nor even in Howard Zinn's *A People's History of the United States* (New York, NY: HarperPerennial, 1995). The omission in Hakim's 11-volume series is particularly egregious, as she notes that 20,000 inhabitants left North Carolina and moved west from 1790-1815, but fails to explain that the majority were Quakers seeking to find a place where their former slaves could live in safety. Most settled in southern Ohio and Indiana.

5   There are several reasonably good children's and young-adult biographies of Levi Coffin. One recent one is *Levi Coffin, Quaker: Breaking the Bonds of Slavery in Ohio and Indiana* by Mary Ann Yannessa (Richmond, IN: Friends United Press, 2001). A retired librarian, Yannessa now serves as a speaker for the National Underground Railroad Freedom Center in Cincinnati, which is scheduled to open for visitors in the summer of 2004 (www.undergroundrailroad.org). In the meantime, one can visit Levi Coffin's house, often known as the "Grand Central Station of the Underground Railroad", in Fountain City, Indiana (www.visitrichmond.org/UndergroundRR.html). (Aliyah and I did.) A fine children's book account of the Underground Railroad in which white people are seen as allies who help people along the route to freedom is Jeanette Winters' *Follow the Drinking Gourd*. New York, NY: Dragonfly Books, 1988.

of whites who worked (and continue to work) for equal justice for all. And the reason he suggests for this omission is that such individuals, viewed by children as models, pose a direct threat to an ethic of compliance.[6]

There are ways to remedy this. Learn, with your kids, about those who, in the song of history, like Harriet Tubman and Levi Coffin, have been willing to put themselves at risk for others. These are people like Andre Trocmé, the French pastor who convinced his small, conservative town to hide Jews from the Nazis [there is an excellent book about this called *Lest Innocent Blood Be Shed: The Story of the Village of Le Chambon and How Goodness Happened There* by Philip Hallie (New York: NY: HarperPerennial, 1994)]; or King Christian X of Denmark, who courageously told the Nazis after they invaded that "there was no Jewish *problem*", thus signaling an organic movement on the part of Danes to save their entire Jewish population during World War II. Or Dorothy Day, who gave up her career as a journalist to found the Catholic Worker movement, setting up houses of hospitality for the poor during the Depression, and calling upon Catholics to oppose nuclear proliferation. Or Myles Horton, founder of the Highlander Center in the 1930s, a popular education center organizing for environmental and economic justice in Appalachia, and for struggles in the South for equality and voting rights. (www.hrec.org). Or perhaps the most famous graduate of the Highlander Center, Rosa Parks, who, as we all know, refused to move to the back of the bus, and helped transform America as a result. Or Sarah Grimke and Virginia Durr, southern belles—the first in the 19th Century, the second in the 20th—who found ways to cast off expectations of family and friends to further the joint causes of civil and human rights.

How about Millard and Linda Fuller, to cite more recent heroes, who gave up a successful business and law careers without any real plans for their futures, and ended up forming Habitat for Humanity a decade later? Or Lois Gibbs, housewife and mother of two, who led a battle against local, state, and federal governments to force a cleanup of Love Canal which, in turn, resulted in the creation of the Superfund used to clean up of toxic sites across the U.S.? Or Janusz Korczak, the Polish-Jewish educator, author, doctor, and progressive orphanage director, who refused to leave his charges even when they were transported to the Warsaw Ghetto and finally to the death camps? Or, to go back further in time, try Robert Carter III

---

6   Loewen, James, *Lies My Teacher Taught Me: Everything Your American History Textbook Got Wrong*. New York, NY: Touchstone Books, 1996.

(1728-1804), a fabulously wealthy contemporary of both Washington and Jefferson in Virginia. Carter owned 16 plantations and 70,000 acres, but, taking the principles of the 18th Century Baptist Church seriously and considered a traitor to his class as a result, freed all 500 of his slaves in 1791, 72 years before the Emancipation Proclamation.[7] If you need to find books for the kids about people like this, or to help them think about acting more creatively in the face of injustice and conflict, check out the annual Jane Addams Children's Book Award winners (www.soemadison.wisc.edu/ccbc/addams/list.htm).

Create your own "Giraffes" hall of fame: enshrining not just people who are selfless (of course, that too is to be prized), but those are have actually stuck their necks out and put themselves at risk to further the common good.[8] And be on the lookout for such people in your community—you'll be surprised how many heirs to Harriet Tubman and Levi Coffin there truly are, if you are willing to search hard enough. Share with your kids the Talmudic tale of the 36 Righteous Men (update it to "people"!). In this traditional Jewish tale, there are 36 righteous people in the world in every generation who usually go about their business anonymously, but without whose saving presence, the world would become a desolate place. (This folktale, incidentally, served as the basis of the Hollywood movie *Men in Black*.) Go on a hunt for them!

* * * * *

I hated 11th-grade English. The high school English teacher, Irish Miss McDermott (I've changed her name, though, bless her soul, she must be long dead by now) was known to eat adolescent boys for breakfast along with the whiskey of her ancestral home. Flaming red hair, and a temper to match. Anyway, here we were, all these science nerds at our specialized science high school, and they made us read the most awful stuff (all of which I now adore): *Ethan Frome* and *Silas Marner* and *Vanity Fair*. I mean this was the mid-60s in New York City and there was no James Baldwin or Ralph Ellison or LeRoi Jones, no, this was *English* class.

Of all the books I read in the 11th grade, the absolute worst, as everyone agreed by overwhelming consensus, was *Giants in the Earth*. In the first 20 pages, nothing happens! Some oxen pull a bunch of carts across fields

---

7   www.npr.org/programs/watc/features/2001/antijefferson/010901.antijefferson.html.

8   Check out the Giraffe Project (www.giraffe.org). While most of their materials are organized for use in school classrooms, their website will be helpful in working with kids to find examples of giraffes in your own communities.

where there are no roads, one excruciating step after another, against a changing sky. Bleak. No trees. No houses. No people (except for those in the wagons, and they seemed particularly uninteresting).

For the next three decades, I made fun of this book, and Miss McDermott. Five years ago, as an experiment to see whether my prejudices might be confirmed, I went back and reread it. It is spectacular! (I don't know whether to blame my initial impression on the quality of high school English teaching, or the state of my adolescent intellect, or both.) Written by Ole Rolvaag, a Norwegian immigrant and itinerant who was later to become the first professor of Scandinavian studies at St. Olaf's College in Minnesota, *Giants in the Earth* is about the original immigrant settling of South Dakota.

Now this was tough stuff for us. My high school class was about 90% Jewish (speak of segregation!), with an admixture of Asians, a few African-Americans and Hispanics, and some nondescript "others". We did have one really tall, very blonde young man in my homeroom class named "Arne Johanson". My "western" relatives lived in Cranford, New Jersey, and we only saw them at weddings and funerals. I suspect that until the day she died, my grandmother couldn't tell Indiana from Iowa (and might have thought one was the capital of the other). It didn't affect her ability to function quite well in the world one whit. Yes, it is all a matter of perspective.

But I think what Miss McDermott was driving at (though at the time, I'm sure I couldn't tell) was to move us past the melting-pot stereotypes we all had of each other, and to show us that we all came with our own distinct and quite marvelous histories. *Pay attention to the particulars.* And that we could celebrate each others' history and culture and would come out the better for it.

In my experience, children best take in new learning about race and religion when their parents themselves are truly excited to learn about unfamiliar histories, cultures, and practices, as well as their own. And so I began to put together a highly idiosyncratic reading list (mostly novels) geared for homeschooling *parents* to provide food for thought about the various cultures and traditions that make up modern America and the experience of immigration and assimilation. They are all, without exception, a very good read! Teenagers will love many of the books on this list as well, which, taken together, will greatly enhance their understanding and appreciation of a diverse society and world. So here they are in no particular order. Start by finding two books—one reflective of the song of your own ethnic and cultural heritage, the other foreign to your personal experience. I invite all of you to contribute to this list-in-progress—write me at shantinik@earthlink.net and share your favorites in this genre.

- *The Joy Luck Club* by Amy Tan (New York, NY: Putnam Publishing Group, 1989). This is really a collection of mother/daughter stories, linked by the narrative device of a *mah jong* game, rather like a Chinese-American *Canterbury Tales*. Tan explores the secret places in the hearts of immigrant parents, their hopes for their children that are tied to successful assimilation, coupled with a wistfulness and not a little bitterness and sense of loss that accompanies this success. A bit more demanding, but perhaps even more salient in its depiction of the Chinese-American divide is Tan's *The 100 Secret Senses* (New York, NY: G.P. Putnam & Sons, 1995).

- *Giants in the Earth* by Ole Rolvaag (New York, NY: Harper & Brothers, 1927). This is the magnum opus of a true towering giant of American literature. Rolvaag's novel is about the settling of South Dakota by Norwegian immigrants in the 1860s, set against the inhospitable bleakness of landscape and weather. You will be haunted by unsettling images and by language stunning in color and texture. It would be hard to overestimate the power of this novel. It was originally written in Norwegian, and then translated with the aid of the faculty of St. Olaf's College in Minnesota, where Rolvaag became a professor and where, today, the library is named after him. There is a "next generation" novel, *Peder Victorious* (Lincoln, NE University of Nebraska Press, 1982), which, however, lacks the overwhelming power of the first volume.

- *Sula* by Toni Morrison (New York, NY: Alfred Knopf, Inc. 2002). This is an early work by the future Nobel laureate, revolving around the relationship between two girls growing up in a desperately poor Black neighborhood in Ohio, and the separate paths their lives take. Morrison's work is highly evocative of the dark realities of survival in what, for some minorities as well as whites, may feel like a harsh and unforgiving world.

- *Lost in Translation: A Life in a New Language* by Eva Hoffman (New York, NY: E.P. Dutton, 1989). This is a highly literate, articulate, and introspective memoir recounting the immigration of a Polish-Jewish teenage girl to North America in the 1950s. Hoffman, a former *The New York Times Book Review* editor, is particularly adept in her intense examination of the special difficulties which come with having to learn to think and feel in a new language, and about the agonizing process of recreating oneself within an initially alien culture.

- *Roots* by Alex Haley (Garden City, NY: Doubleday, 1976). I am amazed when I find adults who have not read this book, so if you haven't done so yet, it's time! Haley's book is the most important, most imaginatively realized work of non-fiction of my generation. It put African-American history on the map and into the consciousness of all Americans, both Black and white, and spurred the search for roots among writers from racial and ethnic groups of all kinds. And, once started, it is almost impossible to put down! I have also already recommended the two-volume set *I was Born a Slave: An Anthology of Classic Slave Narratives*, edited by Yuval Taylor. You will find here the narratives by Frederick Douglass, Nat Turner, William Wells Brown, and several dozen others, including the original narrative that provided the raw material for Harriet Beecher Stowe's *Uncle Tom's Cabin*, by far the most widely read and most influential American work of fiction in the 19th Century.

- *World of Our Fathers: The Journey of the East European Jews and the Life They Made* by Irving Howe (New York, NY: Harcourt Brace, Jovanovich, 1976). This is a superb history of the immigration of almost an entire people to America's shores between 1880 and 1945, where they quickly took up residence as cobblers, peddlers, tailors, diamond merchants, teachers, and Broadway tunesmiths. It is written with verve by an accomplished literary critic. Howe is well attuned to Jewish immigrant aspirations, both for themselves and their families, and for their new land.

- *The Peaceable Kingdom* by Jan de Hartog (New York, NY: Atheneum, 1972). A first-class and very colorful fictionalized account of the trials faced by early Quakers in 17th Century England, and their experience of the "Holy Experiment" in trying to form a new and very different commonwealth as they carved out a place for themselves in the New World in what is now Pennsylvania. It gives a sense of what America might have been had earlier settlers truly struggled with their consciences in their relations to both native peoples and slavery.

- *Obasan* by Joy Kogawa (New York, NY: Anchor Books, 1982). This is a highly acclaimed novel detailing the evacuation, relocation, and dispersal of Canadian citizens of Japanese ancestry during World War II. David Guterson's excellent *Snow Falling on Cedars* deals with similar historical material within a U.S. context, but Kogawa's telling, making use of personal narratives, dreams, fairy tales, song lyrics, and official documents, is the more moving fictionalized account. The book also provides a sensitive portrayal of the clash and melding of cultures, values, religious beliefs, and communication styles. Teenage girls will especially appreciate this work as an account of growing up. It would be a fine companion book to *The Diary of Anne Frank*.

- *A Yellow Raft in Blue Water* by Michael Dorris (New York, NY: Henry Holt & Co, 1987). This is a fierce saga of three generations of Native American women beset by hardship and bound by kinship, set on a Montana reservation and in the Pacific Northwest. Raw in language and brutally honest in approach, Dorris' book invites invitation with the works of Toni Morrison about the African-American community. It gives perhaps an unbalanced portrayal, given the cultural revival underway in many American Indian communities today.

- *Spirits of the High Mesa* by Floyd Martinez (Houston, TX: Arte Público Press, 1997). A "young adult" novel, Martinez' celebrated fictional account of growing up in New Mexico and the gulf between Anglo and Hispanic/Indian culture in the post-World War II period is told with passion and humor. Without preaching, Martinez captures the divide between the seductiveness of progress and the optimism of the early 1950s and loyalty to centuries-old village traditions and to the land that are an almost totally forgotten part of the American heritage.

- *My Name is Aram* by William Saroyan (New York, NY: Dell Publishing Co., 1991). A sunny, lightly humorous collection of stories (one of many) of growing up as an Armenian-American in Fresno, California. The general goodwill and deft lightness of touch of this and most of Saroyan's other work (he was also an excellent playwright) is quite remarkable, given that the backdrop for later Armenian immigration during the time of Saroyan's coming of age was the Armenian holocaust in Turkey during World War I.[9] In some ways, Saroyan's work is reminiscent of Mark Twain, with deep truths adroitly revealed in the most entertaining of fashions.

- *The Spirit Catches You and You Fall Down* by Anne Fadiman (New York, NY: Farrar Straus & Giroux, 1997). If there is any single book

---

9   See www.armenianholocaust.com. The word "genocide" was first used to describe the mass extermination of the Armenians, and provided the model for Hitler's later actions against Jews and Gypsies.

that demonstrates the importance of appreciating, understanding, and coming to terms with other cultures, it is this extraordinarily moving work of nonfiction. Fadiman has taken the story of the trials and eventual death of a young Cambodian Hmong girl at the hands of the American medical system, and transformed it into a tragedy of Shakespearean proportions, with writing that plumbs the depths of human feeling. You will not be the same after reading it.

- *The Healing Wisdom of Africa: Finding Life Purpose Through Nature, Ritual, and Community* by Malidoma Patrice Some and L.M. Some (New York, NY: J.P. Tarcher/Putnam 1999). Some. An evocative and eloquent account of the traditional healing practices of the Dagara people of West Africa, told by a gifted healer now teaching in California. Some opens the world of spirit to those weighed down by western rationalism, without excessive preaching or moralizing. The author himself was "kidnapped" by French Catholic missionaries at the age of 4, and so had to return to his ancestral home to have his sense of human possibilities reinvigorated. An earlier work, *Of Water and the Spirit: Ritual, Magic, and Initiation in the Life of an African Shaman* (New York, NY: Putnam Publishing Group, 1994), details Some's initiation into the competing worlds of western sensibility and traditional African wisdom.

- *Fasting, Feasting* by Anita Desai (Boston, MA: Houghton-Mifflin, 2000). This is an accomplished, subtly told story of bridging the worlds between Asian-Indian and American culture, and of a generation still caught between them. After reading this unsentimental tale, one comes away understanding a vanishing India better, while at the same time having been treated to a view of American culture as if through the surgical eyes of a foreign anthropologist.

- *The Fortunate Pilgrim* by Mario Puzo (New York, NY: Scribners, 1965). Through his authorship of *The Godfather* and the movies based upon it, Puzo is probably more responsible for the negative stereotypes that Americans hold about Italian-Americans than any other individual. And that's too bad, too, for his earlier work, loosely based on the immigration experience of his grandmother, is a spellbinding portrait of a family determined to survive in America.

- *Ramayana* translated by William Buck (Berkeley, CA: University of California Press, 2000). There are now more than a few novels dealing with the Asian Indian experience in America. However, it is almost impossible to come to any real understanding of Asian Indian culture, traditions, and worldview without at least a passing knowledge of this millennium-old epic. One could almost say this is the Indian version of *The Iliad*, but it is a lot more, as images, folk-tales, and personalities from the epic pervade Indian consciousness. There are many translations available, but none will provide the kind of pleasure afforded by the Buck, so accept no substitutes!

And one special book for last:

- *Life on the Color Line: The True Story of a White Boy Who Discovered He was Black* by Gregory Howard Williams (New York, NY: E.P. Dutton, 1995). A moving memoir, told without overt moralizing, by the Dean of the Law School at Ohio State University who grew up white in Virginia in the '50s, but Black when he and his family moved to Muncie, Indiana. Williams' school records were specially marked so his teachers would know he was "colored". He was instructed by school officials not to show any interest in white girls, but scandalized the audience at his school graduation by walking down the aisle with a Black one. A first-person account of the social invention of race.

* * * * *

There are many ways to gain information, all of which are "basic skills" with which our children should be equipped if they are going to embrace the song of the world fully. They need to learn how to undertake critical or analytical research, starting with their own concrete questions, and develop the tenaciousness often necessary to question a text and coax a melody out. They must learn how they themselves and the artifacts of their lives are part of a dynamic web of relationships with other people, other cultures, with the world of work, and with the earth itself. They need to develop the imaginative sense to gain insight into the new and unfamiliar through literature, music, and the arts. These skills all play a role in enabling children to recognize the world as their home, and the world's song as their own.

There is yet another basic skill that is necessary, and that is the ability to elicit information about the world from other people. There is a world of experience out there to be grasped, once one learns to seek it out, and to become an engaged listener. Whether it is because I am a native New Yorker, or something constitutional, I am not sure, but this has always been a challenge for me.

In another book I am currently editing, my friend the storyteller Doug Lipman reports on a series of games he has developed to help teach children interviewing skills.[10] The trick, he emphasizes, is for kids to learn that rather than working from a set of questions to be answered, the goal is to complete a story-picture in one's own mind. Another way of looking at this would be to say that one has to move from the brittleness of "fact", to the fluid boundaries of "the world". Doug works with children to interview elderly residents in the community by teaching the importance of open-ended questions, the twists and turns interviewing may take if it remains flexible and open to change in the flow of discovery, the hidden mysteries that can often be found in the most mundane, and the fact that all events and narratives have a "before" and "after" that can enhance and enrich understanding. Put the "social" back in "social studies"!

As I have suggested elsewhere in this book, conversation and dialogue lie at the basis of all learning. It is modeled on external conversations a child may have with other adults, beginning with her parents, but which eventually become internalized and, if successful, enrich the child's life well into adulthood. And, might I add, that with honest dialogue anything remains possible, and, as any diplomat would add, dialogue provides the fundamental prerequisite of peace?

* * * * *

We have tomorrow
Bright before us
Like a flame.

—Langston Hughes, "Youth"

We live on an underachieving planet.

There is an extraordinary passage in the first book of Homer's great song *The Odyssey*, especially moving in the new, modern translation by Robert Fagles,[11] (terrific for homeschoolers and intrepid schooling souls alike). In it, Zeus berates humankind for blaming their misfortunes on the gods. Recalling the miseries brought on by the Trojan War, Zeus says, "Ah, how shameless—the way these mortals blame the gods. From us alone, they say, come all their miseries, yes, but they themselves, with their reckless

---

10 Lipman, Doug, "Games to Teach Inteviewing," in Cox, Allison M. & David H. Albert, eds., *The Healing Heart~Communities: Storytelling to Build Strong and Healthy Communities.* Gabriola Island, BC: New Society Publishers, 2003.

11 Homer, *The Odyssey*, translated by Robert Fagles. New York, NY: Viking Press, 1996.

ways, compound their suffering way beyond their proper share." He reminds the other gods that the war and all the attendant suffering was caused by men reaching beyond their rightful portion, though knowing full well that it would ultimately end in their own total ruin.

We are blessed or cursed, both individually and as a species, with a biological and environmental heritage, though through science and technology we are forever pushing at its outer limits. But within these limits, we, as human beings have choices to make regarding who we are, and how we are to be towards one another. History is a record of these choices—both positive and negative—that explains who we are today.

Social studies should teach children that we, and they too, have choices, that nothing is written in stone, and that knowledge of our world is not limiting. Placed in the proper context, it cannot fail but lead to greater freedom as they become *singers*, the authors of future history. Social studies must always be placed in a larger social, political, economic, and ecological context, not so the kids will grow up and feel constrained to embrace the same set of political beliefs that their parents hold (indeed, I am looking forward to decades of friendly disagreements)—if anything, it is so they feel grounded enough and free enough to choose not to!

When I was a young teen in New York during the days of the Civil Rights Movement, a young teacher took it upon herself to explain to us that ignorance breeds prejudice. I doubt it was part of the curriculum, and I applaud her to this day for the courage to step beyond its state-mandated bounds. But with the hindsight now of a half century of experience, I have come to the tentative conclusion that what she had to say, on balance, is not true, or at best is only a small part of the truth. Ignorance does not have to breed prejudice; but *prejudice virtually always breeds ignorance*. When my children lack information about the world, chances are that unless there are barriers placed in their way, they will want to remedy the deficit, and if I provide the tools, they will try to do just that. If our homeschooling efforts have been successful, our children will have come to a recognition that *ignorance represents opportunity*. I find myself increasingly following the example of my kids in that regard, and I think these three chapters are ample evidence of the kinds of quests on which my ignorance has led me, and with a messier house as one of the results, as I reshaped my priorities. But my experience of the world has often been that it is prejudice that prevents adults from undertaking such knowledge quests upon ourselves, and it is the luxury of ignorance that allows us to reconfirm ourselves in own comfortable, if poorly informed, prejudices.

I would be disingenuous if I were to suggest that I didn't have a homeschooling agenda for my children when it comes to social studies. It is a *moral* agenda with which I want my children to go out and meet the world, and that is this: that they will personally choose moral and ethical principles which are also principles of justice, that is, to promote a world in which any individual would agree that the rules of the game are just regardless of the position within it she happens to occupy. Call it the societal equivalent of the Golden Rule.

But I don't expect my preaching at them incessantly about virtues or values is likely to be an effective way to ensure they arrive at that point. We are definitely not joining the "virtue of the month" club. In a contemporary culture that sometimes appears unhinged from its ethical moorings, I want to make sure my children are prepared to ask uncomfortable and disquieting questions, and to have the courage to seek out the answers for themselves. To quote the teacher I never had, "The only stupid question is the one left unasked."

Coda

So here I am, standing, in my gray sweater, gray pants, gray socks, and black walking shoes. Quakerwear! No, no religious overtones here—I just happen to like wearing gray. (In my house, January 1st is also called "Gray Sweater Day"—the kids know that rather than watching football games, I almost always go out to the mall, my once-a-year visit, for the New Year's Day Sale, and almost inevitably come home with—you guessed it—a gray sweater.) And, increasingly, it matches my hair and moustache. It's not that I am trying to fade away into the woodwork (which isn't gray in any case); it's just that I choose to call attention to myself in other ways. You can already tell if you've read this far that I'm no shrinking violet, and certainly not a gray one!

I would be overdressed if I were at my Friends Meeting, but I'm conscious of being underdressed here. There are men in rust-, bright green-, and maroon-colored suits and black-and-white wing tip shoes, women slightly less showy (or so it seems to me, given that I am contrasting myself with the men) though especially noticeable are the broad-brimmed and beribboned hats, boys in white shirts and skinny black ties, girls in pastels. We are all standing. No one told us to stand, but remaining seated is next to impossible.

Aliyah is on the stage, dressed in red. They're *all* dressed in red, and she is squeezed, all 13 years and 95 lbs. of her, down in the front row on the left between two very large, very big-boned women, and she is smiling, they are smiling, they are *all* smiling, 60 of them strong, all in bright red dresses. They are all smiling, and swaying, and there can't be room for another sound to fit inside the building.

These are the "Women of Praise", the extraordinary women's gospel choir of our local African-American Baptist Church. Aliyah had heard them once five years earlier, and when an announcement came that the Women of Praise were holding a three-day choir workshop, we agreed to drop everything else from her schedule so that she could join in. And they are delighted to have her.

We are known here. We have participated in interfaith events with New Life Baptist, attended on Sundays following the spate of African-American church burnings some years ago and raised money for rebuilding, and have friends from the church throughout our community. New Life Baptist is also, ironically, probably the most racially integrated church in Olympia, with 10-15% of its membership, and some its officers, being

white. I doubt that there is any mainline church in our town with an equivalent number of African-Americans attending, or in leadership positions.

But none of this matters as I am standing, swaying with the *vamp* of
the choir, the finely honed yet highly improvisational call-and-response,
memories of an oral tradition reflecting generations of chains and mana-
cles, now come alive in freedom:

> I go to the rock of my salvation,
> I go to the stone that the builder rejected,
> I run to the mountain,
> And the mountain stands by me.

And we are "Standing.... Standing.... Standing." And the mountain
stands by me, as I am embraced by the song of the world. In my gray
sweater.

Praised be.

Armand Berliner

No one ever learned anything.

I mean adults, of course. We kids went to school, and had to learn whatever they told us to learn, whether we liked it or not. But no adult ever learned anything, or at least not voluntarily. Or so was my experience.

While I was in grade school, I became (oh, horror of horrors!) a "latchkey kid", because my mother was off learning to become a school-teacher. Now mind you, I couldn't imagine what it was exactly that she was learning, and couldn't fathom what could possibly take so much time! After all, hadn't she been to school herself? She could remember what it was that teachers did. If she asked, I thought, I might have been able to help her, for didn't I see what they did every day? Anyway, I never really did discover from her what it was she was learning, and since her future job required it, it certainly wasn't voluntary.

From what I could tell, my father never learned anything. He never read a book. He read the sports pages of *The New York Daily News*, or maybe he just looked at the baseball standings. Oh, he did have a subscription to *National Geographic*—I think it was for the pictures.

Of course, none of my teachers ever learned anything. Information sprang out of their heads as from the cranial cavity of Zeus. Eventually, I would discover that a lot of the information was wrong, but they never seemed to question it, so there couldn't have been much learning taking place. Or at least if there was, I was never witness to it.

None of my relatives ever learned anything. They were too busy work-ing—fixing storm windows, making ladies' hats, selling wastepaper baskets and men's suits and haberdashery, waxing kitchen floors, and, perpetually, dusting. No one played the piano, took art lessons, carved fishing lures, messed with motors, or invented improvements to the Veg-o-matic. And I had no older siblings or even cousins who could have suggested other possibilities.

Indeed, there was some dull recognition within that little cloud of my childhood that entertainment—and the ability to purchase it—had replaced learning. Why wrestle with learning to play Chopin when Liberace would always do it better, and one could now afford a 15" color TV and see him on the Ed Sullivan Show? Why mess with oil paints when you could buy an "original Morris Katz", a work by the New York painter whose great claim to fame was that he could polish off a complete painting (using oils and wadded-up toilet paper, I kid you not) while you waited in under five minutes?[1] (We had three, $95 for the set—and they looked pretty good to me, much more classy than a velvet Elvis.) Learn a foreign language? The grandparents had all struggled so hard to learn English (perhaps voluntarily, but certainly not very well), so why would one want to do that? Didn't they speak English in every place that really mattered anyway?

Learning was highly prized, make no mistake, but never for itself. Learning that was something other than directly instrumental to some other end was odd or even slightly freakish—why would one want to learn something that could not be expected to lead to increased consumption? I know my characterization sounds somewhat harsh, and it really shouldn't. For in this post-World War II generation, with the scars of the Depression still remembered if not fresh, it was consumption, symbolic of freedom from want, and the future expectation of consumption that was the hallmark of the American dream.

And I learned that learning was a highly circumscribed activity. I learned that I would be given learning tasks when the teacher was ready, that I would be judged upon the basis of whether I performed these tasks correctly and on time, that both my parents and teachers would be well satisfied when I completed the tasks and that I would be rewarded for it, and that when so completed, learning was done. (I did have one early—and rather disastrous—flirtation with the saxophone, which ended my involvement in music for almost two decades, but that's another story.) And between school, homework, and a strong and time-consuming dose of religious education after school and on weekends—all intended to be instrumental to something of which I had very little inkling—there was not much time left for anything else.

Now let me be clear: I *was* learning things all the time. I just didn't

---

1   Morris Katz (b. 1932) claims to be the world's most prolific painter. As of this date (2003), he had sold more than 225,000 oil paintings (including the three my mother owns), the largest body of saleable work by any painter in world history, outpacing Picasso. On July 15, 1987, he made 103 painting in 12 hours and sold 55 of them on the spot, donating the proceeds to the Boy Scouts.

But wait—there's more! You can send a photo of any of the paintings and a check for $50 and Mr. Katz will send you *by insured priority mail*:
- a signed Certificate of Approximate Value, PLUS
- a signed 8" x 10" original painting, PLUS
- a 2-hour video of Morris Katz International TV Talk shows, PLUS
- additional reproductions of Morris' original paintings and his bio.

Check it out at www.morriskatz.com.

think of it at the time as learning. Besides playing stickball (where I learned negotiating skills), and collecting postage stamps (where I learned geography, and something of international history and politics, as the map of Africa was being redrawn on a biweekly basis, and stamps of occupied World War II Europe had overprintings on them), I read voraciously, an activity highly encouraged by both of my parents. My father had a small credit-and-collections route that he ran one Friday evening every month, and he would always take me along. At the end of the route, we would go to my favorite malt shop, where they had a rotating rack of the Golden Guide nature books. I got to pick one out to take home on each visit.

Soon my room was full of little guides—about snakes and amphibians I had never seen, flowers that didn't grow anywhere near me, trees that I couldn't identify from the pictures, butterflies with painted colors! (all we had in our neighborhood were cabbage-whites and an occasional sulphur), and birds that weren't pigeons, robins, or little brown birds that I now recognize were some kind of sparrow. Rocks and minerals must have all been dug out of our backyard years before we moved in, and the crushed gravel in the alleyway behind the house didn't look like anything in the minerology book. Even though we had moved to Queens, this was, after all, still New York City!

I dimly remember asking my parents and my teachers an occasional question related to what I found in the Guides, only to find out that, when they didn't just brush me off, they were as much a blank slate as I was. These Golden Guides could just as well have been describing the surface of Jupiter from the little anyone around me seemed to know.

My favorite among the Golden Guides was the one on stars. I was absolutely fascinated by it, and perhaps aided in my fascination by the fact that, on my well-lit New York City street, for the most part I couldn't see any!

I think my incipient infatuation with astronomy came about because I was the first kid in second grade to memorize the order of the planets. This was going to be very important if I was to assist in the national effort to defeat the Russians. I cut out my pictures of the planets dutifully, though I was wholly unaware at the time that I was a "man on a mission". What is interesting about this is that I am quite confident that none of my elementary school teachers had ever actually *seen* a planet except by accident (other than earth, of course, and earth wasn't *really* a planet, was it?). No one in school during the 13 years of my public school education ever suggested that we could actually view them in the sky (was that where they were, except for earth?), and I suspect not a single one of my elementary school teachers would have known where to locate them. And school was, after all, a daytime activity, so the ignorance of the teachers was perfectly safe! In short, these planets had no more reality attached to them for me than the Roman gods and goddesses for whom they were named. (I do remember taking a trip to the Hayden Planetarium, but the sky never looked anything like it did there, and nowhere, to this day, have the dots been connected for me so that I can identify Leo the Lion or Sagittarius the Archer in the celestial flesh as it were. But at the age of 46, on October 31, 1996, in front of Top Foods supermarket in Lacey, Washington, I saw Saturn for the first time!)

Ah, yes, Armand Berliner. Don't worry, I'm getting there. Beginning at age eight, for 19 days every summer, I attended a sleep-away summer camp in upstate New York. It was kind of a "fresh air" camp for poor kids from New York City (this was my first recognition that someone would actually consider us poor), who could escape the asphalt heat for a few health-giving weeks in "the country".

The first days of my camp experience were absolute misery. My eyes itched, my nose ran and was rubbed raw—I actually lost a camp boxing match because the judge thought my nose was bleeding, when it was just hay fever! I lost my voice entirely, which was a problem, as I was to be the villain in the camp musical, and I was soon to become infamous for my pre-pubescent rendition of Kay Starr's "Rock'n'Roll Waltz". (Over the next several years I managed to perfect a wonderfully hoarse Rex Harrison imitation.) I was homesick, and for some reason particularly upset that the camp was surrounded with barbed wire on all four sides.

And so I sat to the side of the ball field with the sun beating down as other kids were playing, with tears in my eyes, thumbing through the pages of my Golden Guide Stars book, which I had brought with me (along with Reptiles and Amphibians). A junior counselor, a decade my senior and not from my own cabin, approached me. Short, with the thickest black-rimmed eyeglasses I had ever seen, and black hair. A deep scarlet sweatshirt that said "Rutgers" on it. He asked to see my book and, as I remember, turned over a couple of pages, handed it back, and walked off. I don't even think we had a conversation.

That night (or was it the night after?), long after I had fallen asleep, he came into my cabin, woke me up, and whispered for me to put on my slippers and my jacket over my pajamas. Out we went. He had set up his telescope! Now, I don't recollect the first thing about what I saw—I frankly don't even remember looking through the eyepiece. But I do remember a moonless night sky under which mountains slept, owls hooted, and green-black forests snored, a concave carpet above my head that was alive and electric with stars, and right there, they were there, millions of them, right there, for me! They were there and I was here and we were all alive, here and there, and they—the telescope and the mountains and Armand Berliner and his black-rimmed glasses and the song of stars—they were there and alive, they were there, for me! And I shivered, and my nose ran and I didn't have my handkerchief, and it didn't matter.

I don't recall a thing about what Armand Berliner said to me that night. There is certainly no reason to believe that it was especially profound. In fact, I don't recollect having a single conversation with him over the next six years of our bare acquaintance. I didn't pursue any interest in astronomy whatsoever until I was in my late 40s.

But we shared a secret between us. And that was enough. I had been initiated into a secret and holy fellowship, with its own religion. The main tenet of this faith is that the world is an open book, spine bent and pages ready. Fed by its own consecrated streams, there is a subterranean river that I glimpsed that night for the first time, a world where people gather, in ones and twos or more, and partake of the sacred texts of gods and of nature, of people, and of themselves, unfettered by anything that the state can standardize, or the corporation buy and sell. We are free in those places—you and I—far from the triumphant jackbooted march of education, along riverbanks and upon clandestine islands where magic flutes and magic bells lay claim upon our minds.

That night I learned what learning is all about. And I have not forgotten.

* * * * *

My wife and older daughter Aliyah together built an 8" reflector telescope when the latter was 9, the details of which (with pictures) can be found in my book *And the Skylark Sings with Me* (www.skylarksings.com). I now have a general idea of where to find heavenly bodies—I know what an *ecliptic* is, and where to locate the visible planets, and if it wasn't for all those *trees*.... My night-time driving has definitely suffered. I am now aware, because I look out for such information as part of our homeschooling mission, that the dominant color of the universe is coffee (www. pha.jhu.edu/~kab/cosspec/), and that it is awash in sugar molecules (www.southpole.com/headlines/y2000/ast20jun_1.htm?list). I already knew where to find the Milky Way.

When made sensible of the vastness of space for the first time, most people feel themselves very small. Just the opposite happened to me. It had nothing to do with space, but rather with there being, if but most briefly, a mentor, one who through having voluntarily elected to learn something new, was expanding his own definition of who he was, and had shared that possibility with me. I think that is what mentors are supposed to be. Sadly, it took me several decades of recovery from my own school-based *successes* to truly figure this out for myself. It was never taught in school. Good teachers or bad, there were never any mentors.

And so, recently, I went on a search for Armand Berliner. He wasn't hard to find. He has, after all, a rather unusual name. I recalled his Rutgers sweatshirt, and at the time was impressed that he was from New Jersey, that being to me a rather exotic locale, it being the home of my westernmost relatives whom I only saw at weddings and funerals.

He now teaches mathematics at the New Jersey Institute of Technology, and there he was on the Institute webpage, complete with Rutgers degree, and a picture sans black-rimmed glasses. Hail the wonders of ophthamological science!

Aliyah and I took a special trip down to Florida (where Armand has a vacation home) just to say thanks. He doesn't know that was really why I made the trip (he does now! I managed to make the excuse that I was on a homeschooling speaking tour, which I was, but I had arranged it specifically for this purpose) There we were, two aging, graying, *short* men, drinking grapefruit juice. He claims to remember me vividly from four decades earlier—maybe he is still mentoring me, for that is what a mentor would be supposed to say, isn't it? But I probably shouldn't doubt him—after all, I remembered *him*, didn't I? We shared old stories (things do look different, depending on whether one was 8 or 18, both sets of perspectives clouded by time), information about our respective telescopes, family pictures, a little bit of religion (mine having changed since then), and his having spent 30 more years involved in summer camps. I told him I had finally found it in my heart to forgive the counselor who hadn't explained to the boxing judge about my red nose. And I said thanks, though being less than fully emotionally forthcoming, I'm not sure I conveyed the essence of the thing, my gratefulness of his having shared a little piece of his *inner* universe with me. Hence partially the reason for this essay.

So what has all this to do with homeschooling? Simply this: the fact that you have taken on full responsibility for your children's education does not mean that you have to be—or even should be—the sole source of it. That's what schools do, and leave our children with a shrunken sense of

Aliyah (with Dragon) in *The Magic Flute*, August 2002. photo: David H. Albert

what community is supposed to be about. If you do your job well, your kids should be allowed to come to the conclusion early that there are plenty of places in which your own knowledge and experience are, well just not that deep. And even if it was, you may not always be the one in the best position to share from it. There will come a point—there *always* comes to be a point—when your children will look at you askance in any case. If they do not come to realize that there are other people—adults even!—with passions and dreams as well as knowledge and experience—and ready to share them, the world can become a cold, dark, and cynical place.

* * * * *

O Isis and Osiris, grant the spirit of
wisdom to the two newcomers!
You who direct the wanderers' steps,
strengthen them with patience when in peril.
—Sarastro's Aria, Act Two
Wolfgang Amadeus Mozart, *The Magic Flute*

Aliyah and I, together, are singing in Mozart's *The Magic Flute* this summer. Hence the flutes and bells. This will be the first time I will have been on stage since summer camp 39 years ago. My greatest peril is singing flat on the high notes!

We have both found new mentors (in this sanctum, our "Isis and Osiris"), the founders of our budding local opera company Opera Pacifica (check us out at www.operapacifica.org). Robert (Papageno the birdcatcher) is a 55-year-old realty instructor and broker (who grew up about three miles from where I did in New York City—serendipity strikes again!), who put his operatic career on hold several decades ago. He says he now sings better than he did back then, and can no longer wait. Claudia is a retired 727-airline pilot who, it is said, can play most of the musical instruments known to humankind, and, while based out of Las Vegas, used to entertain on the piano in the expected venues. But opera is her first love, and she, too, can no longer wait! They've recently returned from China where they recorded a CD of French and Italian operatic arias with a Beijing symphony orchestra. I am in awe, and a little abashed in honing in on *their* passions and dreams, even as we sponge off their knowledge and experience.

As for Aliyah and myself, we are 14 and 52 respectively (an age at which I can finally lay claim to playing with a full deck!)—both good ages for operatic debuts. The best we'll ever have. Wish us luck, and tell us to break a leg!

Flow II—
The Teenage Edition

If the future doesn't come toward you, you have to go fetch it.
—Zulu Expression

"We always used to go explore new and interesting things together—museums, tide pools, astronomical observatories, Now he just wants to sit at home. And he won't try anything new—even food!"

"She used to love to play her cello, and we loved it so much just to listen to her. And we bought her a good one. Now she won't practice any more, no matter how much we cajole (or swear!), and she wants to quit the youth orchestra."

"Those computer games! I don't what he sees in them. He just plays them over and over again. And it's not that he's learning anything new from them—he mastered them a long time ago, and doesn't seem to want any new ones. And don't dare ask him to clean his room!..."

"He thinks he's such a tough guy. Big front, big exterior—it's like he's wearing a suit of armor. Sometimes he frightens me a little. We can't seem to talk anymore, though he gets on great with his uncle."

"She used to have so many friends, and was on the telephone all the time. Now, I almost have to remind her who her friends are! And she used to be so generous—now it seems it's always 'me, me, me'."

"He plays innumerable games of solitaire, hour after hour. I can't see what he finds in it. And then he sits and counts the stones in his rock collection. He doesn't really examine them; just counts them. And he's become secretive. It's driving me crazy!"

"She says she's bored! Can't figure out why—she has every book, every compact disc, every computer game, a slew of musical instruments, everything she wants. If she needs something else, we get it for her—no questions asked. And not only is she bored, but everything we suggest is "boring"! Makes us just want to throw up our hands!"

"Everything has become some kind of drama, even down to the weird clothes she wears. And it's not like they are the same clothes as her friends'. And those hats! She even tries to wear hats to the dinner table!"

"I just don't know what happened. He used to be such a nice kid. Now, sometimes I feel I hardly recognize him."

I have heard all these comments and more from parents attending my lectures and workshops, from perfect strangers who come to talk with me at my book table, from friends whose children are homeschooled or in public or private schools. I've become a good listener. I've heard these anxious descriptions often enough so that I immediately know what the ages of the kids are—early teens (12-15 year olds).

Ah, teenagers—a different species, we may be tempted to say. Only thing is—they're not. Our culture has come to view teenagers as simply "children with hormones", difficult to understand, bound to get themselves into trouble, and if we only managed to lock them up for several years (or perhaps a decade), maybe the risks would pass, and they'd turn into, well, they'd turn into us!

Nor are they simply "adults in training". Indeed, one of the problems with the way we treat young teenagers is that we tend to view them as seeds germinating in the hothouse, which are to be kept locked up and free from all external contact with rain, wind, and the soil which are soon to be central elements of their eventual homes. And, like the seeds in a hothouse, they have no "market value".

Consider how relatively rare it is to hear parents express pride in the accomplishments of their young teenagers. With younger children, one is always hearing comments about how cute they are, or funny, or (most often) how precocious. With older ones (16-18), it's often about how well they are preparing for their futures—what kind of college they will go to, or how committed they are to their religion, or, again, how precocious they are (especially if they are athletes or scientists-to-be). On the whole, we tend at best to view young teenagers as *diseased*, usually not fatally of course, as we have faith somehow that they'll *get over it*.

Unfortunately, as we are all too well aware, many never do. As older teenagers and as adults, so many people carry over traits—emotional, intellectual, and spiritual dependence; unmindful impulsivity; a lack of an ethic of personal responsibility—that, under healthier cultural circumstances, would have been better left behind in childhood. Much of this, I would suggest, is rooted in a lack of sensitivity in contemporary culture and society for the special needs of young teenagers.

As a student of history and cultures, when I see a condition like this, I have learned to do a scan of other times and places to see if they have something they can teach us. And indeed, when we look at cultures and civilizations around the world over the past three millennia— from the most "primitive" to the most "advanced"—we find the same lesson. The ages 12-15 are a time for learning how to participate in the adult world, for apprenticeships and mentoring, for ritual initiations and rites of passage, for *vision quests* and *walkabouts*, for emergence into a new self beyond the confines of family and peers.

We can, of course, reject this wisdom, but, I believe, we do so, and have done so, at great peril. Just as the butterfly requires different food from the butterfly larva, the young teenager requires a different set of experiences. Those representations related to me by anxious parents at the beginning of this chapter are a reflection of *hunger*. And it is a hunger that parents, by themselves, are unable to satiate.

A young person reaching the ages of 12-15 is foremost fixated upon the future, specifically, *her own* future. She has already learned (usually between the ages of 7 and 10) that the artifacts of her life have a history of which she or her parents have no firsthand knowledge and experience, and that living things (including parents and grandparents) age and eventually die. She has also learned (usually between the ages of 10 and 12) that much of our lives is governed by conventions over which we have no control (but many of which can be learned just as effectively from her own peers as from anyone else).

But where does that leave her? She knows, perhaps but dimly at first, that there will be a time when her parents or family will no longer be there to filter experience for her, and that she will not live with us forever, regardless of how hospitable we currently happen to be. And there comes a point at which peers no longer provide the nourishment necessary to further her on her voyage of self-discovery.

And so there he is, ready and prepared to uncover his future, and his place in adult society, but is fed a steady diet of family and peers, and is still hungry. And he lets you know it in ways to which you as a parent do not take kindly (and are, objectively, "unacceptable"). He sits among the cornucopia or the flotsam and jetsam—depending on your point of view—made possible by modern industrial civilization—books and videos and music and television and computer games—and is *bored*. They do not feed any sense of who he is meant to become. He counts objects mindlessly, plays solitaire, repeats the same old computer games, seeking within them as if by divination some indication of what the future holds. If he were in school, he certainly wouldn't find it in his homework.

She knows inwardly that it is time to put away childish things, but has no source of information beyond peers and family as to which things these are. Perhaps the cello is among them. She has never met a classical musician. More critically, perhaps, she has never met an amateur (other than maybe that same old-maid teacher she has had since she was 7, and who teaches for money) who carries a love of playing music on into adulthood. Certainly not among her uncles and aunts. What good is the cello, really, and why would she want to spend an hour a day in the music room, when there is no future in it?

The young teenager stands at the threshold, on the margin, at the boundary. Cultural anthropologists have a word for this threshold state—*liminality*.[1] Among most traditional peoples, during this liminal phase the individual is neither a member of the group she previously belonged to nor is she a member of the group she will join following passage through the stage. Having spent their entire lives in the company of their parents (or extended kinship groupings), boys (and sometimes girls) are removed from their previous settings and placed under the care of an older man or women—*never* their own parents—and are taught and trained in the ways of the community to which they will soon receive full membership. They may be subjected to various ordeals or humiliations, and undergo various tests, before a ritual reintegration into the society of which they will now be fully a part. Among some peoples, teenagers are considered to have died

---

1   The term was coined by the folklorist Arnold van Gennep (*Rites of Passage*, 1909), but is now most closely associated with the work of the cultural anthropologist Victor Turner, (*The Forest of Symbols: Aspects of Ndembu Ritual*, 1967; *Dramas, Fields and Metaphors: Symbolic Action in Human Society*, 1974, among others).

as children and are now reborn as men and women, given new names, and then "reintroduced" to their families and friends.

Among the Plains Indians of North America, it would not be uncommon for the young man to undergo a "vision quest". Following tutelage in the skills and discipline necessary to survive in the wild and as a member of the tribe (which might require several years), the young man would be left on his own in a remote place to discover his true nature in nature itself, and a view of his own future. Guided back to the tribe and for the first time aware of his own name, he is now ready to take on the mantle of authority and authenticity of a new self in adulthood. Similar customs were common about the aboriginal peoples of Australia (the origin of the "Walkabout"), or among the tribes of central and eastern Africa, where initiation might include long periods of ritual seclusion.

This special status and training provided in the liminal phase of adolescence was once common among European peoples as well. They might be attached to religious practice—the *bar mitzvah* among Jews being the most obvious example. Here, the young adolescent is taken under the wing of an older man or men and tutored in the practices and observances of Jewish ritual life and study.

More commonly, tutelage took the form of apprenticeships. Contracts would be drawn up between family and craftspeople, merchants, or artists, with expectations assumed on all sides. On the one hand, youth were usually assigned the most menial of tasks—they were seen as a pool of cheap labor. On the other hand, it was assumed that the masters would eventually impart their special learning and trade secrets to the young man (with very rare exceptions, apprentices were always male), as the viability of trades depended upon the development of new talent to take the place of old (or "not-so-old", as life expectancy was much attenuated before the 20th Century). The young teenager was thus recognized as having economic value to the entire society, both in the present and in the future.

In all of these societies, parents had a continuing responsibility for the physical well-being of their children. Disciplinary functions, however, were no longer the domain of parents, but were passed from them to other members of the adult community—whether other relatives, elders, mentors, and masters. The expected norms and codes of conduct expected of the youth were no longer those of the immediate family, but of the larger community and society. A friend of mine—an elder in the Skokomish Tribe in Washington State—notes that vestiges of this division of functions still exist among his people on the reservation. When a young teenager requires discipline, the parent will alert an aunt or uncle or other extended family member to the need, which will usually be met through a teaching story or fable especially chosen for that purpose. (In extreme situations, the youth may be subjected to public shaming, usually through the cutting of his hair!) The child is expected, at this age, to be growing out of full dependency upon parents, and the point of separating discipline from parenting is to not threaten that natural attachment which should be maintained into adulthood.

The young person *in limen*—on the threshold—is threatening. He is *supposed to be*—that is his role. Betwixt and between position assigned and arrayed by law and custom, convention and ceremony—he calls into question *everything*. The community is called upon to answer, but in doing so, must rethink its own values and commitments, and ways to express them. "Because" is no longer a sufficient answer to "Why?"—no adult, upon gaining entrance into a community of equals would be expected to accept such non-answers to questions about mores and norms, and youth can no longer be expected to either. In this role, youth is both a force for social integration and for social change at the same time.

* * * * *

When I was a child, I spoke as a child, I understood as a child; but when I became a man, I put away childish things.
    —Paul, *First Letter to the Corinthians* 13:11

This essay is not a brief for changing society, nor even for reforming education. Needless to say, I see need for both. And I like to believe that if everyone cared as deeply about the education of their children and acted upon it as homeschooling parents do, many of the needed changes and reforms would simply take care of themselves. To me, this is not a strategy, but simply a statement regarding where we, as a society, now find ourselves.

The reality is that our children are growing up in society *as it is now*. So the question I seek to address is, given what we know about the needs and gifts of young people, how can we feed our children's emerging sense of themselves so that they can become empowered, responsible, life-satisfied adults?

I guess the first thing one must consider with a young teenager is to provide them the opportunity to put away *what they consider to be* childish things. This can be hard on parents. We remember the first time Beth got the little solo in the Christmas recital put on by her children's ballet school, or Marcus sang in the kids' choir at church, or Susie was entranced by the crystal-making possibilities in her chemistry set, and our eyes were bedazzled as we imagined Beth dancing in the New York City Ballet, Marcus bowling over audiences in the San Francisco Opera, and Susie as a famous Chicago heart surgeon. Well, all of these are possible but, ultimately, these choices will have to be made by our children themselves, even if our own visions are dashed. And, really, our visions were just that— the odds of any of them becoming reality were rather long to being with!

The fact that the kids put aside activities or aspirations as childish does not mean they won't come back to them later, sometimes with renewed vigor, and with new meaning and as part of a self-chosen identity. What may be more important to the child's voyage of self-discovery is knowing that she is growing into new authority and responsibility for steering the boat.

She will grow anyway, but the question is whether this will occur in the context of a healthy family and community life. I have often suggested that especially when their children reach age 12 or so, parents should actively ask whether there are activities the kids want to give up. Sometimes, paradoxically, this will drive the children to renewed effort; other times they will be grateful for the open invitation. Trial separations or short-term contracts between parents and child to continue pursuits can help ensure ongoing dialogue.

I have also suggested that when young teens decide to put aside activities that they previously found satisfying, families should celebrate the decision. Making choices like this is a sign of growing up. Hold a karate exhibition for the retiring devotee, and invite her family and friends. Ditto with the retiring violinist, etc. Last summer, I made this suggestion to a mother concerned that her homeschooled son no longer wanted to play the piano. The boy studied hard enough to play a single piece of music really well. The family sent out invitations requesting family and friends to come to a farewell concert. The young man played his one piece, and then was feted for the commitment he had made up to that point, and presented with a cake and several compact disks of music he had grown to love. The mother reported back to me that it was a watershed event in opening up improved and more mature dialogue in her family around her son's educational aspirations. Her son was no longer a *quitter*, but a *graduate*.

In homeschooling circles, the term "deschooling" is commonly bandied about. It is usually applied to the needs of children who have been taken out of school by their parents when the latter have seen the kids lose their zest for learning. The parents are then disappointed when the child does not quickly recover her lost curiosity about the world and head off on knowledge quests of her own, or, alternatively, does not respond well to the parents' curricula plans for her. Deschooling is based on the notion that the child has been wounded by the "socialization of learning" that has really been the primary curriculum of the early grades. The child has learned to sublimate her own learning desires, and has learned that the only worthwhile tasks to be undertaken are those assigned by the teacher, on a timetable designated by the teacher, with the successful completion of those tasks to be judged by the teacher. The chief lesson to be gained is not any of the content (indeed, sometimes the content is truly laughable), but the importance of compliance. The child has also been socialized into believing that anything learned outside of this compliance context is not worth knowing, or at least is of lesser value. Parents are then surprised to learn from the experience of other homeschoolers that it may take six months to a year or even longer for these wounds to heal and for the fires of curiosity and spontaneity to be re-ignited.

While the term is usually applied to situations when the child has left school, it may surprise some to learn that I have been asked to consult on homeschooling circumstances where a similar deschooling process is called for. Often what has happened is that the parent has imposed "school at home", sometimes commencing when the child is as young as three, with little open to the child's desires, until at age 11 or 12 the youth is now reasonably "well-schooled". But left to his own devices, he is totally at wit's end. He has begun to rebel against parental expectations, but, unlike in school situations, there is no dodging the teacher's unyielding gaze, and no stratagem of deceit or wiliness to effect even a temporary escape. It doesn't help that the only people he has ever looked toward for approval for everything else in his young life are his parents. He expresses no interests of his own, yet seems bored and frustrated at the same time, and, above all, confused, for he has learned the lessons of compliance and dependency only too well, only to have it now implied that this is no longer sufficient. And Mom, sensing something is really wrong, feels defeated, and can only think of ways to enforce more of the same.

So anxious mothers have asked me, "Can I undo what I have done?" And the answer, of course, is no, but you can view what you have done as preparation for what you together are now about to do. I suggest holding a family gathering, and at it, saying, "Son, I am proud of you. You've learned all this reading and writing and math (and science and history and what-have-you) really well. (Review with him what he now knows.) And then add something like, "It's time for all of us to graduate, to start a new chapter in your education, one in which you take equal responsibility. I am here to help you find new ways to explore the world, when you are ready, and to assist you in finding new people to explore it with, and to prepare for a future that is really yours." Another occasion for a big cake!

You'd be surprised, though. Deschooling for families that have always homeschooled is even tougher than for parents who have taken their kids out of school. It is especially hard for moms (or stay-at-home-dads), who now have to find new things to do with themselves. I advise a big project, like wall-papering the entire house! (And if you're lucky, Junior might eventually decide to join in....)

* * * * *

It is almost impossible to grow up. Most people just get older, and they find parking spaces....

—Maya Angelou

The young teen might decide to continue to advance her studies as she grows out of childhood, instead of putting them aside as childish, if she is provided the opportunity to put aside childish ways of knowing and learning instead. The reciprocity between teacher/mentor and student may now emerge as the centerpiece of education. The perfectly competent music teacher (or math tutor, if there was one) may need to be discarded in favor of a new one simply because she *was* the childhood teacher and had been chosen by the parents. The young teen needs more opportunities to select her own teachers if only because the relationship more freely entered into should more closely reflect the possibilities of a future of which she only now has the barest inkling. Dad-the-math-whiz may no longer be suitable as in years past, because while he can provide the requisite knowledge and skill, he can open up but cannot himself provide the opportunity for his daughter to find her way in the larger world of mathematics (or anything else!), which is now precisely what she needs. The need for change and for the young person's inclusion in the process of educational choice should now also extend to selections of curricula and learning approaches, even down to the time of day during which one undertakes to learn.

To see how *not* to nurture a young teen, look to the public middle school model (grades 6-8, or, in areas where there are junior high schools, 7-9). At a time when the child requires more freedom, the school dictates a greater need to control, accomplished through expanded monitoring and testing, and more intrusive invasion into the child's private life (we excuse it by the name "homework"). In a period during which a child requires more attention paid to the highly individual and specific rhythm and character of her being, the school gets larger, the classes get larger, the learning clock more regimented, the teaching less rather than more personal, the demands of external authorities to "cover material" more compelling. We can see the hidden hand here: the middle school model is built upon the need to have children "mature" into compliance (excused by the current administrative need for it) rather than into the responsible exercise of freedom.

It is no wonder then that, deprived of the sustenance required (or fed inappropriately), many a teen rebels. For rather than promoting the inner independence and individuality of the child, her growth and integrity, the demand is placed upon teachers—who find little in the way of recourse—to follow the lesson plan. Of course, as we are all too well-aware, when assisting young teens in expanding their discovery of learning's intrinsic rewards is forced to play second fiddle to feeding their fact-registering apparatus, more often than not neither is achieved. And when middle schoolers find themselves cut off from their first hesitant steps of participation in the adult world, they can and do find an outlet for free "adult" expression in the world of their peers to which they are confined, in sex, drugs, and alcohol.[2] The kids don't have a primary need for sex and drug abuse education (I say this despite the fact that as part of my professional work, I help to ensure that it is provided); they need opportunities to understand how their learning prepares them for vital participation in a world for which they will soon become responsible.

I cannot express strongly enough my belief that unwillingness to learn—which, as the learning capacities atrophy does indeed become inability to learn—is itself *a learned behavior*. It reflects the development of a personality that feels powerless and alone, fearful and anxious. It is a personality that has been traumatized, as often by rewards as by punishments, trapped under conditions where the development of an autonomous sense

---

2   The President of Bard College, Leon Botstein, in arguing for the abolition of high school as we know it (and for college entrance at 15 or 16 for those requiring it), notes that the American education system was designed at a time when the average onset of puberty was between 15 and 16. In the late 1990s, it had fallen to 13. This was not a significant problem before 1950, when fewer than half of all Americans completed more than 9th grade. Given this new reality, it would seem surprising how low the levels of adolescent sex and drug use really are. But, insists Botstein, "The challenge, therefore, is to find ways to engage the early onset of adolescence and its attendant freedoms and habits", at which American education has failed dismally. See Botstein, Leon, *Jefferson's Children: Education and the Promise of American Culture* (New York, NY: Doubleday, 1997).

of self is suspect, and within a culture that only honors such development in the breach. It is a personality which, instead of growing through the excitement of discovery, has learned to conform to a ceaseless barrage of petty rules or, if creative enough, to develop strategies of deceit as necessary defenses to get around them with the least modicum of effort.

* * * * *

Rewards and punishments are the lowest forms of education.
—Chang-Tzu

Motivation is the key to the development of talent, and we all know it. It is no secret that the reason so many talented young people do not become skilled scientists, able craftsman, or gifted artists, or that those with less talent struggle with the rudiments of verbal and mathematical literacy, is not because they can't cope with the required challenges, but that they don't want to put out the effort necessary to learn.

Motivation always presupposes a future, for in its development lies the understanding that the attainment of goals often requires overcoming obstacles and challenges placed in one's path. But when goals or even choices are unclear and futures cloudy, motivation can be difficult to maintain.

The young teen must thus be given the opportunity to converse with the future, actually many futures, to find the one (or ones) that fit. It is not so much that, as in Renaissance times, he will be making an irrevocable commitment to a career path (indeed, these conversations don't have to be about career paths per se at all), but rather that they provide the motivation to continue the knowledge quest.

The lack of these conversations shows up even among academically talented students. I have a friend who is the admissions director of a leading, selective, (and pricey!) liberal arts college. Over lunch, he told me how, in conducting interviews, he had learned not to ask about career goals. "When Quincy was still on television," he noted, "every third science applicant wanted to be a forensic pathologist. Currently, it's criminal defense attorneys. The fact is that the closest most of these kids have ever gotten to a forensic pathologist or criminal defense attorney is Jack Klugman or grandson-of-Raymond-Burr."

For these conversations with the future to take place fruitfully there have to be guides—mentors, those who are actively engaged in these futures. It is easy to forget how recent the rift between practice and formal instruction is. The idea that the role of the teacher would be reduced to purveyor of information would have been thought absurd even two centuries ago. And contemporary teachers are often purveyors of *stolen goods*, because they fail to practice the very skills they attempt to convey to their charges. (School music teachers are occasionally a rare exception to this truth; they are also quickly disappearing from the scene.)

A mentor must be able to convey the joy that accompanies encounters with both the hardships and challenges of the tasks she undertakes in her chosen domain. This can only come through full participation in it—either as career or as serious avocation—so that the transmission of information and skill has a deeply personal context. Does it surprise anyone that to this day, despite their many faults, the best private schools find amusement in the idea that one should be allowed to teach young teenagers solely by virtue of possessing a teaching certificate?

Again, we can look to the experience of pre-industrial Europe. The journeyman craftsman or artisan, like the junior fellow at the university, could carry on a trade, but was forbidden to teach. It was not that the journeyman or junior fellow lacked skill in the domain. Rather it was that they were still so involved in making their own way into the future that they would be less capable of conveying what it would actually be like to occupy it. The master mentor, it was assumed, could go beyond the mere purveyance of knowledge and skill to seek out that spark to make learning come alive.

In our supposed rationality as a culture and as a society we have become fundamentally irrational in the way we seek to educate young adolescents growing into adulthood. Somehow we have come to believe, against our own experience, that learning is a function of the way material is organized and the internal logic of its presentation, and that information is best conveyed via inoculation—brief, highly specialized programmatic presentations that take no account whatsoever of the particular reciprocal relationship between teacher and student. In the past 150 years, we have witnessed the subversion of the paradigm of the teacher as wise and knowledgeable elder and seen it replaced with the civil servant trained to ensure social control. We should not be so surprised when we see so many of our children at sea.

The true mentor enables the conversation with the future by the very fact that, in some very palpable sense, she is a stand-in for the child's own future. The young teenager, by living if only partially in the world of the mentor, learns not necessarily to creatively think like the mentor, but to taste the fulfillment—the love of the craft and its ideals—which may come from actually using the skills to be acquired and having learned to think creatively at all.

So where do you start? Well, I must forewarn you: there is a vast store-house of helpful mentors waiting for your call! Does your child think she might be interested in law? Don't have her watch TV: call a local judge. Last summer, after spending months learning about the Bill of Rights, my older daughter (13 at the time) spent a week in a local courtroom watching and analyzing a carjacking trial. (We failed, however, in setting up a debriefing with the judge. Next time....) Thinking about veterinary sciences? Find volunteer opportunities at the local animal shelter, and be sure to schedule them for when the vet comes through. Ask for a chance to spend a week sweeping up in an auto mechanic's or violin bowmaker's shop. Have your son take a minister out for lunch, or ask whether he can shadow him for a week. If you live in a small town, have your daughter call the mayor, or the guy who owns the local hardware store, or the president of the local YMCA (they may all be the same person!) You and your son and daughter have all of these special opportunities: you're homeschooling!

Can't seem to make a connection through family, friends, or acquaintances for this purpose? My advice is "Let Your Fingers Do the Walking". Go *shopping for mentors*, and assume it will require at least three times the amount of time necessary to buy a new car. You can provide the most amazing experiences for your kids by following their interests into the Yellow Pages and calling people you've never met. My general experience is that people love to talk to others who are interested but ignorant about their business or craft: after all, you can't contradict them! And who knows where it may lead?

In some cases, if you're lucky—and manage to get out of the way—the kids by themselves will seek out adults who will share their own interests and passions. Almost like clockwork, when my younger daughter Meera passed her 12th birthday, she went from a seeming complete lack of interest in the adults around her, to an almost obsessive hunger to know all about them. She befriended a local (and childless) librarian (whom she had known in passing at our Friends Meeting for a decade) who volunteers at the local animal shelter, and the librarian's husband, recently returned from a peace team fact-finding mission to Israel/Palestine. She joined a cousin of my wife who organizes a monthly adult Jewish-Moslem dialogue group in town (Meera being neither). Having attended a jazz concert, she struck up a relationship with the saxophone player who is confined to a wheelchair as a result of childhood polio, and who has assisted her in educating herself about jazz, as a supplement to her more classical piano studies. And, having read a book about polio as an outgrowth of this relationship, she has started up a written correspondence with the author who, as it turns out, lives only about 90 minutes from our home. Virtually all of Meera's reading and writing projects over the past six months have been linked in one way or another to these burgeoning relationships.

This is likely to play havoc with your curricula plans. Last fall, a homeschooling mother approached me at a conference. It seems her 13-year-old son has decided he wants to be an architect some day (he has been the block-building champion of the living room since he was 3), and managed to find an architect who would let him help out in the office for a whole month! His mother, concerned about upsetting their normal home-schooling routines, was particularly worried that her son now wanted to study geometry "out of sequence" with the store-bought math curriculum. I told her she should be thrilled rather than worried, but that she shouldn't take my word for it, because it was her son's education and it was his opinion that really counted, not hers and definitely not mine! But she might let her son ask the architect his opinion, and let him be the arbiter. What a nice "problem"!

* * * * *

I have lived on the lip of insanity,
Wanting to know reasons, knocking
On a door.
It opens.
I've been knocking from the inside!

—Rumi[3]

Ultimately, we are brought back to the flow idea. This is seemingly somewhat of a paradox, for even as the young teen is fulfilling the need for conversations with the future, the flow idea places stress on the deriving of fulfillment in the present moment.

But underneath there is no paradox at all: the future-seeking of the young teen will not be denied, and it is this very future-seeking that provides the impetus for skill-building. Rather, what we have is a precarious balancing act, between the playful aspect of seeking new challenges and the work necessary to overcome them.

As we have found earlier in examining the concept of flow, if the challenges are too demanding, attempting to overcome them becomes

---

3   Rumi, Jalal Al-Din, *The Illustrated Rumi*, translated by Coleman Barks, illustrated by Michael Green. New York, NY: Broadway Books, 1997.

overly frustrating. More commonly (and one can easily see this in middle schools, and among some homeschooling parents), the challenges are put on hold, the child "incubated", and boredom sets in. Often the only way out for the child, if he has not "matured into compliance", is dare-devil behavior.

Occasionally, we are told by pop psychologists, this reflects what the child perceives as a lack of caring on the part of adults. Perhaps, but I think more often it is a result of the wrong kind of caring, an over-protectiveness that fails to take account of the child's needs for a new kind of nourishment, and the failure of the child to find suitable adult challenges into which to mature.

I was on a panel several years with an extraordinarily articulate young man, age 20. He related how, at the age of 16 and a high school dropout, he had worked himself up from the time he was 12 to head a business grossing $1.5-million. He supervised over 35 employees, was responsible for all hiring and firing decisions, and for his employees' health and safety. He was responsible for the purchase of and payment for all products at wholesale to be sold, for setting up and maintaining all distribution networks, for advertising, for setting prices, and for dealing with competitors. He handled all finances, and made all decisions about expansion plans, all this until he had to put the business on hold as he found himself in state prison. He was a midlevel cocaine dealer. Now he was expected to be thankful for the opportunity to sweep floors at Burger King.

Clearly he had gone down a wrong road. He had chosen his mentors poorly or there were few available to him from which to choose. Putting aside ethical considerations, his chosen field of endeavor entails more risk than is healthy for a young teen. But the barely concealed pride with which he told his story spoke volumes about both his yearning for and his satisfaction in having learned as a young teen what was necessary to be a leader in his own, if somewhat limited, world. (P.S. I knew he wouldn't be long for Burger King. Last I heard, he made his living going into middle and high schools—dropout and all—to lecture about alcohol and drugs. He has never left his professional field—and now he and I are in the same one!)

We are faced with another paradox: she won't try anything new, even as her actual capacities for dealing with the new seem to be expanding. But look more carefully. What is really happening is that the young teen is dealing with the new, confusing, and somewhat terrifying all the time—the truth of her new self knocking from the inside. This can make young teens extremely glum, for as the literary critic Walter Benjamin once wrote, "To be happy is to become aware of oneself without fright." And to be sure, there *is* fright! Perhaps in the first inklings of a new self-awareness, the child-man wrestles with the paradox of the Tao Te Ching:

> *In the pursuit of learning, every day is something new acquired.*
> *In the pursuit of Truth, every day something is dropped.*

I like to think of young teens as blue hard-shelled crabs who are in the process of molting. The haughty disdain and diffidence on the surface is often a cover for the tenderness and even fear to be found beneath. In the proper safe environment, and provided the necessary nourishment, she will be free to cast off the shell. Without them, she will be unable to carry over that spontaneity—the gift of childhood—into a fulfilling adult life.

Or, I am now reminded by Aliyah, like snakes before they shed. Because before they slither out of their old skins, their eyes cloud completely over, and they have no clue as to where they are going!

Hannah Arendt once wrote, "Education is the point at which we decide whether we love the world enough to assume responsibility for it and by the same token save it from the ruin which, except for renewal, except for the coming of the new and the young, would be inevitable…and where we love our children enough not to expel them from our world and leave them to their own devices, nor to strike from their hands their chance of undertaking something new, something unforeseen by us, but to prepare them in advance for the task of renewing a common world." And, truly, it is working with young teens that we irrevocably make that decision.

And so we are confronted with paradoxes. Except we are not. We are confronted with *miracles*. The time of the great turning is no less than the miracle by which our children learned to take their first few halting steps, or tie their shoes, or make out their first few words from the jumble of letters. Only here they are confronting a new body, a new sense of self, new intellectual and emotional capacities, new intimations of a future into which we ourselves, ultimately, are refused entry. The doors are opening for our children: we must stand back in awe of these wonderful, brilliant, brash, annoying, headstrong, foolish, scary, fearful, complicated, paradoxical perfect beings, and allow them to step on through.

Cilia!

T hey want to get rid of cilia!" exclaimed Aliyah, a frown deepening across her 13-year-old face as she speed-read the article.

"Cilia, too," I repeated, putting down the sports section.

"Well, cilia are the whole reason for paramecium. How is anyone going to talk with a scientist? What are we going to say—"little wavy things"?

"How about flagella?" I suggested, then remembering—stupid me—that those are found among a different class of critters entirely.

"No, they are getting rid of flagella, too!"

Ali was reading a May 2001 article on a new, highly publicized guide "Designs for Science Literacy" published and promoted by the American Association for the Advancement of Science. The recommendations, being sent to every school board, school administrator, and school superintendent in the United States, are designed, according to Andrew Ahlgren, Project Associate Director, "to assist education leaders, teachers, publishers, and developers in assembling instructional materials for kindergarten through 12th grade that are coherent and relevant." The goal, says Ahlgren, is to change the curriculum so that even basic science education "is challenging and meets global standards."

"No right-angle trigonometry?" She was now really steamed. "How will we build anything? And, look, they removed the Periodic Table, and acids and bases. How is anyone going to understand acid rain? And no more oxidation, respiration, aerobic or anaerobic…."

"Well, I guess we'll simply have to talk about breathing."

"And they are getting rid of mitochondria. How can you study evolution without mitochondria?"

"Hey, Ali, this is not my idea," I reminded my daughter, intending to cool down the conversation. "Why don't you write them a letter?"

* * * * *

"How is anyone going to talk with a scientist?" was the question that stuck in my craw. I might have added how could one understand fully the public controversy about the teaching of evolution, or how could one as act as a responsible citizen to curb air pollution?

The point is, maybe our kids are not supposed to be scientists, or even involved, responsible, thinking citizens. John Taylor Gatto notes that public education is aimed solely at preparing youth for the jobs of tomorrow. And we know where those jobs are. According to Gatto, citing U.S. Department of Labor statistics, the occupation most widely held by Americans, as well as the job that has had the largest growth in the past 30 years is—I kid you not—Wal-Mart clerk. Second is McDonald's burger flipper. Third is Burger King flipper. And close behind? Schoolteacher.

Now, it should be emphasized, the major requirements for all four of these jobs are the same. The first, and by far the most important, is one has to show up, preferably on a regular or predictable basis. The second is compliance—one does what one is told in an expected and predictable manner, without asking too many questions (don't ask where the clothes are made, what's in the burger, or how they came up with that asinine standardized test question!) The third—really just an extension of the second—is that one doesn't rebel. Only one of these job categories currently requires higher education, but I expect that will change. Within five years, I would not be surprised to find community colleges offering associate degrees in burger flipping, er, I mean "fast food technology management". And in some states where the teacher shortage is most acute, the higher education requirement for schoolteachers is now being waived. Soon, all four of the jobs may be interchangeable.

The education standardization movement across America has occurred without any meaningful public discussion of what those standards should be, or what they mean. You can be sure they have nothing to do with excellence, which is why anyone who suggests the obvious is likely to be viciously attacked. And don't dare to ask to see the test questions! Maybe the whole point is that "we" ("Moi?") *need* Wal-Mart clerks, rather than scientists, computer people, or mathematicians. Professor Dudley R. Herschbach of Harvard University, 1997 Nobel Prize Winner in Chemistry, is a Board member of the New Calculus Project, a national effort to re-evaluate the teaching of mathematics. He is quoted in my high school alumni bulletin as arguing that teaching students more than the four basic mathematical operations is not necessary for most occupations. It is cheaper, after all, he says, for American industries to import mathematicians and scientists from other countries. (The idea that mathematics, or chemistry for that matter, might actually be a thing of intrinsic beauty seems never to have crossed his Nobel Prize-winning mind, but then he teaches at Harvard, and he probably believes that we mere mortals are not capable of experiencing this beauty, or that we are not worthy of it.)

What this means for public education is that students in schools without access to advanced or "college-level" courses, will become second-class citizens. They will lack the common vocabulary that could allow them to become conversant with scientists or scientific issues, or active, informed citizens. We all know where these schools are, and the predominant skin colors, ethnic makeup, and incomes of the families of the kids condemned to them. The public schools will then have accomplished one of their major aims: to find "objective" ways to limit the opportunities of those that attend them. (Mathematics, and in particular algebra, is used as an especially insidious "gatekeeper", and is, according Robert Moses—a major leader in the Mississippi voting rights struggle in the 1960s—the new "civil rights battleground". See his book *Radical Equations: Math Literacy and Civil Rights* (Boston, MA: Beacon Press, 2001), or check out the Algebra Project website at www.algebra.org).

Of course, the officials at the American Association for the Advancement of Science claim that their priority is simply to "improve" science textbooks.

* * * * *

So what does all this mean for homeschoolers? For one thing, it means we have to learn more emphatically to turn our backs on, and our hearts away from, the work of the "Standardistas".[1] These standards are developed without any regard to the needs, interests, passions, or aspirations of your own or any other individual child. The Standardistas care more about Wal-Mart than they do about your kids, or mine.

Not all children will want or need to go to college. Not all kids will want to learn trigonometry or read *King Lear*. Instead of focusing, as the Standardistas do, on our children as a collection of deficits, as empty boxes waiting to be filled, we could do the one thing we know we can do better than the schools ever can, and that is *listen to them*, and act upon what we hear. And we can teach them—and model for them—that the art of learning is a beautiful thing in itself, and one that they can carry with them into a fulfilling adulthood.

Now I'll be the first to admit that I haven't had a paramecium wave a ciliated "hello" to me in over 35 years. Or at least I haven't noticed. It is not one of those beautiful conversations with which I have been blessed.

---

1 The term was coined by renegade retired Vermont schoolteacher Susan Ohanian. Her book *What Happened to Recess and Why are Our Children Struggling in Kindergarten* (New York, NY: McGraw Hill, 2002) is a must-read. Check out her website at www.susanohanian.org.

But I've had others, and I sorely wish I had been afforded the opportunity to have them earlier. And this leads me to a clear conclusion, and it is the opposite of that suggested by the American Association for the Advancement of Science. Once your child acquires a passion—whether it is auto mechanics, horses, or high-energy physics—provide her with the opportunity to acquire all the vocabulary. All of it—forget "developmental appropriateness"—*all of it*. There is no need to wait, and there is a need that you don't!

Don't get the impression that I'm referring only to older kids. I know there are educators, for example, who suggest that when we read to our children (at younger ages), we should try to find books that are just a little bit ahead of our children's current vocabulary. Well, I say bunko![2] Children generally learn vocabulary by swimming in a world where the "level" at which the language being spoken around them is always far in advance of what they might otherwise be expected to know, and they manage to maintain their buoyancy, thank you. Research has shown that the average five-year-old (as if there is such a thing as an "average" five-year-old—I've never met one, and I bet you haven't either) knows approximately 10,000 words, vocabulary having increased exponentially from around 250 words at 18 months. She will gain another 2,000-3,000 a year until her vocabulary at age 18 will be approximately 40,000 words. With more good reading and good conversation, her vocabulary will just keep growing. (The same studies, by the way, indicate that in classrooms, children are formally introduced to no more than 300-500 words a year, and since they may already have known about half of them before being "taught", they are obviously getting well more than three-quarters of their vocabulary from somewhere else!) She didn't learn these words by having conversations around her intentionally dumbed down to what it is presumed she can understand. So if your child has an interest and a passion, engage her with the best you and the world have to offer, rather than some strained calibration of "what she is ready for". Talk "up" to your child and, where necessary, provide the tools and scaffolding whereby she can make the reach. If you listen hard enough, she'll make known to you quite clearly how far she is prepared to go.

And if you're stuck and can't figure out where your child's interests lie? That's an easy one: read what interests and excites *you*.

Doing so will soon enrich her conversation with the world of auto mechanics, horse breeders, and physicists, and will enable her to try on

---

2   A technical term, also referred to as "hokum".

futures for herself. The problem (actually just one of the long litany of problems) with modern schooling is that we wait too long to allow our children to have these conversations. So long, in fact, that many of our kids are inured to boredom, and come to view such conversations with haughty disdain (a cover for fearfulness) long before they might have had them. Sadly, many never do.

Consider for a moment: what did George Washington, Benjamin Franklin, and Admiral David Farragut have in common? In their younger years, they were allowed to follow their passions well beyond what might have been considered their expected capacities based on their chronological ages (if anyone even thought about such things), and certainly in no orderly fashion as divined by education bureaucrats (of whom, in those days, there were thankfully few.) George Washington (no intellectual giant, whatever his myriad other virtues) first attended school at age 11, and the first subject in mathematics he ever studied was trigonometry, because he wanted to be a surveyor. Benjamin Franklin knew virtually everything there was to know about printing presses by age 12. David Farragut went to sea at age 10, fought in the War of 1812 at 11, and was given his first command of a ship at 12.

And, by gosh, do you know? They all managed to have "reasonable futures" even without having ever attended Hamburger University.[3]

---

3 Check this one out: www.mcdonalds.com/corporate/careers/hambuniv/index.html. They even have 30 full-time hamburger professors! Have the burgers improved much recently?

The <u>Success</u> of Public Education

A Tribute to John Taylor Gatto on the Publication of the 10th Anniversary Edition of *Dumbing Us Down: The Hidden Curriculum of Compulsory Schooling*

> *The right to express our thoughts, however, means something only if we are able to have thoughts of our own; freedom from external authority is a lasting gain only if the inner psychological conditions are such that we are able to establish our own individuality.*
> —Erich Fromm, *Escape from Freedom*

As its editor and former publisher, I would have liked to flatter myself into believing that John Taylor Gatto's book *Dumbing Us Down* was both his first book and his most popular. Unfortunately, and by a long stretch, neither turns out to be true. That will come as a surprise to many, who are most familiar with *Dumbing Us Down* in its earlier green-and-black cover incarnation, or with John's two more recent books *The Underground History of American Education* (that's the big, fat one) or *A Different Kind of Teacher* (a blue hardcover).[1]

John's first work was a set of Monarch Notes. Some of you may remember these from high school, a way to get by in English class without doing the required reading! At any rate, Gatto's first book was published in 1975, a Monarch Notes guide to the late Ken Kesey's *One Flew Over the Cuckoo's Nest*.

John related to me once, after affixing his signature on my copy—with handwriting only a hair more legible than my own (we must both have had Mr. Lucas in the 6th grade and still not recovered from the experience)

---

1   Gatto, John Taylor, *The Underground History of American Education*. New York, NY: Oxford Village Press, 2001, and *A Different Kind of Teacher: Solving the Crisis of American Schooling*. Berkeley, CA: Berkeley Hills Books, 2000.

that the Monarch Notes guide, still in print after 26 years, has actually sold hundreds of thousands of copies, making it by far his most widely read work. But all John ever got out of it was a Burmese cat. If you ever get the opportunity to attend one of his talks, make sure to ask him about it.

Anyway, this Monarch Notes guide—the only book of Gatto's likely to be read by students undergoing their slow death in what passes for "educational institutions" these days—is an incendiary work. And not only because of its black-and-red cover.

Kesey's magnificent novel, as well as the excellent movie featuring a young Jack Nicholson (not recommended until you've read the book!), is the story of a rebel—one Randall Patrick McMurphy—who finds himself (or rather finds a way to get himself) inside a state psychiatric institution in the 1960s. Once within, he discovers himself bound by a web of rules, procedures, and protocols—really, kid gloves—behind which stands an iron fist of violence and repression, all designed of course for "the patient's own good". In scene after scene, McMurphy probes against the boundaries of the forces that stand behind the institution—"the Combine"—which comes to be symbolized by "The Big Nurse" who controls the ward, and ultimately holds the fate of each of the patients in her hands. Let me not ruin the book for you. I suggest you go out and read it, alongside your teenager if you have one, or, if you've read it once before, read it again with new eyes.

Kesey's novel takes place against a backdrop of relentless institutional conditioning. While meetings on the ward may seem to be democratically organized, and while inmates—no, here they are called "patients"—are urged toward accountability, one quickly realizes that there is no democracy at work in the asylum, and that accountability is a sham. Inmates are tracked, without their consent, into well-demarcated groups as acutes and chronics—and further subdivided into walkers, wheelers, and vegetables (we all do remember being grouped into Bluebirds and Robins in first grade, don't we?). The highest value to the Combine is neither democracy nor accountability, but *compliance*, pure and simple, and its favorite strategem is divide and conquer. And if that doesn't work, there are always drugs. Hmm.

I doubt that a set of Monarch Notes has ever been heaped with literary praise before, but Gatto's are much deserving. His description of the Keseyan institutional world contained in this incendiary set of crib notes, (he even quotes Che Guevara—"Educate your enemy, don't kill him, for he is worth more to you alive than dead"), is as compelling as the novel itself.

He describes the Combine that controls this little world as "an all-powerful, earth-girdling, brain-destroying association of technocrats…intent on building a world of precision, efficiency, and tidiness…a place where the schedule is unbreakable." "In such a world," writes John, "there is neither grief nor happiness; nobody dies—they only burn out and are recycled; actually, it is a rather safe place, everything is planned—there are neither risks nor surprises." Gatto continues that within this little world, "Words and meaningless routines insulate people from life itself, blind them to what is happening around them, and deaden the moral faculties." The defense to this charge, ironic of course as John notes, is that the Big Nurse delivers charity baskets to the poor. Pivotal to Kesey's novel, according to Gatto, "is the cataclysmic revelation that the inmates of the asylum are not committed but are there of their own free will." And the way they are controlled, ultimately, is through guilt, shame, fear, and belittlement. Double hmmm.

And now, Gatto, in telescoping the next 25 years of his own career, tells us the way out. "The way out of the asylum," he writes, "is literally to throw out the control panel, on a physical level smashing the reinforced windows, on a symbolic spiritual level becoming independent of rules, orders, and other people's urgencies." "Self-reliance," concludes John, "is the antidote to institutional stupidity."

We should all express our gratitude that John took his own advice, and, beginning with *Dumbing Us Down*, has undertaken to tell us what life is really about "on the inside", as if, in our heart of hearts, we didn't already know. Like Chief Bromden—the supposedly deaf-and-dumb Indian in the novel who finally finds his own voice—he managed to steal away. Well, perhaps that's not the best possible description, for John has made rather a big splash! And I have been privileged to have helped the resultant wave along.

* * * * *

When I first read what was to become *Dumbing Us Down* in manuscript back in 1990, it provided an almost unique answer to a conundrum I had not been able to figure out for myself. My older daughter was two at the time—long before my own previous book *And the Skylark Sings with Me* was even a glint in my eye. I was beginning to read up on education writers, both those who occupied the deep left end of the pond (that's where to this day you'll usually find me) and those who swam in a "less sinister" direction.

What was most striking to me at the time, and remains so to this day, was how much they both occupy the same pond. Their descriptions of the world of public education closely parallel each other, even if they view underlying causes differently. They all emphasize what seem to them to be the obvious deficiencies of public education. More often than not, though with different points of emphasis, they note the boredom, the mindless competition, enforced social and economic stratification, the lack of real engagement—academic or otherwise, the brutality and violence, the "soul-less-ness" that characterizes what passes for education these days. From Alfie Kohn (liberal) to Thomas Sowell (conservative), they wax poetic about the shortcomings of modern schooling, though their antidotes are often worlds apart. And all my friends had stories they could remember as inmates—oh, sorry, I meant "students"—of being shamed, embarrassed, harassed, brutalized, drugged, inflicted with boredom, or just plain ignored, and they remembered these experiences far more vividly than anything they were ever ostensibly taught.

And yet the idea that schools are failing didn't make any sense to me. After all, the schools are run by highly paid and educated public servants, hired by local elected school boards—my neighbors, staffed by people pre-pared in our graduate schools of education where they were, in turn, taught by faculty trained at our elite private universities such as Yale or the University of Chicago. Teachers are honored, school administrators with salaries well in excess of $100,000 receive merit-pay raises, the school boards continue to get elected, the electorate continues to vote to give the schools more money, the graduate schools of education get bigger. If these are failing institutions, they sure have a funny way of showing it!

John provided, and continues to provide the key to understanding this conundrum. Central to this understanding is the fact that *schools are not failing*. On the contrary, they are spectacularly successful in doing precisely what they are intended to do, and what they have been intended to do since their inception. The system, perfected at places like the University of Chicago, Columbia Teachers College, Carnegie-Mellon, and Harvard, and funded by the captains of industry, was explicitly set up to ensure a docile, malleable workforce to meet the growing, changing demands of corporate capitalism—"to meet the new demands of the 20th Century," they would have said back then. The Combine (whoops, slipped again!) ensures a workforce that will not rebel (the greatest fear at the turn of the 20th Century), and that will be physically, intellectually, and emotionally dependent upon corporate institutions for their incomes, self-esteem, and stimulation, and will learn to find social meaning in their lives solely in the production and consumption of material goods. We all grew up in these institutions and we know they work. They haven't changed much since the 1890s because they don't need to—they perform precisely as they are intended.

What do the captains of industry really care about? That public education be public. In other words, that we (and not they) pay for it. Corporate institutions have unloaded their basic training needs on to us, and we voluntarily pay to forge the chains of our own servitude.

So far, so good. But the obvious question that follows from this is, if educational institutions are so demonstrably successful, why are we always hearing about their failures? And here John might have provided the answer, for in his aborted career before becoming a New York City schoolteacher, with Monarch Notes a decade away and this new edition of *Dumbing Us Down* almost four, Gatto was an advertising copyrighter, "a young fellow," (he writes in "The Green Monongahela"), "with a knack for writing thirty-second television commercials." The copywriter knows that to sell a product or service, one must create the perception of need, and the palpable feeling that this need can only be filled exclusively through the purchase of the particular snake oil or service being offered. The simplistic notion that "our schools are failing" easily translates into a limitless demand for more resources for the institution and its supports—for books, for teachers, for computers, for real estate (and hence book publishers, graduate schools of education, computer manufacturers, and real estate developers), as well as for more time—more pre-school, more homework, longer school years, the end of recess, and semi- (and soon fully) compulsory summer schools. And to the copywriter's delight, it is a zero-sum game. Not only is there an endless stream of consumers with little or no institutional memory and absolutely insatiable demand, but the truth is that no matter how much is expended in the educational marketplace, 50% of the schools will remain "below average", with those branded as poor performers changing from year to year, and those above the mid-point fearing, above all, that they will fall into the abyss. And the copywriter has done his job for, it is universally believed, the only response to a fall into submediocrity is to buy one's way out.

This stratagem is extraordinarily elegant but so transparent that it always runs the risk of being seen for the confidence game that, at bottom, it is, except that it gets translated down to individual children. In other words, the Combine preys upon our maternal and paternal instincts. And so the latest iteration of "education reform" (the fifth such set of reforms in my brief lifespan) comes with new (actually old) testing strategies where it can be ensured that large majorities of children will regularly "fail", either in comparison with each other, with those in another school, or with children living in the much more productive economies of Tunisia or Slovenia. The "answer" to those deficits, and the perpetual dissatisfaction they engender, is simply more of the same, rather like "the hair of the dog that bit you".

The reforms are never completed. To do so would require admitting failure, or worse, that the failure is not failure at all, only a continuing round in the socialized enforcement of intellectual and emotional dependency, of which John writes so eloquently. In the meantime, it is like requiring our children to live in buildings that are never finished, and never to be, and being forced to breathe in the noxious fumes and dirt and dust from the never-ending construction.

Our children deserve the opportunity to come up for a breath of fresh air.

* * * * *

> A general State education is a mere contrivance for moulding people to be exactly like one another: and as the mould in which it casts them is that which pleases the predominant power in the government, whether this be a monarch, a priesthood, an aristocracy, or the majority of the existing generation in proportion as it is efficient and successful, it establishes a despotism over the mind, leading by a natural tendency to one over the body.
> —John Stuart Mill, On Liberty (1859)

Fresh air is going to be difficult to find.

Dan Greenberg, founder of the Sudbury Valley School—a successful, 30-year-old learning community based on the principles of self-initiated learning and democratic self-government (www.sudval.org) has written that leading educators, business leaders, and government officials share a virtually unanimous agreement regarding the essential features of an education that would meet the needs of society in the 21st Century. He sees consensus on seven points:

- As society rapidly changes, individuals will have to be able to function comfortably in a world that is always in flux. Knowledge will continue to increase at a dizzying rate. This means that a content-based curriculum, with a set body of information to be imparted to students, is entirely inappropriate as a means of preparing children for their adult roles.

- People will be faced with greater individual responsibility to direct their own lives. Children must grow up in an environment that stresses self-motivation and self-assessment. Schools that focus on external motivating factors, such as rewards and punishments for meeting goals set by others, are denying children the tools they need most to survive.

- The ability to communicate with others, to share experiences, collaborate, and exchange information is critical. Conversation, the ultimate means of communication, must be a central part of a sound education.

- As the world moves toward universal recognition of individual rights within a democratic society, people must be empowered to participate as equal partners in whatever enterprise in which they are engaged. Students (and teachers) require full participation in running educational institutions, including the right to radically change them when needed.

- Technology now makes it possible for individuals to learn whatever they wish, whenever they wish, and in the manner they wish. Students should be empowered with both the technology and the responsibility for their own learning and educational timetable.

- Children have an immense capacity for concentration and hard work when they are passionate about what they are doing, and the skills they acquire in any area of interest are readily transferable to other fields. Schools must thus become far more tolerant of individual variation, and far more reliant on self-initiated activities.

Nice list, yes? Gatto shares Greenberg's vision of what education should be like (and is supportive of all ventures that would bring it to fruition, even for the few), but having spent the better part of three decades in the trenches, he has a far more realistic, if darker, view of the purposes toward which public education is directed. He views school (as he writes in the *The Underground History of American Education*) "as a conflict pitting the needs of social machinery against those of the human spirit, a war of mechanisms against flesh and blood that only require a human architect to get launched."

Let's put it plainly: in Gatto's view, the Combine needs dumb adults, and so it ensures the supply by making the kids dumb. Seen from this perspective, it is clear that Dan Greenberg is wrong. While there is always a need for a highly circumscribed number of technocrats to replace themselves, the Combine has only limited use for hundreds of millions of self-reliant, critical thinking individuals who engage in conversation, and who determine their own needs as individuals and communities free of the Combine's enticements and demands. And when such individuals exist, the Combine fears them. It may occasionally pay lip-service to their value, but it ultimately has no real use for artists, dancers, poets, self-sufficient farmers, tree lovers, devoted followers of what it views as non-materialist cults—Christian or otherwise, handicraft workers, makers of their own beer, or, for that matter, stay-at-home moms and dads, all of whom, when they endure at all, do so at the margins and on the periphery of the social economy. What the Combine needs, most of all, is Wal-Mart clerks and burger flippers, and dedicated but low-paid government-employed "foreign service officers", proud of their titles as teachers, who prevent the restless natives from rebelling while the extraction of resources and capital, human and otherwise, continues unabated. And, in the final analysis, while it employs the most extraordinary of spin-doctors and apologists, the Combine makes no compromises and takes no prisoners, not until it has colonized every nerve ending—every synapse and every habit of mind—as much as it has swarmed over every square centimeter of this good earth.

But the strategy doesn't work entirely. For every McMurphy who, as in *Cuckoo's Nest*, has had his brain fried (literally so in the novel), there is the possibility of a Chief Bromden who escapes. There are weeds growing in the cracks in the highway that will not be stamped out. We are here— the weeds—you, I, and Dan Greenberg, and the author of our incendiary book. There are now a million homeschoolers, and there will soon be another million homeschool alumni. And with us, maybe, just maybe, and unlike any of the other abortive alternative school movements of the past century, will come the power—with enough weeds grown up into tall trees—to block the highway as the Combine with engines blazing moves down our path.

John implies through his writing, his life, and his witness, that he does not believe individual solutions are likely to be the answer to larger societal-wide problems—they may not by themselves destroy the Combine. But he has also demonstrated, and the new 10th Anniversary Edition of *Dumbing Us Down* celebrates, that we can only stand to gain by protecting and enlarging those meager zones of freedom for ourselves to inhabit—to widen the cracks in the pavement—and to begin to recapture that common energy, creativity, and imagination with which we are endowed by Great Nature as children, and which holds out the promise of better times to come.

On Forgiveness

Blessed are You, Oh Lord our God, Ruler of the Universe,
who commanded us to forget what we forgot,
and to forget that we have forgotten it.

I wrote the above in the form of an ancient Hebrew prayer, and even had a Jewish friend of mine translate it into Hebrew. While I am extremely well-traveled, somewhere along the line I developed a phobia about forgetting things when leaving for an extended trip. My kids are amused watching me check my pockets for the plane tickets three or four times, open my luggage again *just one last time*, feel in my jacket *yet again* for the address book and my reading glasses, and walk out the door with a deep breath.

Funny thing is, in 30 years I have never forgotten anything of significance. Sure, I have arrived in places and discovered there are items I would have preferred to have brought with me. Most of the time, I am able to make up for this deficit one way or another. It has never been debilitating. If pure rationality were a cure for phobia, I would have moved on a long while ago.

Somewhat more recently, the prayer has come in handy for more general purposes. I do forget things, though not much that most people would notice. I hypothesize that my oversized "thought-a-rama" of a brain has become overloaded, and I haven't discovered a way to install an expanded hard drive. Actually, I find that I don't really forget anything. Rather the slides in the memory carousel don't pop up into the viewer quite as quickly as they used to. I will want to drag up something arcane (like the administrative capital of Dalmatia—this actually came up over the weekend as Aliyah and I participated in a workshop to learn Dalmatian choral music at the Northwest Folklife Festival) and find that I can't locate it immediately in rummaging around among the synapses. I'll say my little prayer, let it go, and ten minutes later the answer will make its appearance on the screen (Zadar! though Split was the site of the Roman capital during the reign of the Dalmatian-born Roman Emperor Diocletian). I'm still Mr. Know-It-All—I just know it all a little more slowly! Of course I don't understand whether this means my IQ is declining, or I am affected by particular foods eaten four hours earlier or impurities in the air supply, suffer from the long-term after-effects of medications or vaccinations received half a century ago, or am simply becoming a lazy underachiever who is not working up to his potential.

Another problem is that I keep on learning new stuff, which probably presses down heavily on the pile of the old. My brain is like spanakopita (though I would have much preferred Napoleon cake.) My tests scores, if tests were regularly administered to 52-year-olds, would definitely suffer.

"Your brain sounds like my room," comments Aliyah, reminding me she has just lost a piece of her Queen of the Night costume that she needs on Saturday night.

"Right," I mutter. "A real archaeological dig. Try the upper Pleistocene layer."

Upper Pleistocene. Is that where I live? "Fossils are numerous and complete (thank you!), and there is an even greater geographical range. But time scales are shorter and morphological contrasts are less marked." No wonder I'm not any good with names and faces.

This is all simply a reminder, I guess, that I am less than perfect. Or more accurately, *less than less than perfect*. I flatter myself into thinking that the less perfect I am, the more interesting I become. The final determination in this regard, however, dear friend, must be left up to you.

* * * * *

While I was growing up in a conservative Jewish household, I learned about a particular custom (one which we didn't observe) called *tashlich*. *Tashlich* is a ceremony that takes place on the afternoon of the Jewish New Year (*Rosh Hashanah*).

The word *tashlich* means "to cast away". The ceremony is very simple. One walks down to a body of water (preferably a moving one, and one with fish) and empties one's pockets into it (bread crumbs having been placed there for this explicit purpose). The bread crumbs are supposed to represent our sins being cast into the water, usually accompanied by a recitation from the Old Testament Book of Micah (7:18-20): "And You will cast into the depths of the sea all their sins." The fish, not being able to close their eyes, represent God who never sleeps and who can see into our hearts. The sins are to be swept away by the currents. (This is not a practice that easily lends itself to greater ecological understanding, for who knows where trash dumped in a river is likely to wash up?)

Tashlich occurs in a larger context. In the 30 days prior to the beginning of the New Year (*Rosh Hoshanah*, metaphorically, being considered the time during which God decides whether to inscribe individuals in the Book of Life for the coming year), people are required to seek forgiveness from those they have wronged, and to compensate them if appropriate accordingly. God, having given humans the power to wrong each other, has surrendered the power to forgive these wrongs. And, in their power to forgive each other, human beings are empowered to act as if they are God Himself.

In the ten days following *tashlich*—known as the Days of Repentance—people are called upon to repent of their sins. But now we get down to the crux of the matter, for the remaining sins must be only those committed against God, rather than against other human beings, for as already noted, God has no power to deal with the latter.

The culmination of this process is *Yom Kippur*, considered the holiest day in the Jewish calendar, also known as the Day of Atonement. It is a fast day. In one of the strangest and most misunderstood of all Jewish observances, it begins with a prayer in Aramaic, "*Kol Nidre*", which takes the form of a legal brief. *Kol Nidre* means "all vows", and in it, the petitioner—taking the persona of an attorney standing before the Most High—declares that all vows, obligations, oaths, and pledges are hereby to be declared null and void.

But now here comes the interesting part. The vows to be annulled are not those made with other human beings—these supposedly having already been dealt with by the proper parties—nor those with God—these have also already been dealt with, but promises one makes to *oneself*. And the obligations and pledges to be voided are not those which have occurred in the previous year, *but those which will be undertaken in the next*.

The psychological reality addressed by this extraordinary prayer is fear of failure. Just as a human being may have failed in the past, so he or she may be convinced that failure will occur in the future. This can, of course, become a self-fulfilling prophecy, for instead of thinking of oneself as a basically good person who occasionally errs, one may begin to imagine oneself as a failure from whom little should be anticipated. Hence, the ceremony embodies the necessary faith that one could look forward to being forgiven *prospectively*. It doesn't let one off the hook; on the contrary, one becomes a human being from whom more can be expected.

It is said that the early rabbis were hostile to this concept. It seems to fly in the face of the oft-repeated Biblical injunctions against the breaking of vows, and the power being reserved to priestly institutions to annul them, and only on the basis that they were undertaken without full awareness of their implications or consequences. But human beings will out, and must find the strength of "at-one-ment" within themselves. Human being are not perfect: we are, after all, only human! Faced with a choice in the Garden between the Tree of Life and the Tree of Knowledge, Eve in her naïve wisdom chose the Tree of Knowledge, and that means we must find ways to come to terms with the gap between who we are and who, in our best moments, we know and expect ourselves to be. And, no, no thought or action can ever be undertaken by a human being with absolute foresight of its implications or consequences. In short, we do the best we can.

And wouldn't it be wonderful if we could find ways to act—in exercising our God-like powers—by forgiving both ourselves and each other in advance, *prospectively*?

Come to think of it, isn't that what love is supposed to be all about?

* * * * *

"So how do you expect me to learn anything if you keep teaching me?"
—Eight-year-old homeschooler

What does this all have to do with homeschooling? I would suggest absolutely everything.

It is my experience that, as a group, we homeschooling parents are tremendously hard on ourselves. We are often hard-driven to work in what we perceive to be our children's best interests and, more often than we care to admit, we often wonder whether or where we have failed them, *or will*.

Another way of viewing this is to say we hold ourselves accountable. We can't play the blame game. We can't blame schools or schoolteachers, or even the government, as we have rescued our children from their clutches. We can't blame the TV; most of us learned long ago that we can indeed turn it off! We can't blame the books or the curriculum; we chose them. We can't blame the food; we prepared it ourselves. And so who or what is left but us? And, as I am always reminding homeschooling parents who come to me for advice: "Don't worry: whatever you do, you scar 'em for life!"

We also don't have the luxury of schoolteachers. We don't walk away after nine months, remembering only those charges who gave us the greatest pleasure or the largest heartburn, but taking long-term responsibility for neither. No, these kids are ours, and there will be no opportunity to walk away.

And perhaps even this understanding understates our accountability. For we may have the luxury of having more than one child, but rare is the child with more than one set of parents. We are the only ones they've got. Homeschooling abuts the most complicated set of relationships—that between parent and child. One doesn't have to be a devotee of Freud to realize how central this relationship is to our life choices, who we are and who we will become. It is fraught with need and expectations on both sides, some of which may go unfulfilled, as we each feel our way. And each relationship, even within a single family, is absolutely unique.

As parent-teachers, we may begin with a nagging belief in our own inadequacies, as we carry around the burden of societal messages. From our own school-based education (often reinforced by our parents and families), we learned that we were little more than a collection of deficits. We learned either that we were failures, or potential failures, and, if the latter, to fear failure far more than to love learning. We learned strategies to deal with our learned fear of failure, ranging from passive invisibility to slavish compliance, committed small acts of subversion, and determined the utter hopelessness of rebellion.

And we learned that happiness was conditional upon the approval of others. The deficits must be filled by something—preferably material—from outside ourselves. Hasn't our culture made it quite clear that there are any number of trained and certified professionals who, having never met our children, are much more expert in educating them than we are?

So it shouldn't be surprising if we carry this burden forward in dealing with the education of our children. The problem facing each of us is unlearning how to *teach*. We learned it in school, and discovered that in a culture of lovelessness absolutely anything—and everything—should be the center of the educational enterprise but the child herself. Lesson plans, curricula, standardized tests, comparisons with other children, school buildings, national goals and objectives—anything and everything but the child herself.

I neither expect nor even desire that we should forgive our educational institutions for the way they have drained and continue to drain the vitality of our children, and the vibrancy of our communities. Educational institutions do not have souls, and so would not appreciate our forgiveness in any case.

But it will do us well to find ways to forgive those who forged the chains inside these institutions. By finding ways to forgive, you will free yourselves of the shackles, and maybe, just maybe, be able to forgive yourself, *prospectively*.

Forgive the teacher who gave you "A's" when you were bored, and "C's" when you were being creative. Forgive the teacher who taught you to love dodge ball, or to hate it. Forgive the teacher who wouldn't let you go to the bathroom, and shamed you before your friends. Forgive the teacher who punished an entire class of people because they sat in the same room as an individual who had committed an imagined misdeed, or for your whispering to a friend. Forgive the teacher who rewarded you, already over-weight, with food, and then made fun of you in phys. ed., setting a pattern with which you are still wrestling. Forgive the teacher who rewarded you with gold stars for reading, thus ensuring a love of gold stars and a sure knowledge that reading could only be instrumental, and never to be valued for itself. Forgive the teacher who after nine months could still not pro-nounce your name properly, or didn't even know it. Forgive the teacher who didn't read your essay because she couldn't get beyond the way you wrote your cursive "f"s. Forgive the teacher who ignored your question because it didn't fit into the lesson plan. Forgive the teacher who made light of the fact that you were being sexually harassed and, later, sexual-ly abused, in the hallway. Forgive the teacher for lining you up in size places, thus reminding you daily how very short you were, and setting the stage for your being constantly picked on as a consequence. Forgive the teacher who taught you that learning was punishment, and that if you "mis-behaved", you would be required to do more of it. Forgive the "good" teacher who made you feel happy, and trained you to become wholly dependent upon her and upon others for your happiness. Forgive the teacher who taught you that cooperation and cheating were synonymous, and that neither was a good way to approach a task, and that competition was the only law of life. Forgive the teacher who cared more about dead white Egyptians than about you, and made sure you knew it. Forgive the teacher who failed to protect you or defend you, or keep you out of harm's way.

They were only doing their jobs. I have learned that forgiveness is eas-ier, maybe only possible, if one releases any expectations that it will ever be any different. Let your muscles relax and your skin go slack, and the fish hooks can be removed one at a time from your body, and maybe from your soul as well.

My dream for homeschooling parents is that we will see our jobs dif-ferently. My dream for homeschooling parents is that we will see ourselves as part of an army—an army of fearless warriors of love. The reality is that it is *not* such a hard world out there for children who have parents who have learned that love and listening go hand-in-hand. Our children don't have to make up for the shortcomings of our educations—we can forgive and let it go. They don't have to learn, as we did in school, that love—like other resources—is scarce and conditional. We can forgive and teach that love is abundant, and that the most important resources—those that are to be found inside them…and us—are infinite.

To forgive does not mean to forget. Tell your children stories of what your education was like, and ask them to forgive you when you act toward them in a manner about which you should know better. Explain to them that the ways of slaves and prisoners die hard. Ask them to help you deal with your infirmities, and your blind spots, *and your forgetfulness*. Remind them that you are still in recovery, and are most assuredly less than perfect. Or even less than that.

Take a deep breath…and relax. Nature has provided each and every child with the raw materials and ineradicable thrust to undertake the journey of original seeking, and nature has provided each and every parent with the capacity to nurture our children along the way. The rest is simply a matter of technique. Approach your children with open hands, and open heart, and empty pockets, and let them show you the way.

There is a river. At least once a year, take a walk with the kids down to its banks. Don't throw anything in. Just sit and watch the water as it ripples by….

There is a fountain that was not made by the hands of men.

The Violin Bow

I spent most of yesterday looking at violin bows. I must have tried 50 or 60 of them at my favorite luthier's shop. Some were light chestnut in color, others red maroon, still others a dark, rich brown. There were octagonal and round ones. Some had buttons (the piece that tightens the hair) made of nickel, others silver, and still others gold, and they could be in either one or three parts. Frogs (that's what one holds when playing) were of ebony, or ivory, or tortoise shell (I could never in good conscience own one of these last two; some of the ivory ones came from mastodon or woolly mammoth tusks which, when one considers that the donors are extinct, pose fewer ethical questions than if they came from elephants), with slides (attaching the hair to the frog) of abalone or oyster shell. Grips on the bow itself were of gold, or silver, or nickel wire, or plastic; the really fancy ones had whalebone (I thought those had only been used for 19th Century corsets!). Some of the bows were lighter and some heavier, fatter or skinnier, flexible or stiff, heavily arched or straight.

"There are actually 157 different kinds of Brazilian hardwood," said my luthier friend, "even though we usually only talk about two of them." He showed me some of the various types.

And so I started trying them out. For the first ten minutes, they all sounded alike. Then, as if a veil was lifted, they began to reveal their individuality. Some were sweet and some grouchy, some were best played loud, and others softly. Some showed themselves off well in brisk passages, where others were almost uncontrollable.

"Of course, there is the matter of the wood itself," explained my friend. "A product of nature. Some pieces have small knots in them, others have variable densities, still others grains that are uneven. No two pieces are alike. So there's always that." I nodded, and continued to separate the proverbial wheat from the chaff, the black sheep from the white.

"But that's where the bowmaker comes in. He has to know what to do with each particular stick. It is almost like he can listen to the wood before it is worked. Some bowmakers have that special knack—it is as if their own nature knows the music in the wood and can bring it out. For others, it's rather more hit and miss. But the music is already there."

By this time, I've narrowed down my choices to five or six, though I'm beginning to wonder whether any of these is better than the very first one I eliminated.

"And," he went on, "no matter how good the bow is, it won't be the right one unless it brings out the best in your violin. The opposite is true, too. It's rather like a marriage," he chuckles.

I'm trying to figure out whether the one I'm playing now is scratchy because it doesn't have enough rosin on it, or because the bow is tip-heavy, or is it that I'm just not holding it right? This is not the first time that this question has crossed my mind. My friend senses that I'm getting a little frustrated.

"They'll sound different depending upon the environment in which they are played," he says, explaining that I can take some home on trial. The entire stringed instrument industry, I've learned over time, runs on trust.

He sees that I'm taking turns among three bows now, two of them new and rather fancy, and an old, rather pedestrian-looking one, with plain and somewhat tarnished fittings. "You can't always tell by the fittings, "he says. "Sometimes you find a real sleeper, just waiting for the right time to open up."

He takes the three bows from me. "You know, you can tell which bow is going to be most alive without even playing it. I'll show you." He grips one of the bows in his right hand. "You just tap the tip on your palm and you can feel the vibration through the stick." He has me try it. "It's all about the vibrational capacity. You are just freeing up the music that is already there. Ooo, this is a good one," he says, tapping the older, non-descript-looking bow. "I know the maker. I've even visited him in Bubenreuth (a German town famous for violin-making). The interesting thing is that he himself is a trombone player."

So I've decided to take the three bows home for a couple of weeks. And then I ask him, "Is there any way to coax greater vibrational capacity out of the bow?"

"Just hold it more lightly," he says, handing me the receipt. "The music is already in the bow. The more gently you hold it, the finer it can sing."

Index

vocabulary, 236

About the Cover Artist

Brianna Kathleen Thomas did the cover art when she was thirteen years old. She is homeschooled and she loves to make pictures with Plasticine and write fantasy and adventure stories.

She lives with her Mom, Dad, her sister Molly, and her two brothers, Kieran and Aidan. She also lives with her spunky cat, Scarlet and her dog, Griz, plus an assortment of gerbils.

About the Author

David H. Albert holds degrees from Williams College, Oxford University, and the Committee on Social Thought, University of Chicago, but says, "the best education he ever received he gets from his kids." He writes a regular column—"My Word!"—for Home Education Magazine, and his work has appeared in scores of magazines and journals worldwide, ranging from Life Learning Magazine to the Journal of the American Philosophical Society. He is also author of *And the Skylark Sings with Me: Adventures in Homeschooling and Community-Based Education* (New Society Publishers, 1999), and editor of the two-volume set *The Healing Heart~Families: Storytelling to Encourage Caring and Healthy Families* and *The Healing Heart~Communities: Storytelling to Build Strong and Healthy Communities* (New Society, 2003). As founder of New Society Publishers, he was both editor and publisher of John Taylor Gatto's *Dumbing Us Down: The Hidden Curriculum of Compulsory Schooling*, and more than 100 other titles. He was also a founding member of Co-op America and the National Association of Socially Responsible Businesses.

David lives in Olympia, Washington with his partner Ellen and two wonderful daughters, Aliyah (age 15) and Meera (12). When he is not learning with and from his kids, writing (mostly stories), making music, or raising funds for child welfare or community development projects in India, he serves as Senior Planning and Policy Analyst for the Washington State Division of Alcohol and Substance Abuse. David is also an active member of the Religious Society of Friends (Quakers), and moderator of the Quaker Homeschooling Circle.

David is available for speaking engagements or workshops in your community. He invites your comments as well. Write him at shantinik@earthlink.net or visit his website at www.skylarksings.com